The Azores : or Western Islands : a political, commercial and geographical account ...

Walter Frederick Walker

THE AZORES:

OR

WESTERN ISLANDS.

A POLITICAL, COMMERCIAL AND GEOGRAPHICAL ACCOUNT,

CONTAINING WHAT IS HISTORICALLY KNOWN OF THESE ISLANDS,
AND DESCRIPTIVE OF THEIR SCENERY, INHABITANTS, AND
NATURAL PRODUCTIONS; HAVING SPECIAL REFERENCE
TO THE EASTERN GROUP CONSISTING OF

ST. MICHAEL AND ST. MARY,

THE FORMIGAS AND DOLLABARET ROCKS;

INCLUDING SUGGESTIONS TO TRAVELLERS AND INVALIDS WHO MAY
RESORT TO THE ARCHIPELAGO IN SEARCH OF HEALTH.

WITH MAPS AND ILLUSTRATIONS.

BY

WALTER FREDERICK WALKER,

*Fellow of the Royal Geographical Society; Member of the Society of Arts;
Member of the Society of Biblical Archæology; Corresponding
Member of the Geographical Society of Lisbon, &c.*

LONDON:

TRÜBNER & CO., LUDGATE HILL.

1886.

LONDON :
PRINTED BY LAKE BROTHERS,
3, WESTMINSTER CHAMBERS S.W.,
AND 7, SUFFOLK LANE, CANNON STREET, E.

PREFACE.

—◆◇◆—

Les longs ouvrages me font peur :
Loin d'epuiser une matière,
On n'en doit prendre que la fleur.
La Fontaine.

THIS little work, devoid of any scientific or literary merit, has been penned solely in the hope that it may prove useful to those contemplating a visit to the Western Archipelago, and especially St. Michael, the " Insula bella " of the group, for it is now 44 years since Bullar's " Winter in the Azores, and Summer at the Baths of the Furnas " *—the last work in our language purely descriptive of these delightful islands, first appeared, and many changes have taken place in the intervening time, even in that land of slow progress.

I have endeavoured to adhere, as closely as possible, to the salutary precept laid down by La Fontaine, and to fill these pages with such matter only as an intending visitor might seek to learn. For much of the information herein given, relating to the early history of the islands, I am indebted to the laborious compilation ("Archivo dos Açores") of the learned Dr. Ernesto do Canto, and to the ably written "Observações sobre o Povo Michaelense" of Senor Arruda Furtado. I must also express my deep obligation to my talented friend, the Baron Das Laranjeiras, for the two

---

* In 1870 a valuable work on the " Natural History of the Azores," by F. du Cane Godman, was published by Van Voorst, and in the May number of " Fraser," 1878, a very able and accurate account of the islands appeared from the pen of R. M. D.

excellent and faithful drawings he kindly made for me, and which I present exactly as received from him. I have, lastly, to thank the Proprietors of the " Graphic " for the illustrations taken from photographs they have permitted me to reproduce.

I can only add that, independent of the many objects of interest to the scientific and the curious which these islands present, they possess many attractions to certain classes of invalids, from the mildness and salubrity of the climate. Situated, as they are, in mid-ocean, they enjoy an even temperature, such as is vainly sought in the constant and capricious changes of our treacherous northern isle. I have, in the course of this work, sufficiently indicated the conditions of climate which prevail, and pointed out such as render the islands unfavourable for the cure of some of the " ills which human flesh is heir to." Whatever labour I have bestowed on the following pages, I shall consider well repaid if their perusal shall diffuse a more prefect knowledge of the islands among the travelling community, and at the same time afford a guide to the restoration of that inestimable blessing—health.

LONDON, 1886.

MAPS, ILLUSTRATIONS, AND
ISLAND MELODIES.

ISLAND MELODIES.

CONTENTS.

—◆◦◆—

Introductory Chapter.

Descriptive and Historical—Means of Access.

```
* * * And Uriel to his charge
Returned on that bright beam, whose point now raised
Bore him slope downwards to the Sun, now fallen
Beneath the Azores ; whether the prime orb,
Incredible how swift, had thither rolled
Diurnal ; or this less volúbil Earth,
By shorter flight to the east, had left him there,
Arraying with reflected purple and gold
The clouds that on his western throne attend.
```
" Paradise Lost," Book IV.

The archipelago of the Açores, or as our sailors prefer to call them, the Western Islands, occupies a longitudinal but irregular line in mid-Atlantic of some 400 geographical miles in extent, running W.N.W. to E.S.E., and situated between latitudes 36° 59′ and 39° 44′ north, and longitudes 25° 10′ and 31° 7′ west of Greenwich.

St. Michael,* the largest, which lies nearly E.N.E. and W.S.W., in 37° 46′ north latitude, and 25° 12′ west longitude, is distant about 700 miles west of the coast of Portugal, and 1,147 from the Lizard.

Flores, the most western of these islands, is 1,680 miles from the shores of Newfoundland. They may, therefore, be said to belong to Europe, their nearest mainland.

They consist of nine islands, São Miguel, Santa Maria, Terceira, San Jorge, Pico, Fayal, Graciosa, Flores and Corvo ; also of two groups of rocks known as the Formigas and Dollabaret, with an aggregate area of about 700 square miles. According to the last census of 1878, the population of the Açores amounted altogether to 259,790, made up as follows :—

---

* St. Michael's, San' Miguel or São Miguel, as it is variously written.

São Miguel, 119,933; Santa Maria, 6,338; Terceira, 45,026; Graciosa, 8,321; San Jorge, 18,272; Fayal, 24,962; Pico, 26,396; Flores, 9,662; and Corvo, 880.

The whole of them, with the exception of Santa Maria, which appears to lie outside the focus of disturbance, show evidences of comparatively recent volcanic activity. The stratified rock identifies them as of the Miocene period, and, if carefully sought for, there are abundant signs of the effect of the Glacial epoch in the deep grooves and striations to be found on several of the islands and more especially at Terceira. The earliest writers on the Açores concur in attributing the origin of the name to the presence, when first discovered, of large numbers of a species of hawk or buzzard *(falco buteo)* which the Portuguese called "açor."

Their inhabitants are Portuguese, and they are subject to the Crown of Portugal, but at the time of their colonization, in the middle of the fifteenth century, a great influx of Flemish blood took place. In 1433 these islands were bestowed by King Duarte upon his brother Prince Henry (the Navigator) as a reward for his re-discovery of them. A sister of this Prince, the Infanta Isabel, having married Philip III., the Duke of Burgundy and Count of Flanders, received and sheltered at her Court many members of noble families who sought her protection from the persecutions and wars which then devastated the Low Counties.

Many of these refugees found their way to Portugal, and through his sister's influence, Prince Henry employed some on board his ships of discovery, others as colonists. One of these, Jacome de Bruges, a man of considerable wealth, was appointed in 1450 Captain Donatary of the island of Terceira, on condition of his colonizing it. Sixteen years later, at the period of a severe famine in Burgundy, we find the Duchess Isabel actively engaged in fitting out an expedition under Jobst Van Huerta, Lord of Moerkerchen, numbering over two thousand souls, for the purpose of colonizing Fayal and Pico, of which he became the first

Captain Donatary. San Jorge, and some of the other islands to the west, were also peopled by him; so that in 1490 there were several thousand Flemings settled there, attracted by large grants of land and other advantages. One of the earliest colonists in Fayal was the celebrated Martin Behaim, the traveller and geographer. He, with Diogo Cão, discovered the river Zaire or Congo, remaining on the west coast of Africa some 18 or 19 months. Returning to Lisbon, he married in 1486 a daughter of Van Huerta, and took up his residence at Fayal. A pupil of Regiomontano, the discoverer of the metheoroscope and astrolabe, Behaim was able to impart to the Portuguese navigators the use of these instruments. He left Fayal in 1490 and proceeded to his native place, Nuremberg, where he constructed his famous terrestrial globe. On setting out for his island home for the last time, he was captured not far from Antwerp by an English vessel and taken a prisoner to London, where he lingered on a bed of sickness for three months.

This remarkable man, the friend of Columbus, and who earned from the Emperor Maximilian the title of "the most widely travelled of all Germans," died in Lisbon in 1506.

Horta, the capital of Fayal, is to this day still named after its founder Huerta, and a few miles inland is a beautiful valley known as " O Valle dos Flamengos," or the valley of the Flemings, where these people for many years lived entirely apart from the Portuguese settlers, indeed, so greatly did they outnumber the latter, that the island was called "Ilha dos Flamengos." A constantly increasing immigration from Portugal, however, caused them towards the end of the sixteenth century to lose, not only all trace of their speech, but even of their ancestral origin. In Horta itself there is a half ruinous quarter, known as "a rua velha," or the old street, with a few dilapidated cottages inhabited by fishermen and their families, who for generations have never left the spot, and are averse to mix or intermarry with the other inhabitants of the town. Where they originally came from none can now tell, but they differ in physiognomy, dress, manners, and, to some extent, in language, from the rest of the town-folk. Are these singular looking islesmen the degenerate descendants of Van Huerta's followers, or must we look to a much earlier date for an explanation of the presence of this colony in Fayal? In Oporto and Aveiro, we find small communities of equally remarkable people, and alone of all the seaward inhabitants of Portugal using the narrow "Biga" and "Saveira" boats —peaked high in the bows and stern, and painted in brilliant colours, which so astonish a traveller in northern Portugal. Mr. Consul Crawford, in his charming book on that country, thinks these are the remnants of Phœnician immigration. There is no evidence to show that these people ever penetrated into these seas, and on none of the Açores were any inhabitants found at the time of their discovery by the Portuguese. It is therefore probable that the ancestors of the "rua velha" dwellers came from the banks of the Douro, in the wake of the Portuguese and Flemish settlers, and have ever since, to a remarkable extent, preserved their individuality.

Of all nations in Europe, perhaps the Portuguese spring from the most heterogenous elements. In the array of ancient hordes who successively overran the country, we find the Iberians, Celts, Celtiberians, Phœnicians, Lusitanians, Carthaginians, Greeks, Romans, Goths, Visigoths, Burgundians, Moors, and, in more recent times, no small leaven of Hebrew and African blood. Up to 1534, the Azore Islands were under the jurisdiction of the military Order of Christ,* of which Prince Henry was Grand Master,

---

* Established in 1319 by Dom Diniz, and is the only order in Europe representing the ancient Templars. When, at the instigation of the infamous Philip the Fair, of France, a Papal Bull was issued suppressing the order, King Diniz, to his lasting honour, refused to carry out the cruel edict in his dominions,

but they were subsequently incorporated in the Crown possessions, and attached to the Bishopric of Funchal in Madeira, and their inhabitants began then to enjoy more beneficial influences from the immediate government of the kings, for prior to this they had been much neglected and abandoned to the rapacity of successive governors, eight years sometimes elapsing before a vessel visited them from the mother country. Well might they have said :—

> We dwell apart, afar—
> Within the unmeasured deep, amid its waves —
> The most remote of men ; no other race
> Hath commerce with us.

At the earnest solicitation of King John III., a separate Bishopric of the Açores was created in November, 1534, by Paul III., the episcopal see being established at Angra do Heroismo, the capital of Terceira, partly in consequence of the political importance the island derived in those days from its almost impregnable position, but more especially from a singular error in the Papal Bull, as we shall presently observe. The discovery, too, of India in 1497, by Vasco da Gama, and of Brazil in 1500, by Pedro Alvares Cabral, gave Terceira at that time a great commercial importance, as it became the port of call for all the homeward-bound fleets of Spain and Portugal; so that in the Bay of Angra there were often as many as one hundred merchantmen at one time re-victualling and repairing after their lengthy voyages.

Paul III. really meant to establish the episcopal see in the island of San Miguel, as being the " largest and most notable of all the islands called Açores," but by a remarkable

---

but so far complied with the wishes of the Pontiff as to change the name to that of the Order of Christ, their vast estates and privileges in Portugal remaining, however, intact. The Templars are said to have possessed 19,000 manors in different parts of Europe. In Portugal they had no less than 21 towns and villages, and 454 commanderies or benefices. The Sovereign became the constant Grand Master of the order, and received therefrom an annual revenue of 40,000 crusados. The "Commenda de Christo" to this day is the commonest decoration in Portugal.

instance of Papal fallibility in matters geographical, Angra, the capital of Terceira, was in the Bull made the capital of San Miguel, and the fortunate Angrenses have ever since lived under the spiritual protection and blessing of their bishop.

The following is an extract from the Bull referred to : "Et inter alias Insulas eidem ecclesie funchalensi pro ejus diocesi assignatas Insula Sancti Michaelis nuncupata, in eodem Mari Occeano sita, ceteris, dos Açores nuncupatis, illi adjacentibus Insulis Maior et notabilior, ac magno Christianorum populo referta et munita, existeret, et in illius parte, quœ Angra nuncupatur, inter alias una insignis parrochialis ecclesia sub invocatione Sancti Salvatoris dicta, &c., &c.

Translation : "And among other islands subject to the diocese of Funchal, there was one named the island of San Miguel, the largest and most notable of all the islands called the Açores, inhabited by many Christian people ; and, in the part of the same island which is called Angra, there was erected a renowned parochial church, under the invocation of San Salvador, &c., &c."

It is the duty of the Azorean bishop to occasionally visit the islands under his jurisdiction. It so happened that after one of these periodical visitations to Pico, a few years ago, the pilchard fishery, until then abundant, suddenly ceased, the fish apparently abandoning the coast; this was unfortunately attributed by the simple-minded people to the presence of the bishop, who was waited upon by a deputation of fishermen, who civilly, but firmly, requested him to immediately leave the island : "Ja não queremos saber de bispo, o que precisamos são chicharros !" "We care nothing for bishops," said they, "what we want are pilchards !"

Santa Maria, as well as San Miguel, received their first inhabitants from the provinces of Estremadura and Algarve, in the south of Portugal—Terceira by people from the neighbourhood of Oporto, and it is extraordinary how the

latter have preserved the characteristics at present dis-
tinguishing the inhabitants of Minho and Douro. These
peculiarities have earned for them amongst the other
islanders the sobriquet of "rabos tortos," in allusion to the
singular curl of the tails of their dogs, a savage breed of
Cuba-mastiff stock, and indicative of a stubborn and un-
forgiving spirit.

Fayal, Pico, and San Jorge derived most of their
first inhabitants from Flanders.

Besides these, the donatarios of the different islands
brought with them numerous slaves of either sex, both
Moors and Negroes, and we find a whole ship-full of Hebrew
families carried over there by an accident in 1501. Fleeing
from the persecutions of the Inquisition in Portugal, these
wretched people, to the number of several hundred, shipped
on board a caravel for Barbary, but being driven by stress of
weather to the Azores, they were at once made prisoners,
and having been bestowed by the King as a present on
Vasqueanes Corte-Real, were condemned by him to perpetual
slavery.

The Spanish dominion, too, of 60 years, could not but
tend to fuse many of the two nationalities; thus we have
several distinct races colonizing these islands, now scarcely
distinguishable in their descendants.

Until 1832, a Captain-General ruled over the destinies of
the Açores, but on the 4th June of that year this all-powerful
office was abolished by Dom Pedro, and they then became a
province of Portugal, with Angra as the political capital.
On the 28th March, 1836, another decree was passed,
dividing the group into three administrative and fiscal
districts, i.e., the district of Ponta Delgada, consisting of the
islands of San Miguel and Santa Maria, with Ponta Delgada
as capital; the district of Angra, comprising the islands of
Terceira, São Jorge, and Graciosa, having Angra for capital;
and the district of Horta—including the islands of Fayal,
Pico, Flores, and Corvo, having Horta for their capital;

each division under the administration of a civil governor, who is responsible to the Lisbon government for his acts, and generally loses his appointment on a change of ministry. Each one of the districts, for the purpose of electoral returns to the Cortes, constitutes a separate centre; that of Ponta Delgada, known as the oriental, or eastern, sending four members; Angra, as the central, two members; and Horta, as the occidental, or western district, also two—in all, eight members for the entire group.*

The climate, though humid, is healthy, mild and equable, the thermometer seldom rising above 75°, or descending below 50° Fah., or 24° and 10°, C. São Miguel is in point of area, wealth and beauty, the most important of the archipelago.

Before proceeding to a brief description of that island and its dependent Santa Maria, we will first observe that the Açores are reached from London (calling at Dartmouth) by the excellent steamers of the London and West India Line, sailing twice a month, and calling at St. Michael to drop passengers, provided three berths at £10 each be engaged; they also touch at the island homeward bound from the West Indies, for cargo and passengers. Agents in London—Messrs. Scrutton and Co., 9, Gracechurch Street, E.C. Also during the months of November to March, by British steamers engaged in the orange trade, sent from England direct—generally from London, Hull or Cardiff—and all the year round by a bi-monthly service of Portuguese mail steamers from Lisbon, owned by the Empreza Insulana de Navigação, consisting at present of the " Funchal " (s.s.), sailing from the Tagus at 10 a.m. on the 5th of every month, calling at São Miguel, arriving on the 8th or 9th; Terceira, 10th; Graciosa, 11th; São Jorge, 11th; Pico, 11th; Fayal, night of the 11th, in

---

* All Spanish and Portuguese colonies or islands, however distant, are divided into provinces, as if they formed contiguous portions of the continent.

winter morning of the 12th, and Flores, 13th; returning viâ the same islands excepting Pico.

The second steamer, the "Açor," leaves Lisbon at 10 a.m. on the 20th of each month, calling first at Madeira, where she arrives on the 22nd of each month, then at Santa Maria, 25th; São Miguel, 26th; Terceira, 27th, and Fayal, 28th; returning viâ same islands.

The accommodation on board these steamers, although heavily subsidized by the Portuguese government, naturally contrasts but indifferently with that experienced in the Royal Mail Packets from Southampton, and the cuisine is entirely Portuguese; the shorter voyages, however, to and from Lisbon, and the few days rest in the Lusitanian capital, are important considerations to travellers suffering from *mal de mer*; but to those who like the sea, a passage direct would be found much less irksome.

PASSENGER FARES.

			£	s.	d.
Lisbon to Madeira	.. .. ..	27$000 =	6	0	0
,,	São Miguel, or Santa Maria	30$000 =	6	13	4
,,	Terceira	31$000 =	6	17	9
,,	Graciosa, S. Jorge, Fayal or				
	Pico	32$000 =	7	2	3
,,	Flores	34$000 =	7	11	2

Agent in Lisbon—Snr. G. S. Arnaud, Caes Sodré.

The fruit steamers from England direct take passengers to St. Michael or Fayal, for £10 each, everything included.

Agents in London—Messrs. Collings and Co., 16, Philpot Lane, Eastcheap; Messrs. Tatham and Co., 9, Gracechurch Street.

Chapter I.

Our onward prows the murmuring surges lave;
And now our vessels plough the gentle wave,
Where the blue islands, named of Hesper old,
Their fruitful bosoms to the deep unfold.
Mickle's " Camöens."

ABOUT the fourth decade of the 12th century, a series of
remarkable voyages were undertaken by a celebrated Arabian
navigator, Sherif Mohammed al Edrisi, a native of Tetuan,
who, besides discovering the Cape de Verd, Canary and
Madeira islands, would seem to have penetrated as far as
the Açores. He is said to have constructed, at the request
of Roger II., King of Sicily, a silver globe, weighing 400
Greek pounds, on which the lands he visited, and all the
then known parts of the world, were carefully laid down,
but unfortunately, this most interesting work soon afterwards disappeared, the descriptive manuscript written in
the year 1153, in Arabic, alone remaining; this was translated into Latin in 1691, by Hartmann, and in it we find,
after a description of the "Insulæ Canarides," mention
made of nine other islands to the north of these, and in the
western ocean, one of which he calls "Raka,"* i.e., of birds,
for it abounded in a species of eagle, or raptorial bird. He
describes the islands as covered with forest, and the co-
incidence of nine of these to the north of the Canaries, and
the existence at that time in large numbers of the very bird

---

* Huic insulæ proxima est insula Raka, i.e., volucrum. Ferunt in hac insula
esse genus auium aquilis rubris similium unguibusque instructarum, quæ belluas
marinas venantur et comedunt. Ab hac insula eas nunquam recedere affirmant.

which subsequently gave its name to the group, goes far to confirm the opinion of the learned Hartmann that the islands in question were really what he calls the Occipitres, or Açores, and looking at the distances which separate them, not only from each other, but from the nearest mainland, we cannot but be struck at the hardihood of these early navigators.

Either in translating from the Arabic, or from original discrepancies in the chapter devoted to the " Insulæ Maris Atlantici," it is much to be regretted that the various groups treated of, the Cape de Verd, Canaries (which Edrisi calls by their real name of Insula Chaledat or Fortunate Islands), Madeira, and Açores, seem inextricably mixed up; thus, in the same paragraph relating to the latter, the island of Sahelia* is mentioned as once possessing "three cities of equal size, much peopled, the inhabitants of which were now all slain in civil wars." Ships came from distant parts to these cities for the purchase of ambergris, purple dyes, and stones of divers colours; no doubt one of the Canary group is here meant, for we know that they were peopled, and that the Syrians, Carthagenians and Romans, are said to have sent their ships to trade with the inhabitants of these islands, a handsome copper coloured race of Asiatic type, who in more recent times became troglodytes, living in grottoes and caves; the mention, therefore, of several populous cities at the time of Edrisi's visit is interesting.

Petrarch, too, thus writes to the Genoese in 1351 :— " You, whose ships have free course in the ocean and in the Euxine, and before whom peoples and monarchs tremble. From Tapobrana to the Fortunate Isles and Thule, to the extreme confines of the northern and western world, your

---

* Hinc vehuntur ad insulam Saheliam. Longitudo, eius 15, latitudo 10 dierum spatium comprehendit. Olim in hac insula tres urbes extabant parvæ quidem, sed populosæ, quarum incolæ autem bellis intestinis fere omnes perierunt. Ad has usque perueniebant nautæ, atque emebant ambarum et lapides diversi

pilots safely guide their crafts," showing that the Genoese in those days already traded with the Canaries. Their visits must have commenced between 1291 and the date of Petrarch's address, for the Genoese attribute the discovery of the Fortunate Isles to an expedition under Tedisio D'Oria, which sailed in that year into the Atlantic, but never returned.

On none of the Açores have traces ever been found of the presence of man, anterior to the arrival of the Portuguese, although several circumstantial, but purely apocryphal stories, were rife in the 16th century, respecting an equestrian statue which stood on a promontory on the north-west extremity of Corvo, bearing on its pedestal a cuniform inscription, which, however, no native philologist, or Champollion, had been able to decipher. The historian, Damião de Goes, writing in the first half of the 16th century, mentions this statue in full belief of its existence. In 1800 the Governor of Terceira, Count de Almada, received instructions from his Government to cause minute search to be made for any traces of it, but without result. Seventeen years later we find Antonio José Camões writing: "Truthful tradition asserts that on a formidable rock to the north-west of the island the perfect figure of a man on horseback could be discerned, with one arm extended as if pointing towards the west," but after a lapse of several years, Brigadier General Noronha, who spent some time in the island investigating the matter, and the traditions connected with it, came to the conclusion that the report originated "in some optical illusion." I am inclined to believe, however, that its true solution is to be found in the pages of Edrisi, for in his account of the Canary Islands the following passage occurs:

"There had been erected on each of these islands a statue hewn out of stone, and a hundred cubits high; over each statue was set a brazen image beckoning towards the west with its hand; there were six of these statues."

Ibn al Vardi also says : " Dans chaque île il y a une statue haute de cent coudées, qui est comme un fanal, pour diriger les vaisseaux et leur apprendre qu'il n'y a point de route au-delà." It is clear, therefore, that Corvo, the smallest and most northern island of this archipelago, must in remote times either have been inhabited by the same race who peopled the Canaries—a very unlikely hypothesis—or that the fable of the equestrian statue must have been coined from the above passage of Edrisi, of which there appears more than presumptive evidence. It is interesting to re- member that these statues in the Fortunate Islands were regarded in those early days as the work of Dzou-el-Qarnayn, the Hercules of the Arabs.

Could these romancers have heard, as Plato narrates, that the great statue of Poseidon in Atlantis was surrounded with the lesser statues of one hundred Nereids? Or was the idea associated with the Phœnician Astarte, which, at the prow of their boats, always pointed the way with an ex- tended arm?

Damião de Goes was in the service of King Dom Manoel from 1510 to 1521; he wrote the famous "Chronica do Principe D. João III.," and in it mentions the statue as follows :—" In the island of Corvo (discovered subsequent to 1460), or as it is sometimes called Island of Màrco, as it is used by sailors to demark any of the others when making them, there was found on the top of a hill on the north-west side, a stone statue placed on a ledge, and consisting of a man astride on the bare back of a horse, the man being dressed, and having over him a cloak (" capa com bedêm "*) but bareheaded, with one hand on the mane of the horse, and the right arm extended, the fingers of the hand folded, with the exception of the index finger, which pointed to the west. Dom Manoel ordered a drawing of this statue, which

---

* " Bedêm " is a Moorish word, and signifies a peculiar-shaped cloak which was worn by the Moors in wet weather.

rose in a solid block from the ledge, to be forwarded to him, after seeing which he sent an ingenious man, a native of Oporto who had travelled much in France and Italy, to the island of Corvo in order to remove this antiquity, who, when he returned, told the king that the statue had been destroyed by a storm the previous year. But the truth was that they broke it through ill usage, bringing portions of it, consisting of the head of the man, and the right arm with the hand, also a leg and the head of the horse, all of which remained for some days in the wardrobe of the king, but what was afterwards done with these things, or where they were put, I could not discover. These islands (Corvo and Flores) were bequeathed to Pero da Fonseca, who visited them in 1529, and was told by the inhabitants that on the rock below where the statue rested, some letters were carved. Owing to the place being dangerous and difficult of access, he caused some men to descend by means of ropes, who took impressions of the letters (which time had not altogether effaced) in wax, which he took for that purpose ; but the impressions were much obliterated when they reached Lisbon, being almost without form ; for this reason, and probably because those present had only a knowledge of Latin, no one could tell what the letters meant."

Although this circumstantial account is given by a contemporary historian of these events, in whose veracity implicit confidence is reposed, we must remember that on this particular subject he simply recorded hearsay reports, There are three points in his account, which in my opinion are fatal to the supposed existence of the Corvo statue. 1st. The situation on a ledge of rock so inaccessible, that in order to enable him to take an impression of the inscription at its base, Pero da Fonseca "caused some men to descend by means of ropes." 2nd. The fact of a statue of such conspicuous dimensions being cut out of the solid rock, horse and man in one piece, and placed in such a difficult locality. 3rd. The " Capa com bedêm," with which the horseman was covered, is a proof that none but Arabs, Portuguese, or Spaniards, could possibly have erected such a statue, even admitting its impossible position, for the Moorish cloak was of pecular shape, and only worn in the Peninsula, and the fact of its special mention identifies the fable as originating in either a Spanish or Portuguese source, as the Moors, supposing them to have visited Corvo, were very unlikely to have selected such a means, forbidden by their religion, of commemorating their presence there. Mr. Ignatius Donnelly, who has spent much time and labour in proving that the Azores, with some other Atlantic islands, are but the topmost peaks of the lost Atlantis, asks, " May not the so-called Phœnician coins found on Corvo, one of the Azores, be of Atlantean origin? Is it probable that that great race, pre-eminent as a founder of colonies, could have visited those islands within the historical period, and have left them unpeopled, as they were when discovered by the Portuguese ? "

The assertion that Phœnician coins were discovered in the island of Corvo in November, 1749, was made by Humboldt in his " Examen Critique," entirely upon the authority of Snr. Podolyn, but uncorroborated by any other testimony. The story, as handed to us by Humboldt, relates that, after a violent storm, the eddying waves uncovered a strongly constructed and dome-shaped dolmen of stone, under which was found an earthen jar containing a number of gold and copper coins, which were taken to a convent, where the major portion were distributed among the curious, some (to the number of nine) being sent to Padre Flores of Madrid, who gave them to Snr. Podolyn.

These coins, according to the illustrations published in the " Memorials of the Society of Gothenberg," No. 1, page 106, bore either the head of a horse, or its entire figure, or a palm, some being considered Carthagenian, others Cyrenean. There is not the slightest corroborative tradition, however, amongst the inhabitants of Corvo, of the finding of these coins, and doubts are cast upon the veracity of the account as related to Humboldt. In none of the other islands have any such coins or ancient relics ever been found, and, like the famous story of the Corvo statue, we must relegate this numismatic "find" to the region of myth.

———————

CHAPTER II.

" ATLANTIS "—SOLON—PLATO—THE VOYAGE OF ST. BRENDAN OF CLONFERT—
MAPS—THE " FORTUNATE ISLES."

> The fair breeze blew, the white foam flew ;
> The furrow follow'd free !
> We were the first that ever burst
> Into that silent sea.
> " *The Ancient Mariner.*"

FOR two centuries. following these surprising voyages of
Edrisi, we hear nothing further of the Açores until we find
one of the group, which from its westerly position and shape
must be meant for Corvo, noted on a Spanish map, dated
1346, in the National Library in Paris.

In 1351, their geographical position is accurately marked
in the famous Portulano Mediceo map, of the Laurentian
Library, in Florence, published in that year by some unknown
Genoese, who must either himself have sailed among them
or heard of their existence from some countryman, probably
the pilot Niccoloso di Reccó, who, in 1341, guided the
expedition sent out by Affonso IV., of Portugal, under
Angiolino del Tegghio, for the discovery of the Fortunate
(or Canary) Islands, where Reccó *had previously been,* and
from whence he may, in former voyages, have visited
Madeira and the more western group. However this may
be, the first really undisputed identity of the Açores is to be
found in the hydrographical chart, bearing date 1385, in
the Royal Archives in Florence, in which the islands of San
Miguel and Santa Maria are laid down, the names given them
being unfortunately illegible. Terceira is named " Insula
de Brazi," from the Brazil wood with which it was supposed
to abound, but which we shall presently see was an error ;

C

while San Jorge, Pico, and Fayal, are named "Insule de Ventura" and "Columbis," a notable circumstance, implying, from the one name "Columbis" given to the two latter, that they were at that time joined, and formed one single island. This remarkable chart bears the following epigraph :—

"Guil (*i.e.*) lmus Solerij civjs Maioricarum" (*i.e.*, native of Soller, in Majorca) "me fecit anno a Nat Domini, MCCCLXXXV."

It is much to be regretted that no descriptive account of the voyage which this map evidently commemorated, or of the persons engaged in it, has been preserved to us. In it no mention is made of the extreme western group, consisting of Flores and Corvo, and it is probable that their re-discovery was due to the brothers Diogo and João de Teive, who, in 1452, twenty years after the first discovery of Santa Maria, by Cabral, came upon them under the guidance of the pilot Pedro Velasco, a native of Paulos de Moguer, who had probably seen the latter island mentioned in the Spanish map of 1346.

We next observe all the islands reproduced on Andrea Bianco's map, dated 1436, belonging to the library of St. Mark.

For a long period, and more especially since the eleventh century, there had existed in Europe vague rumours of undiscovered and unknown lands in the Atlantic ocean. Among the Irish peasantry of Mayo especially, there had long been traditions of a wonderful land in the far west. The successful discovery of the Canaries, Madeiras, and subsequently of the Açores, together with the gradual spread of letters amongst religious orders, had revived these old traditions, and pictured them as actual realities.

Lisbon and Sagres had, since the days of Dom Henrique, become the rendezvous of adventurous spirits, whose earth-hunger had been whetted by the powerful donataryships bestowed upon the fortunate discoverers and settlers of these newly-found islands, and to such a pitch had this desire been wrought that the dangers of the " mare tenebrarum " had lost their terrors, and each fresh expedition was hailed as a " navis stultifera," to bear them away to some new land of promise.

Let us for a moment trace the grounds upon which these rumours were based.

The earliest reference made to the existence of a large island in the Atlantic is probably to be found in the fragment of Theopompus' works composed in the 4th century before Christ, in which the continents we now call Europe, Asia, and Africa, are mentioned as being surrounded by the sea ; but that beyond them existed an island of immense extent, containing great cities, peopled by civilised and orderly nations. Later, occurs Plato's almost identical account of " Atlantis " in his Timaeus and Critias, and later still, Pliny and Diodorus mention the existence of a vast continent to the west of Africa.

Solon, the Grecian philosopher, poet, and Athenian lawgiver, lived 600 years B.C.; he visited Egypt, and appears to have received from the Egyptian priests what purported to be an account of the Island of Atlantis, which was transmitted to his descendant, Plato, and by him preserved in his " Dialogues " written 400 years B.C.

The following are short extracts of this old-world story:—
" Egyptian priest to Solon : ' Many great and wonderful deeds are recorded of your state in our histories, but one of them exceeds all the rest in greatness and valor ; for these histories tell of a mighty power which was aggressing wantonly against the whole of Europe and Asia, and to which your city (Athens) put an end. This power came forth out of the Atlantic ocean, for in those days the Atlantic was navigable ; and there was an island situated in front of the Straits which you call the columns of Heracles ; the island was larger than Libya and Asia put together, and was the way to other islands, and from the islands you might pass

through the whole of the opposite continent which surrounded the true ocean; for this sea, which is within the Straits of Heracles, is only a harbour, having a narrow entrance, but that other is a real sea, and the surrounding land may be most truly called a continent. Now, in the island of Atlantis, there was a great and wonderful empire, which had rule over the whole island and several others, as well as over parts of the continent, and besides these, they subjected the parts of Libya within the columns of Heracles as far as Egypt, and of Europe as far as Tyrrhenia. The vast power thus gathered into one endeavoured to subdue at one blow our country and yours, and the whole of the land which was within the Straits; and then, Solon, your country shone forth, in the excellence of her virtue and strength, among all mankind; for she was the first in courage and military skill, and was the leader of the Hellenes. And when the rest fell off from her, being compelled to stand alone, after having undergone the very extremity of danger, she defeated and triumphed over the invaders, and preserved from slavery those who were not yet subjected, and freely liberated all the others who dwell within the limits of Heracles. But afterwards there occurred violent earthquakes and floods, and in a single day and night of rain all your warlike men in a body sunk into the earth, and the island of Atlantis in like manner disappeared, and was sunk beneath the sea. And this is the reason why the sea in those parts is impassable and impenetrable, because there is such a quantity of shallow mud in the way, and this was caused by the subsidence of the island.*

The first king of Atlantis, Plato continued, was Poseidon, who begat ten children; he divided the island into ten

---

* There are numerous instances recorded of vessels making way with difficulty through floating masses of pumice in the Azorean seas after a serious volcanic or submarine eruption in the neighbourhood.

portions, giving to each of his sons a tenth part; to Atlas, the eldest, fell the largest and fairest portion, and he was made king over his brothers, who ranked as princes.

From him the whole island and surrounding ocean received the name of Atlantis. These ten kings possessed 10,000 chariots. The Atlanteans were apparently sun-worshippers, and erected to the honor of their deity magnificent temples, wherein and about which were placed numerous statues and ornaments of gold, the island abounding in this, silver and other metals. There was abundance of timber for building purposes, also fruit trees and cereals of various kinds, which were systematically cultivated. Cattle, horses and other domestic as well as wild animals abounded. The people, who had attained to a high degree of civilization, employed themselves in building vast temples dedicated to their deities, palaces for their princes, harbours and docks for their ships, their ports being frequented by foreign vessels coming there to trade; their own fleet numbered 1,200 ships. They had numerous fountains, both of cold and hot springs, which they largely used, not only for themselves, but for bathing their horses, of which they took extreme care.

The great plain, in the centre of which their principal city was situated, was entirely surrounded by a protecting moat 1,150 miles in length, 607 feet in breadth, and 100 feet in depth. Many other remarkable things are told us by Plato of this extraordinary island and its inhabitants, but those of my readers who are interested in the subject cannot do better than refer to the able and fascinating work on "Atlantis: the Antediluvian World," by Ignatius Donnelly, where the question is exhaustively handled.

When the Moors, during the eighth century, penetrated into Portugal, they were not slow to discover the advantageous position of Lisbon, as a base for their power and commerce. They accordingly seized the hilly country on the northern bank of the Tagus, and continued to hold it until expelled in the middle of the 12th century by the first king of Portugal, Affonso Henriquez, aided by some 13,000 crusaders, mostly English, who, on their way to Palestine, had accidentally put into Oporto, and afterwards, on the invitation of the King, into Lisbon.

The city, at that time, contained, according to Moorish accounts, from four to five hundred thousand inhabitants, and had, at various periods, sent out expeditions into the Atlantic, with the object either of plunder or discovery. The record of one of these expeditions has been preserved by Edrisi, and is sufficiently curious for insertion here. "Eight Arab sailors put out to sea in a large caravel, with supplies for a lengthened voyage; after eleven days sail with a fair easterly wind, they entered what they describe as a feculent sea, where fetid gases sickened them, and shoals of pointed rocks so terrified them, as to cause them to turn the ship's head to the south, in which direction they sailed for twelve days, at the end of which they reached the island of El-Ghanam, so named from the numerous herds of small cattle which quietly grazed, unattended by shepherds; some of these they killed, but so bitter was their flesh* that they were unable to eat it, and contented themselves by carrying off their skins. Having replenished their supplies of water, which they drew from a spring shaded by wild fig trees, they re-embarked, and continued in a southerly direction for twelve days more, until they arrived off an island which appeared inhabited and cultivated; as they approached, they found themselves surrounded by boats, and were made prisoners and conducted to a town built on the shore. Having landed, they were at once beset by numerous people of a swarthy complexion, tall stature and long, straight hair; the women being specially handsome.

---

* M. Berthelot, the accomplished historian of the Canary Islands, makes mention of a plant growing there (le coqueret) on which the cattle browse at certain seasons, and which imparts a bitter flavour to their flesh.

On the third day an interpreter, speaking Arabic, entered the dwelling where they had been lodged, and questioned them respecting their voyage, their country, and the motives of their coming there. Two days later they were conducted to the chief of the island, who repeated the same questions, and promising them his protection, dismissed them to their lodging. Here they remained a few days longer, until the wind set in from the west; they were then blindfolded and made to re-embark. After a voyage, which they estimated at three days and three nights, they were landed and left on a shore, still blindfolded, and with their arms bound behind; profound silence at first reigned about them, but presently, hearing human voices, they uttered loud cries, and thus attracted the attention of certain Berber people. From these, they learnt that they were two months journey from Lisbon, which they eventually reached after much distress and no little disappointment."

Who can, from this account, doubt that this Arab crew, after a favorable voyage of eleven days to the west of Lisbon, reached the Formigas, and came across evidence of what, to them, must have been an incomprehensible and alarming phenomenon, in the shape of some serious volcanic eruption in their neighbourhood, which drove them southward, until they came to one of the inhabited Canary Islands, from whence they were conveyed to the opposite African coast?

Very remarkable is the account preserved in the Irish annals of the voyage of St. Brendan of Clonfert, who, in A.D. 545, sailed from the shores of Kerry in a well-appointed vessel, accompanied by a few adventurous companions, in search of the "Promised Land."

Keeping towards the south-west, after many weeks' voyage he eventually reached a coast which he proceeded to examine, finding some distance inland a large river flowing from east to west, thought by some writers to have been the Ohio; when returning to Ireland, after an absence of seven years, he appears to have discovered and landed upon one of the Atlantic Islands, supposed to have been Madeira, from its well-known liability to become obscured from view by those approaching it from the sea, by haze. This happy land was said to tantalize the faithful in search of it, by appearing like a Will-o'-the-wisp, and as suddenly disappearing. Many were the vain endeavours made to find this supposed abode of the Saints.

In a chart of the brothers Pizzigani, published in 1367, we find the Madeira group inserted as the Fortunate Isles of Saint Brendan; in another, bearing date 1424, in the public library at Weimar, and in Beccaria's map of 1435.

Christopher Columbus, in his journal, mentions that the inhabitants of Ferro, as well as those of Gomera, assured him that they had seen this island every year appearing towards the west; also that he had met people in Lisbon in the year 1484, who had come from Madeira to solicit a caravel from the king to go in search of this mysterious isle, which every year was seen by them, always in the same direction.

Martin Behaim, also, in his famous Nuremberg globe of 1492, places a large island near the equator, where, he says, St. Brendan spent part of his life, witnessing many marvellous things.

In Cardinal Zurla's map of the middle of the fifteenth century, we find St. Brendan pictured as stepping on to the island of Madeira, which the Genoese of that day believed to be the island that the Saint discovered. So firm was the belief in this mysterious island, that when Dom Emanuel renounced his rights to the Canaries, on the 4th June, 1519, he expressly included in this important treaty with Spain the "Hidden or Undiscovered Island," as it was then called.

In 1526, the two Spaniards, Fernando de Troya and Fernando Alvarez, set out in search of it from the Canary Islands. A similar expedition, under Fernando de Villalobos, the Governor of Palma, started on the same errand some years later. Still undiscouraged, the Spaniards despatched another exploring fleet, under their, at that time, most expert pilot, Gaspar Perez de Acosta, but always with the same result. The hope, however, of ultimate success was kept alive by the gulf stream, aided by the north-westerly gales, invariably bringing to the shores of the Canary and other Atlantic Islands, specimens of strange trees and fruits.

The last of those Canarian expeditions we find undertaken under Gaspar Domingues, as late as 1721, when the search from this quarter was finally abandoned, and not without reason, for closer observations proved that this mysterious land was but the reflex or mirage of the Island of Palma. Meanwhile the Portuguese were not idle; certain unscrupulous monks and others, having from time to time deposed upon oath that they had actually landed upon the Islands of St. Brendan and Sete Cidades, the latter being the name they had bestowed upon Plato's Atlantis, various secret expeditions were ever and anon sent out from the Tagus and Açores. This passion for discovery extended in time to England, for we find John Cabot frequently sailing into the Atlantic from Bristol, in hopes of finding in the distant west the imaginary Isle of Brazil, the name being a Portuguese corruption of the Genoese Braxe, "woody," applied by the latter to some island they had accidently visited in the Atlantic, and which is ascribed to either Madeira or Terceira. The imaginative Irish fancied they could sometimes see this island, which they identified as that of St. Brendan, from the west of Ireland, and it became so far a reality in men's minds as to find a place in all the old maps, from that of Andrea Bianco's in 1436 to Purdy's more modern publication. Amongst the Portuguese themselves, the Island of Terceira had long become identified with the Ilha do Brazil,* from a supposition that

---

* No Brazil wood has ever been found growing in Terceira, but the sanguinho (*rhamnus latifolius*), a tree with a reddish wood, is common in all the islands.

its forests produced the much valued dye-wood of that name. Terceira, in the beginning of the 17th century, had become the centre of cultivation of the *satis tinctoria*, or woad plant, from which, before the days of indigo, a blue dye was made in large quantities, and cargoes of it shipped in a granulated form to England and other places. Could Chaucer be referring to this when he wrote :—

Him nedeth not his colour for to dien
With 'brazil,' ne with grain of Portingale.

Foiled in their frequent endeavours to find this mythical land, the Portuguese seem to have derived consolation in bestowing and perpetuating its name upon that splendid discovery of theirs in South America, which has since grown to such vast importance. We find the Captain Donatary of Terceira, Fernam Dulmo, personally petitioning the King in 1486 to be allowed at his own cost to fit out an expedition, and to be given the captaincy of any new lands he might discover. The governor of São Miguel, Lourenço Vaz Coutinho, complying with instructions sent him from Lisbon in July 1591, dispatched a vessel in search of the new island supposed to lie between Terceira and Fayal. Two years later, news having again reached São Miguel that the island had been really sighted by some boatmen 80 leagues to the south of Fayal, a small Scotch vessel, which happened to be in the roads of Ponta Delgada with wheat, was immediately sent in quest of it, shortly afterwards to return unsuccessful.

In 1649 we also find Frei João da Trindade, of the order of S. Francis, setting out under the auspices of the Crown from Lisbon, in search of this *terra incognita*; but his expedition met with the same ill success, and his death shortly afterwards put a stop to further exertion on his part. In a curious manuscript which he left he mentions that in the islands of the Açores there were very ancient traditions of the existence in their vicinity of other islands still to be discovered and peopled.

The last of these expeditions from the Açores took place in 1770, under the direction of D. Antão d'Almada, the first captain-general of the Açores, appointed by the Marquis of Pombal. After a fruitless wandering to the north of Terceira, the too sanguine discoverers returned to meet with the jeers of the people of Angra. To such an extent was their sarcasm expended upon the authors of this luckless expedition, that the governor found himself obliged to issue a decree to the effect that no one was hereafter even to refer to the supposed island, under heavy pains and penalties—and thus ceased their futile attempt. The spirit of fiction had long held sway in Portugal, as in other lands, and to that fascinating writer, Bernardino de Senna Freitas, we owe the discovery of some curious inedited manuscripts, detailing with considerable circumstance the landing on some of these supposititious and inhabited islands of some Genoese sailors, and subsequently some Portuguese priests. The most remarkable account is in a mutilated manuscript of the seventeenth century, by an unknown Azorean, purporting to be the faithful copy of an entry in the "Book of Antiquities of Barcelona in the year 1444," made by some Genoese who put into that port, bearing on one side the chart of a large island, having many high mountains and numerous undulations. It was given a circumference of 300 leagues, and appeared to be cut almost in half by a large river rising in the mountains. On its northern side was a small islet densely wooded, and on the western side, distant about three leagues, was another. The larger island was said to be seen in clear weather, not only from Madeira, but from the rest of the Açores.

At the back of this chart occurs the following deposition by the Genoese:—"In the year 1444, there arrived in the port of this city of Barcelona a Genoese merchantman, which, having been thrown out of her course and almost lost in consequence of a violent tempest, made the Cape of Finisterre, and was then blown out to sea, subsequently sighting land which was not on the ships' charts, and for which they at once made. Casting anchor in a port where they landed, they found people who spoke the Portuguese language, telling them that they belonged to the Portuguese nation, but that when Spain (then under Roderick, the last Gothic king) was overrun by the Moors, their forefathers, rather than submit to the tyranny of the infidels, had determined to venture on the ocean with their families and chattels, in some vessels which were then in the river Douro, and go in quest of some island which they had heard existed there, and where they might live undisturbed; that, in course of time, they had reached this island, where their ancestors had erected five cities on the sea-shore; that in each city there was a bishop, and amongst these there were two archbishops; that in the interior there were three hundred towns, with numerous inhabitants; that the whole island was very fertile, and abundant in gold, silver and other metals, and produced in large quantities everything necessary for the support of man; that their system of government was to elect one of the above-mentioned bishops as governor of the country, whose powers were those of a king; that they had two hundred men trained as combatants; that the people were law-abiding, and went in fear of God.

"Wine, which was very plentiful, was sold by pint measures, and bread by weight, in the markets. The arms of the governing bishops consisted of a dragon on a flag surmounted by a cross, the dragon being encircled by a cobra; on the flag was also the figure of a saint on an ass, typical of the entry of Christ into Jerusalem, all painted on a blue ground, surrounded by fifteen castles in gold, painted on a crimson ground. Murderers were invariably put to death, lesser criminals being punished by transportation to certain settlements on the coast.

"The inhabitants possess a mine of salt, which they use. Their horses are the best in the world, and all provisions extremely wholesome; of these they have great abundance, and especially of vines."

Such is the account which we find repeated in the pages of Faria e Sousa, Frei Manoel dos Anjos, Pedro Medina, Bernardo de Brito, João Botero, Antonio Galvão, and other early Portuguese writers.

In the public library in Lisbon is to be seen a lengthy manuscript dated the 29th May, 1669, and signed by two Friars (Antonio de Jesus, and Francisco dos Martires) giving a most detailed and circumstantial account of a visit they made to this island in July, 1668, but as the whole narrative bears the imprint of fiction, and was doubtless based upon the above similarly apocryphal account of the Genoese, I abstain from reproducing it.

Such minute accounts, however false, could not but secure in those days many believers in the existence of Atlantis, or Sete Cidades—more especially so, as it figured on nearly all the early maps. We thus find it called Antilia on a map in the Weimar library, dated 1424; in Beccaria's map of 1435, in the library of Parma; also on that of Andréa Bianco, of 1436; similarly on the map of the Genoese Bartholomeo Pareto, of 1455; on that of Andréa Benincasa of 1476, in the library of Geneva; and, lastly, on the famous globe of Martin Behaim, accompanied by the following note:—
" When we go back to the year 734, after the birth of Christ, at the time when all Spain was invaded by the African infidels, the island Antilia, called Septe Cidade (the seven cities) figured below, became peopled by an archbishop of Oporto in Portugal, with six bishops and other Christian men and women, who had fled from Spain on board ship, and came there with their cattle and their fortunes. It was by accident that, in the year 1414, a Spanish vessel approached the island very closely."

Portugal was not the only country where such impositions were practised; in England, George Psalmanazar not only discovered (on paper) and minutely described the Island of

Formosa, but actually published a grammar of the language. His pretended discovery was implicitly believed in for a long time.

Again, so struck was the learned Budaeus with the reality of Sir Thomas More's Utopia, an island supposed to have been newly discovered in America, that he proposed to send out missionaries to convert the natives.

One of the singular beliefs of the Sebastianists is that Atlantis* still exists enchanted at the bottom of the sea, and that El Rei D. Sebastião resides on it. Some day, they think, the spell will be removed, when it will rise again above

---

* Compare Shakespeare's "Tempest," and his account of the Enchanted Island, and Bacon's " New Atlantis " :—" About twenty years after the ascension of our Saviour, it came to pass that there was seen by the people of Renfusa, a city upon the eastern coast of our island, within night (the night was cloudy and calm), as it might be some miles at sea, a great pillar of light, not sharp, but in form of a column or cylinder, rising from the sea, a great way up towards heaven, and on the top of it was seen a large cross of light, more bright and resplendent than the body of the pillar, upon which so strange a spectacle the people of the city gathered apace together upon the sands to wonder, and so after put themselves into a number of small boats to go nearer to this marvellous sight. But when the boats were come within about sixty yards of the pillar, they found themselves all bound, and could go no further, yet so as they might move to go about, but not approach nearer, so as the boats stood all as in a theatre, beholding this light as a heavenly sign." The Governor of the New Atlantis informs the strangers who arrive there that " three thousand years ago, or somewhat more, the navigation of the world, especially for remote voyages, was greater than at this day." He then proceeds to enumerate the different peoples whose ships had visited the New Atlantis, and continues: " And for our own ships, they went sundry voyages, as well to your Straits, which you call the Pillars of Hercules, as to other parts in the Atlantic and Mediterranean seas, as to Pegu, which is the same with Cambalu, and Quinsay upon the Oriental seas, as far as to the borders of East Tartary." The credulity and superstition of mariners are proverbial, and when the rage for maritime discovery was at its height, the reader has only to glance at the pages of Hakluyt, " Purchas his Pilgrims," or " The World's Hydrographical Description " by John Davis, for marvellous accounts of the earth and its inhabitants. It may be noted here, as a proof of the early enterprise of the Portuguese, that Hakluyt published in 1601 the discoveries of the world, from the First Original to the year of our Lord 1555, translated with additions, from the Portuguese of Antonio Galvano, Governor of Ternate, in the East Indies.

the waters, and restore this adventurous prince to his country and long expectant followers, as in the case of the Emperor Barbarossa, who never returned from an expedition to the Holy Land, and was also supposed to be enchanted in a vault under the Castle of Kyffhäusser—

> The splendour of the Empire
> He took with him away,
> And back to earth will bring it
> When dawns the chosen day.
>
> *Rücpert.*

The same belief would appear to have been shared in by our own people in early days, for we find the following inscription on King Arthur's gravestone :—

> Hic jacet Arturus, Rex quondam Rex que futurus.
> Here Arthur lies, who formerly
> Was king, and king again to be

A reflection of this Sabastianist belief still lingers amongst the inhabitants of St. Michael, for they firmly assert the existence of enchanted islands on its N.E. side, where they are said to occasionally appear in white, shadowy form. In Santa Maria, this tradition pictures a knight in armour appearing in ghostly shape, apparently sent to watch for all " female " islands which have once been disenchanted, and the nebulous apparitions to the north-east of St. Michael's are waiting for the disenchanted islands to become once more enchanted, that they may themselves break the chains which spell-bind them.

Chapter III.

We spread the canvas to the rising gales;
The gentle winds distend the snowy sails,
As from our dear-loved native shore we fly.
Our votive shouts, redoubled, rend the sky;
"Success! success!" far echoes o'er the tide,
While our broad hulks the foamy waves divide.

Mickle's " Camöens."

In 1387, Dom João I., king of Portugal, had married the Princess Phillippa, daughter of the Duke of Lancaster, "Old John of Gaunt," by which union there were born: Duarte, who succeeded to the throne on the death of his father; Pedro, the knight errant, of whom we are about to treat; Henrique, better known in England as Prince Henry the navigator, but as the "conquistador," or conqueror, in his own country, to whose energy and perseverance the colonization of the Açores is due; Isabel, afterwards Duchess of Burgundy, who, as we have seen, also assisted materially in the settlement of the islands, and the Princes João and Fernando.

Imbued with a strong desire to travel, Prince Pedro, who was one of the most enlightened men of the day, left Portugal with a suite of twelve persons in 1416, and journeying through Spain and other countries, reached the Holy Land, Constantnople, and Venice, visiting the courts of Hungary, Denmark and England, where Henry VI. received him with distinguished honour, conferring upon him the Order of the Garter, in place of the Duke of Exeter who had died in 1426.

Returning to Portugal in 1428, after an absence of twelve years wanderings, Prince Pedro carried with him to his native country the gift he had received from the Venetians, consisting of a MS. copy of the travels of Marco Polo, a translation of which was issued from the Lisbon press for the first time in 1502, together with a mappa mundi supposed to have been drawn by the great traveller, comprising the then known portions of the world, and from the evidence afforded us including the Western Islands. Stimulated by these valuable acquisitions, Prince Henry, whose lofty and ardent passion for discovery had never slumbered, and had received encouragement from his first discoveries of Porto Santo and Madeira, in 1418 to 1420, now determined to prosecute with energy the search for the islands in the west, which he had seen mentioned in the old charts. In the Portulano map of 1351 (on which the Açores already figured), the islands of Porto Santo and Madeira are laid down as the "Isola de lo Legname," or island of wood (Madeira in Portuguese also means wood or timber), "Porto Santo," and "Isole Deserte," names which the Portuguese preserved. Accordingly in 1431, the Prince directed an expedition to be fitted out under Goncalo Velho Cabral, with orders "to sail towards the setting sun until he came to an island." These words, used by Candido Lusitano, in his "Life of Prince Henry," imply a prior knowledge on the part of that Prince of an island or islands in the west, and go far to confirm the supposition that he was already in possession of a map on which their geographical situation was marked.

Antonio Galvão also mentions that Francisco de Souza Tavares told him that in 1528 the Infante D. Fernando had shown him a map found in the archives of Alcobaça, drawn more than 170 years before, and which contained all the "navigation" of India together with the Cape of Good Hope. That this must have been the map the Prince Dom Pedro had brought with him from Venice appears very likely, for Candido Lusitano, writing on this very subject, says that Prince Henry was heard to observe that the existence of São Miguel tallied exactly with the islands noted in his ancient map.

From the foregoing, it is evident that the date of the first discovery of the Azores, or who the actual discoverers were, must ever remain a *quæstio vexata*; to Prince Henry of Portugal, however, must be awarded the credit of laying down with precision their situation, and of ultimately colonizing them by means of his own private resources.

The vessels sailed from Villa de Sagres in the Algarve, with instructions to bear due west, and, on the tenth day, the voyagers came upon a rugged group of rocks, amid foaming breakers, which they named the Formigas, or Ants; the largest of these, forming a small bay, offered them temporary shelter; but, unable to descry* further signs of land in any direction, Cabral returned chagrined and disappointed to Lisbon. Prince Henry, however, only heard in this narrative a confirmation of his enthusiastic hopes, and despatching a larger and better appointed flotilla in the following year, under the same leader, was amply rewarded for his perseverance; for, on the 15th August, 1432, Cabral bore down upon and landed on the western part of a large and well-wooded island, which he found uninhabited. In commemoration of the day, he named it Santa Maria. Quickly returning to Lisbon with the welcome news, Prince Henry at once conferred on Cabral the lordship of the island, and sending a vessel with cattle and various domestic animals to be let loose upon it, he commanded Cabral to prepare for its complete colonization, which was effected three years later, most of the nobility and leading families supplying representatives and vassals to people the new country. Thus was Portugal's first step firmly planted on this beautiful archipelago.

On the so-called Catalan map of Gabriel de Valseca, dated 1439, the entire group of these islands is laid down, accompanied by what amounts to a certificate of good sea-

---

* The Formigas are distant from Retorta Point, St. Michael's, 33 nautical miles, and to those who have frequently seen Santa Maria from that Island on a clear day with the naked eye, it would seem strange that Cabral, having reached those rocks, should have failed to discover either of the above islands on this first voyage, but at that period they were covered with dense forests over which masses of cloud were perpetually attracted and probably shrouded the highlands from view.

manship on the part of Cabral's pilot, Diego de Sevill, who is said to have *found* the islands, but considerable doubts exist as to their having *all* been visited by him during these earlier expeditions.

In those days, Portugal bestowed upon the original discoverers and colonizers of countries annexed to her Crown the lordships of them, with the title of Capitão Donatario. This post was held in high esteem, as, besides the emoluments attaching to it, the fortunate holder was given plenary powers, which secured him almost despotic sway. These royal decrees or alvaras, as they were called, provided that the Donatarios should have jurisdiction over the civil and criminal courts, wherein the strict letter of the law was to be enforced in all cases excepting death, or the severing of limbs, which prerogatives alone belonged to the Crown.

All mandates issuing from the Donatarios were to be everywhere respected, and a tithe of all taxes levied appertained to them; they were granted the monopoly of the sale of salt, owned all the corn mills and baking ovens, for the use of which contributions in kind were made by the community. Under their sanction only could the cattle and other animals, which had become wild, be appropriated by the colonists, and, finally, they had power of making grants of uncultivated land to whomsoever they pleased, on condition of its being occupied by the settler within five years.

Their privileges were hereditary and descended to the lineal successors of those to whom they were granted; provision being made for regencies in the case of minors.

No wonder then that such comprehensive powers, making of the Donatario a sort of sub-regulus, soon excited court favorites to intrigue for these sinecures, until, culminating in subsequent reigns to a scandalous pitch of abuse and extortion, the time-honoured office was abolished by the Spaniards during their temporary usurpation of the Crown of Portugal, from 1580 to 1640, when these islands also fell under the Spanish yoke.

Chapter IV.

Santa Maria—The Earl of Cumberland—Christopher Columbus—Natural
Features—Products and Manufactures.

> In gowns of white, as sentenced felons clad,
> When to the stake the sons of guilt are led,
> With feet unshod, they slowly moved along.
>
> *Mickle's " Camöens."*

Santa Maria is situated in lat. 36° 56′ north, and long. 25° 12′ west of Greenwich.

It is about seven miles in its greatest, and five miles in its smallest diameter, and contains about 27,000 English acres.

At first sight, it presents a marked physical contrast to the adjacent islands in the absence of those bowl-shaped monticules, the unmistakeable indications of volcanic eruptions, which characterise the latter at every step. On close examination, however, we find a basaltic base and general trap formation, which, with the curious caves in different localities, tell of igneous origin.

The severe earthquakes, which at various periods have wrought such desolation upon some of the other islands, have seldom, if ever, been felt here. This would seem to place Santa Maria outside the focus of these destructive forces. In many localities, the soil consists entirely of patches of a deep red argil, known as *Pozzolana*, a volcanic production much used for making hydraulic cement.*

In exploring the geology of this island, the most interesting features encountered, chiefly on the east side, and at

---

* There are many formulas used, one of the best being—1 part blue lias lime : 2 parts sand ; 2 parts pozzolana : the mixture hardening under water in less than fifteen hours.

Figueiral, Meio-Moio, and Papagaio, are veins of a hard, brittle calcareous rock, rich in fossils of marine mollusca, of a by-gone age, excellent specimens of which are exhibited at the museum of Ponta Delgada. Hartung found and described twenty-three of these, of which eight appear to be identical with existing species; twelve are referred to European tertiary forms (chiefly Upper Miocene), the rest being new species. One of these, *Cardium Hartungi*, is common in Porto Santo, and Baixo. These layers of lime-stone are about 20 feet thick, resting upon, and again covered by, basaltic lavas, scoriæ, and conglomerates.

Like all the other islands of the Açores, Santa Maria, when first discovered, was densely wooded, and the soil for many years produced the richest cereal crops in the whole archipelago; now, except in the valleys, there are few trees to be seen, and these are limited to the candleberry myrtle (*Myrica Faya*), Louro (*Laurus indica*), and Pao branco (*Picconia excelsa*). There are few orange trees, their cultivation being unremunerative, though the quality of fruit is excellent, as indeed is that of every other kind of fruit or vegetable grown here. In the ravines, intermixed with ferns, may be seen the *Phormium Tenax*, or New Zealand flax plant, growing wild and luxuriant.

The loftiest points in the island are Pico Alto, 1,900 feet; Pico do Sul, 1,720 feet; and Pico do Facho, 780 feet high.

That the altitudes of this and the other islands have, since the Miocene period, when they are supposed to have emerged, lost much through constant denudation, seems certain, for valleys have been rendered level with higher ground and once fertile hills reduced into stony heaps by this powerful agent.

It is estimated that the mean altitude of Europe is 671 feet, and that from simple denudation alone the continent would be worn down to sea level in about two million years. Judging from the disintegrating influences their surfaces are ever exposed to, nothing would seem to be able to arrest the much more rapid disappearance of these bare islands, save complete re-forestation or the great upheaval confidently predicted by the late Mr. Darwin, which is slowly in process in these seas.*

Owing to its southerly position and its bare highlands, Santa Maria is frequently visited with drought. In the summer of 1876 all the crops were lost and the inhabitants were driven to great straits, exporting nearly all their cattle to obtain the bare necessaries of life. Many of them, unable to subsist upon the scanty food procurable, emigrated in large numbers to Brazil.

The year 1881-82 was again a bad one, during which 6,172 quarters of maize were imported, the island not having produced sufficient for consumption.

Originally from Estremadura and Algarve, in the south of Portugal, the inhabitants are honest and extremely gentle, and preserve in a greater degree than any of the other Azoreans the singular phonetic characteristics of the Portuguese language of the Mediæval ages, which, though not without certain euphony, is nevertheless a source of considerable amusement to their more progressive brethren on the adjoining islands, who cannot reconcile its soft musical sounds with their own much harsher and cacophonous speech of to-day. On this account they enjoy the sobriquet of " Cagaros," and are considered the " Johnny Raws " of the Açores.

The climate of Santa Maria is equable and exceedingly pleasant, and were it not for the utter absence of accommodation and society, its greater immunity from moisture and damp mists would suit it beyond any of the

* As an instance of the serious damage caused by the heavy rains in these islands, I may mention that during the stormy winter of 1880-81 many of the chief Macadamised thoroughfares in the district of Ponta Delgada in St. Michael, equal to the best roads on the continent, were absolutely cleared of their foundations, the débris being carried long distances until reaching the sea, rendering the roads impassible and forming ruts and cavities, in some places 17 feet in depth, which cost the municipality £2,150 to repair.

others as a winter resort for invalids subject to pulmonary disorders.

The chief town is named Porto, and is picturesquely situated on rising ground overlooking the small bay of Santa Luzia, once defended by three now delapidated forts, mounting some 30 guns, which were necessary to repel the frequent attacks of Algerine* pirates and French corsairs who infested these seas in the 16th century.

The most noticeable of these occurred on the 5th August, 1576, when 300 Frenchmen landing from their galleys during the night, completely routed the surprised and badly armed inhabitants, many of whom were put to the sword. After sacking the town, the marauders made off with their booty. Another attack was made 13 years later by four large and powerfully armed French cruisers; but this time the islanders were better prepared, and under the leadership of their Donatario, Bras Soares, made a gallant resistance, beating off the assailants with the loss of their captain and many of his followers, and greatly damaging their ships.

In the autumn of 1598, the Earl of Cumberland and the celebrated Captain Lister were cruising about these islands, and approaching St. Mary with the intention of obtaining water for their ships, discovered two Spanish vessels laden with sugar from Brazil lying at anchor close in shore; these, Captain Lister immediately proceeded to cut out, losing in the operation two men killed and sixteen wounded—one of the ships however could not be got off, when the Earl himself undertook the task, and, underrating his enemy, lost in killed and wounded eighty men. "The Earl received three shot upon his target, and a fourth on the side not deepe, his head also broken with stones that the blood

---

* The seizure of Constantinople by the Turks in 1453, and the success everywhere attending their arms, caused the Algerine Moors to redouble their piratical expeditions in these waters, demanding unceasing vigilance on the part of the islanders to repel sudden attacks.

covered his face, both it and his legs likewise burned with fire balls." *

In 1493 Santa Maria had the honour of receiving Christopher Columbus under rather peculiar circumstances. On returning from his first discovery of Hispaniola, or Hayti, his caravel, the " Niña," was overtaken by so terrible a storm in mid Atlantic, as to imperil the safety of the gallant little vessel. The intercession of the Virgin having been invoked, the pious navigator and the whole of his crew made a vow that, should they be saved, they would on reaching land walk bare-headed and bare-footed, and with no clothing on save their shirts, to offer thanksgiving at the nearest shrine.

Driven by the storm under the lee of Santa Maria, on the 17th February, Columbus sent one-half of the ship's company on shore, headed by a priest, to fulfil their promise, but the Governor, Dom João de Castanheda, a plain, unsophisticated being, apprised of the unwonted procession, and probably resenting the singular garb, especially in the depth of winter, as an insult to the æsthetics of Santa Maria, ordered the whole of the pious pilgrims, whom he took for a piratical band, to be arrested; meanwhile, a strong wind and sea rising, the " Niña " was forced to slip anchor, and is supposed to have reached S. Miguel, but being unable to find shelter there, returned to her former position on the 22nd, when Columbus held a parley with the Governor, and exhibiting his commission, was able to appease his fears, and obtain the release of his followers. It is said, however, that Castanheda had previously received secret orders from his sovereign to seize the person of Columbus, should he call at the island, and send him a prisoner to Lisbon to be punished for transferring his services and discoveries to the King of Spain; but the wily captain, suspecting treachery, declined to trust himself ashore. The " Niña " finally sailed from the inhospitable island on the 24th February. In the town is a large parish church, the religious orders having been

* Purchas.

represented by three huge convents and a Franciscan monastery, to which belonged the most fertile lands in the island ; these buildings are now mostly occupied as public offices.

The Formigas rocks, about 20 miles to the north-east of the island, offer in calm weather a pleasant excursion by sea, with the additional excitement of capturing a somnolent turtle on the way, or having a shot at a large species of seal (*Phocula Leporina*), which at certain seasons of the year resorts to these rocks.

Almost all of them abound with an esculent mollusk, called by the natives Craca, but known to science as *Balanus tintinnabulum*—plainly boiled, and eaten with the indian corn bread of the country, they form an epicurean feast. It is no easy matter, however, to procure them, for the shells cling so tenaciously to the rocks, that portions of these have to be broken and brought away before the succulent delicacies can be secured ; the natives say that the best are those on which " the sun has never shone."

For domestic purposes there is abundance of water, a perennial spring rising in the very crest of the highest point in the island (an inaccessible rock near Monte Gordo) and dashes with mad career over its rugged sides, forming beautiful cascades on its way to the sea, into which it finally tumbles from over the entrance to a romantic cave, which extends for half a mile into the interior.

Another extensive cavern is nearly one hundred yards in length, and in some places upwards of forty feet high, with lateral branches radiating in all directions and presenting a beautiful sight when lighted up by torches, owing to the numerous pensile incrustations on the roof and sides, gleaming like gems. These stalactites are of calcareous formation, and if undisturbed, assume fantastic shapes, but Vandal raids are now and then made upon them for ornamental rock-work.

In these caves is found a soft, grey earthy deposit, much used by the natives for bleaching purposes.

Several other islets stud the coast, and were formerly the resort of innumerable sea-birds, the eggs of which furnished the old colonists with an important item of food.

The first settlers introduced quail and the red-legged partridge from Portugal, both being now common, and with rabbits and rock pigeons, the latter abounding along the high and inaccessible cliffs, afford capital sport, rendered none the less enjoyable, perhaps, by the physical difficulties of the country which the sportsman has in many places to overcome.

Education is much neglected here, there being barely four elementary schools for boys and one for girls, but even these are poorly attended. The trade of the island is insignificant, the average produce of pulse of all kinds being limited to some 6,000 to 7,000 quarters, and allowing little margin for export. Formerly some 200 boxes of oranges were made up, but these are now reduced to less than half, and are never exported.

The inhabitants have for many years manufactured a common pottery for kitchen purposes, the chief merit of which consists in the graceful amphora shapes of many of the vessels made; these they export to the neighbouring islands, where it is a curious sight to see a large boat arrive from Santa Maria with a huge centre pile of this crockery, the articles being simply placed one upon the other without any packing, yet seldom does any breakage occur.

These vessels are painted, before being baked, with a coating of red ochre, thinly diluted in water, which imparts to them a bright colour and lustre. The clay used is exported to several of the other islands.

The total value of the exports and imports during the years 1881 to 1884 were as follows :—

	1881-2.	1882-3.	1883-4.
Imports ..	£7,792 ..	£5,338 ..	£5,030
Exports ..	4,673 ..	5,661 ..	5,122

The average annual fiscal receipts amount to £1,335, and the total expenditure to £1,348.

The chief exports are wheat, sometimes maize and barley, and from 200 to 300 head of cattle every year, as well as cheeses, butter, eggs, fowls, turkeys, and live partridges.

Some of the best horses in the Açores are bred here, and the cattle are also large and fine-looking animals; they were originally imported from the south of Portugal, and are remarkable for the immense length of their horns. In winter, when green fodder is scarce, cattle are given, and seem to enjoy, the young leaves of the aloe—*agave americana*—which everywhere abounds. This practice also obtains in the Algarve, in localities where pasture is scarce.

CHAPTER V.

Pharos (loquitur) :

> Far in the bosom of the deep,
> O'er these wild shelves my watch I keep ;
> A ruddy gem of changeful light,
> Bound on the dusky brow of night,
> The seaman bids my lustre hail,
> And scorns to strike his timorous sail.
>
> *Sir W. Scott.*

THE cluster of rocks first sighted by Cabral, and named by him the Formigas, or Ants, is situated to the north-east of the island of Santa Maria, at a distance of about 20 miles from Matos.

They are the crests of a submarine mountain which Captain Vidal, R.N., traced to a depth of 200 fathoms, extending $6\frac{1}{2}$ miles from N.W. to S.E., by about 3 miles in breadth. It is on the western margin of this bank that the Formigas occur, occupying a space of 800 yards in length, and 150 yards in breadth.

The southernmost of them, which is 27 feet above low water springs, affords some slight shelter in a bay on the west ; it is in latitude 37° 16′ 14″ north, longitude 24° 47′ .06′ west. The highest, known as the Formigão, or Great Ant, rises out of the ocean like a grim ghost on the eastern side of this bank to a height of 35 feet. The fused calcareous veins, so full of fossil shells, which abound on the east coast of St. Mary's, are also found in the Formigas.

Three and a quarter miles to the S.E. of these occurs a shoal, named Dollabarets, from Captain P. Dollabarets, who first called attention to it in 1788. These rocks are tabular shaped, and at low-water springs have only 11 feet of water on them; they are, therefore, more dangerous in calm than in stormy weather, when the seas break over them.

Cabral had already observed these rocks in 1431, for he called them the Lesser Formigas, and noted them as extremely dangerous, not only because of their shallow depth, but on account of the strong currents between their channels.

During the fierce storms which torment these seas in winter, not only the Dollabarets, but the Formigas, are buried in cataracts of foam; haze and fog contributing to canopy them from view.

If these barren rocks could speak, what a ghastly tale of woe they would reveal! It seems certain that they have been the scene of frequent and fatal wrecks, from which not a soul has survived. Oftentimes floating spars and other portions of wreck and cargo are carried to the neighbouring shores—the silent but certain tokens of some such occurrence; but it is seldom that a boat's crew has preceded or followed them.

It is astonishing that in latitudes like these, so much frequented by ships of all nationalities, not a single lighthouse should have been erected for their protection on any of these perilous rocks. The conscience of Portugal, however, to whom the task properly belongs, would seem at last to have been partly awakened by the reproach of repeated fatalities, for in 1882 a commission was appointed to study the question of lighthouses for the Azores, the result of which was an elaborate report recommending the establishment of three lights at Santa Maria, one on Formigão, the largest of the Formigas rocks, five for San Michael's, three each for Graciosa, Terceira, San Jorge and Fayal, one for Pico, three for Flores, and two for Corvo; the estimated cost of these, including buildings, &c., amounting to £63,437, but up to the present, with the exception of two lights at

St. Michael's, and one at Fayal, little has been done to carry into effect the recommendation of the commission.

These are the only dangerous rocks around the Azores, with the exception of a recently-formed ridge just perceptible on the surface of the sea, almost in mid-channel between S. Miguel and Terceira, and occupying a space of some nine miles in a direction N.W., S.E., and in lat. N. 38° 16′, and between longitudes 26° 41′ and 26° 50′ W. of Greenwich.

This shoal would seem to have been observed in 1749, but it disappeared shortly afterwards until 1882-3, when it again rose—without, however, any previous eruption. It would be interesting to closely watch this apparent elevation of the land, and the vicissitudes which it undergoes.

MAP OF

Chapter VI.

> Thou hast a cloud
> For ever in thy sky ; a breeze, a shower
> For ever on thy meads. Yet where shall man,
> Pursuing spring around the globe, refresh
> His eye with scenes more beauteous than adorn
> Thy fields of matchless verdure ?—*Carrington*.

The first discovery of the island of St. Michael's is
shrouded in complete obscurity ; neither do we know anything of the brave adventurers who first approached its
shores.

Writing of the island, Padre Freire, in his Life of D.
Henrique, says that Prince Henry remarked that its discovery "concordava com os seus antigos mappas," *i.e.*,
agreed with the ancient maps in his possession.

Cordeiro mentions a tradition of a Greek vessel surprised
at Cadiz by a storm about the year 1370, and carried as far as
San' Miguel. Her owner wished to colonize it, and returned
the following year with that intention, but being unable to
again make the island, abandoned the idea. Andrea Bianco,
in his map of 1436, gave the name of Mar de Baga to the Sea
of Sargasso, near the northern border of which the Azores are
situated ; this tends to prove that the Portuguese, prior to
1436, had navigated as far as the Sea of Sargasso, or Baga, as
they called it, otherwise whence was the name derived ? The
vesicles of marine algæ* are like berries or bagos—especially

---

* Quantities of these algæ are, at certain seasons of the year, washed ashore at
Graciosa, particularly at a place called Gruta do Manhengo. The inhabitants
come there from all parts of the island, working day and night, to collect all they
can, the weed containing much potash and soda, and being a rich fertilizer.

those of *Fucus natans*, *F. vericulosus* and *F. bacciferus*, of which the Sea of Sargasso is so largely formed, and which induced the early navigators to call it "Mar de Baga," a purely Portuguese name.

A curious document exists in the archives of the Torre do Tombo, in Lisbon, being a decree of Affonso V., dated the 10th April, 1455, granting a free pardon to Catharina Fernandez, who had been banished some ten years previously, when only a child of 10 or 11 years of age, to the island of "Ssam Miguell" for complicity in some aggravated crime; inferring that the island must have been colonized some time before its reputed discovery in 1444.

That seven out of the nine islands composing the group were known to the Portuguese prior to that date, seems certain, for another decree of D. Affonso, bearing date the 2nd July, 1439, grants permission to his uncle, Prince Henry, to people these seven islands; unfortunately their names are not given, but undoubtedly they were the seven nearest to Portugal, and included all but Corvo and Flores. It is not until fourteen years later that mention is made for the first time of these extreme westerly islands in a decree of the same king, dated the 20th January, 1453, in which he makes grant of Corvo to the Duke of Braganza. It must, therefore, have been between 1449 and 1453* that these two islands were discovered; but so little was known of the archipelago, that in Pedro Appiano's Cosmography, dated 1524, only seven islands of the Açores were mentioned.

Cabral first landed at S. Miguel on the 8th May, 1444, and he returned again with settlers on the 29th September of the same year. It was in the interval between these two dates that the great eruption occurred at the Sete Cidades, mentioned in another place.

It is strange that the spirit of enterprise which dis-

---

* The Portuguese historians fix the date at 1452, and assign the discovery to João de Teive.

tinguished the Portuguese at this epoch, should have rested satisfied with the bald discovery of the one island of Santa Maria, for, although only 44 miles of channel separated it from the neighbouring and larger one of S. Miguel, it took the pioneers fully twelve years before they apparently became aware of its existence; notwithstanding that, during this interval vessels were constantly passing to and fro, bearing a constant influx of new settlers and supplies from the mother country to the isolated but salubrious and fertile colony.

The task of further search was once more committed to Cabral, who, after several vain attempts, at last succeeded in sighting the island on the 8th May, 1444, and, in celebration of the day, named it San Miguel. Landing at a spot on the S.E. side, encircled by a small bay, now known as Povoação, the adventurers penetrated as far into the interior as the thick bushwood and virgin forest permitted, and after collecting what emblems they could of its natural productions, set sail for Lisbon.

Like all the other islands of the group, not a trace of the former presence of man was found in San Miguel by its Portuguese discoverers, and no records have been met with of the time " when wild in woods the noble savage ran." Nevertheless, this island, like Corvo, enjoys its myth of ancient monuments.

André Thevet, cosmographer to Henry III. of France, records in his work published in 1575 a visit he paid to the island of S. Miguel, about the year 1550, and mentions the existence, on the basaltic cliffs on the north side of the island, between Santo Antonio and Bretanha, of caves wherein the first inhabitants found "two monuments of stone, twelve feet in length, and four and a half broad, on which were sculptured the forms of two large snakes, and inscriptions recognised to be in Hebrew characters by a man, a native of Spain, whose father was a Jew, his mother

E

being a Moorish woman. This man was unable to interpret the inscriptions, owing to their being so obliterated by time. He, however, made a copy of them, and Thevet illustrates them in his cosmography, where he proceeds to say that so many people, visiting the caves out of curiosity, lost their lives in them, as to cause the authorities to have the entrance closed up with stone and lime.

This account is held by the islanders as altogether fallacious; but it seems strange that Thevet, who undoubtedly visited S. Miguel about 1550, should have needlessly invented it. The only feasible explanation is, that he must either have heard of, or viewed, the very singular superimposed caves near Relva (so graphically described by Dr. Webster in his book on the island),* on entering which, visitors are cautioned against falling down a deep and narrow cleft, which cuts the upper gallery in two, the ancient monuments of stone having been thrown in by the fanciful Frenchman to spice his narrative.

To secure to his master possession of the country, Cabral formed a small settlement (at Povoação), consisting of a few of his friends and some African slaves whom he had taken for the purpose, giving them instructions to test the fertility of the soil. These poor people were destined to be the terrified witnesses of, perhaps, the most awful cataclysm which has ever overtaken these islands, and by the evidence they were able to give to establish an important date in their ceismic annals which would otherwise have been lost.

S. Miguel, at this time, presented a remarkable appearance

---

* In Purchas' (4th vol., 1625) " Relation of Master Thomas Turner, who lived the best part of two years in Brazil, and which I received of him in conference, touching his travels." Turner, who appears from a description he gives of the hot springs at Furnas, to have visited St. Miguel, says—" In these islands (Açores) in caves were found men buried before the conquest, whole." But, as no " conquest " was ever made of these islands, Turner probably confounded them with the Canaries, where he had perhaps also been, the original inhabitants of which, conquered by the Spaniards, were in the habit of burying their dead in caves.

by reason of two great mountains which, at either of its eastern and western extremities, like two watchful giants, reared their cusps high up into the clouds, forming conspicuous landmarks, and being the beacons which had guided Cabral to their shores. How shall we describe his amazement when, on returning with a numerous following a year later, and in the capacity of Donatario of the joint islands of St. Mary and St. Michael, he saw that the largest of these, on the western side of the island, had totally disappeared, and in its place nothing remained but a circular and apparently hollow cone !

Sailing nearer, the navigators came upon fields of floating pumice and immense trunks of trees. Slowly continuing their course, they arrived at their old settlement of Povoação on the 29th September, 1445, and were hailed with joy by their friends. From them Cabral learnt that four months previously the island had been convulsed by repeated shocks of earthquake, and that almost immediately on the cessation of these, flames of fire had appeared on the summit of the western mountain, which then commenced to vomit forth large stones and to cover the island with hot ashes, until the mass gradually disappeared from sight. These revelations, and the earnest entreaties of the affrighted settlers to be removed from the island, cast consternation into the ranks of Cabral's followers ; but, true to his mission, the gallant navigator commanded all the stores to be landed, and sending away his ships, prepared for its colonization.

From Povoação smaller settlements soon segregated throughout the island, until one of these, situated near the present site of Villa Franca on the south-east coast and offering greater natural advantages, was selected as the chief and capital town, taking the name of Villa Franca do Campo, and becoming the residence of the Donatario, under whose protecting ægis the other villages remained for over seventy-eight years, during which interval no volcanic eruptions or earthquakes of note are chronicled.

Villa Franca, or the Free Town, enjoyed, as its name implies, at this time, certain privileges and exemptions, amongst others complete immunity from fiscal contributions; and, being the seat of Government, it naturally attracted many residents. Its spacious though exposed harbour enabled it to carry on an important trade with the other coast settlements, and we find it, in 1522, a flourishing community of over 5,000 inhabitants.

The immutable decree of fate had, however, been sealed against the devoted town, for, on the morning of the 22nd of October of the above-mentioned year, shortly before day-break, and in the midst of perfect stillness,

> Like that strange silence which precedes the storm,
> And shakes the forest leaves without a breath,

a terrific earthquake suddenly rent the earth, and, upheaving a high hill, which stood to the north of Villa Franca, at a distance of some 450 yards, hurled the mass with irresistible force upon the hapless place, which was completely destroyed. In its ruins perished 5,000 souls, only seventy escaping the fatal catastrophe.

So suddenly did all this happen, and without any premonitory warning, that, from the time the crash was first heard to the moment of the entire demolition of the place, only sixty seconds are said to have elapsed.

This terrible " deluvio de terra," or earth deluge, as the old writers call it, does not appear to have been accompanied by any volcanic eruption, but volumes of water subsequently issuing from the site of the demolished hill, and forming impetuous streams, inundated the country around, and with destructive force, carried everything before them.

The sea, too, filled up the vial of horrors, for a great tidal wave, leaping high up the shore, threatened it with total submersion.

Some half-dozen caravels lying at anchor off the town narrowly escaped foundering, and the effects of the shock were felt far out at sea, in a south-east direction, by the crew of a vessel proceeding to Madeira.

Four shocks of lesser violence succeeded the first, at intervals of two or three hours, and seemed to have travelled from Ponta Delgada in the south, round the eastern side of the island as far as Maia in the north, where several serious landslips occurred. In the valley of the Furnas, a land wave carried huge cedar trees on its crest, and deposited them a considerable distance away. The loss of life at these various places, then sparsely populated, amounted to nearly forty, but the destruction of property, churches, and other buildings was considerable. As soon as the terror-stricken survivors and inhabitants of the neighbouring villages ventured to approach what was now a dreary solitude, where not a vestige of the once flourishing Villa Franca remained, endeavours were made to save what lives still existed, buried beneath the ruins; some few were thus recovered, but of these many were bereft of reason; others had lost all power of speech, whilst, in singular contrast to the surrounding chaos, a little child three years old was found playing with fragments of *débris* that had buried alive her parents hard by. The excavations continued for upwards of a year, the devotion of the survivers sacrificing everything to afford the remains of the victims Christian burial.

We are told that when this search had been nearly completed, the excavators came upon the skeleton of a mounted horseman, with spurs still fixed, and lance poised just as he had been engulphed and mired whilst wending his way into the country.

Undismayed by what had befallen the old town, and probably prompted by additional exemptions conferred upon them by the executive, the survivors proceeded to rebuild a new town, almost upon the ruins of the old one, which, Phœnix-like, soon outvied the older settlement. It now contains upwards of 5,000 inhabitants, and is second only to Ponta Delgada in importance.

Scarcely had the sufferings caused by the great earth-quake been appeased, than another dire visitation befel these poor islanders in the form of a fatal plague, which, accidentally introduced from abroad, in the summer of 1523, committed terrible ravages, and, during the eight years of its duration, decimated the inhabitants of Ponta Delgada and Ribeira Grande. In the former no less than 2,000 persons died; the losses in the latter amounting to more than 1,000, besides great numbers of Negro slaves.

The evil results of slavery, which at this time became rampant in Portugal, and had crept into her colonies (every-where producing a vitiated condition of society, sapping the energies of an industrious people, and intensifying their baser qualities), had been slowly bringing these once virtuous islanders under its baneful influences. To such a pitch had the evil extended, that, in 1531, the Negro population, in many places, far outnumbered the European.

Fearing a revolt and the ascendency of the Blacks (who had the sympathy of, and were instigated, it was said, by the Lusitanian Moors, who had found an asylum in the island), and led on by an ignorant and brutal priesthood, who attributed the recent successive calamities to the anger of an incensed heaven at the presence of these heathens, the frenzied islanders were easily induced to enter upon a war of race and supremacy, in the course of which every male Negro and Arab was savagely massacred—an ignoble deed, which must ever remain a stain in the history of these eminently peaceful people.

It is owing to the presence of these slaves for so long a period, and the introduction of half-breeds from the Brazils, that so many prognathous types are met with amongst the inhabitants of Portugal and her dependencies.

The Marquis of Pombal, the greatest minister Portugal ever had, and the man who dared, during a bigoted and priest-ridden time, to expel the Jesuits from the country, had the courage also, in 1773, to decree the abolition of slavery throughout Portugal and the Colonies, but the corrupt condition into which society had drifted never allowed the enactment to be entirely carried out, and, on the great minister's fall from power, slavery became for a time, as regnant as ever.

As an example of the brisk trade carried on in human flesh, especially during the Spanish interregnum in these islands, we find records of Gonçalo Coutinho, the Governor of St. Michael, contracting with the Spanish Government for the introduction of 4,240 African slaves every year into the Brazilian Colony. This contract was to hold good for nine years, commencing in 1603, the Government receiving a capitation tax in consideration of the same, amounting to 140,000 ducats. A similar privilege had been held by a brother of this Governor, João R. Coutinho, up to 1602, when he died, the Spanish Government receiving as consideration 162,000 ducats. Thus we see that, during the eighteen years of which these contracts treat, no less than 76,320 slaves were conveyed from African ports to the Brazils.

In 1585, two British cruisers, entering the roads of Ponta Delgada, surprised a Portuguese vessel full of African slaves, whom they at once liberated.

According to the inventory of Jacome Dias Corrêa, a wealthy landowner of Fenaes, and dated 1543, we find that the price of slaves in S. Miguel at that time was as follows:

Black slaves and mulattoes, from 17$ to 20$000
Slaves of two years of age   ..   ..   4$000
A mulatta of 12 years ..   ..   ..   10$000

Mares were then worth 4$000; fillies from 1$000 to 2$000; bulls 3$000; cows in calf 1$300.

During the reigns of John I. (1385), Affonso V. (1438), and Sebastian (1557), immense numbers of lives were lost in the sieges of Ceuta and other Moorish strongholds; so much so, that the latter prince was only able by force to get together 11,000 men for his last unfortunate expedition.

It was to replace these men, as labourers in the fields

and for domestic purposes, that Negroes were first imported in large numbers into Portugal, and, in 1521, threatened to outnumber the native population. We find Garcia de Resende lamenting this state of things in a couplet in his " Miscellanea " thus :—

> Vemos no reyno metter,
> Tantos cativos crescer,
> E irem-se os naturaes
> Que se assim for, serão mais
> Elles que nòs a meu ver.

> (We see brought into the realm
> So many captives increase,
> I fear they will us o'erwhelm,
> If this don't speedily cease.)

The following official figures, derived from the Portuguese customs records, give some idea of the extent of the traffic in human flesh from African ports to Brazil and Spanish Colonies, from the year 1807 to 1819, when English cruisers first checked the trade :—

Shipments to Brazil	680,000	
„ Spanish Colonies	615,000	2,194,000
„ other places ..	562,000	
Loss during voyage	337,000	

From 1819 to 1847 :—

Shipments to Brazil	1,122,000	
„ Spanish Colonies	831,000	2,758,000
Loss during voyage	688,000	
Captured by cruisers	117,000	

Total from 1807 to 1847 4,952,000

CHAPTER VII.

A shore so flowery, and so sweet an air,
Venus might build her dearest temple there.

"*Camöens.*"

A GLANCE at the physical character of the island of S. Miguel marks it as the very focus and theatre of igneous activity in this region. Everywhere around are evidences of this in the truncated cones of all dimensions, the scarped and deeply furrowed sides of which, with their immense concavities, tell of the awful power which gave them birth.

All about the sloping flanks of these "basal wrecks" are clearly discernible the regular furrows, in places forming dark ravines, hollowed out by the flowing lava, and constantly deepened by erosion and heavy rains.

In the interior of these cones are precipices 2,000 feet in depth, into which the spectator peers with awe and admiration at the wild grandeur and indescribable beauty of the scene, for, as if regretting her work, and desirous of hiding all evidences of the barren desolation which must have pervaded these spots, nature has clothed these once gloomy wastes in a mantle of rich verdure up to their very summits.

The earliest account we have of volcanic eruptions in this island is of the one which, in 1445, completely destroyed the highest eminence it boasted, situated in its western extremity, leaving in its place a hollow crater upwards of four geographical miles in circumference, with a concavity measuring at its base one and a quarter geographical miles in diameter. The lips of this gigantic cone were ascertained by Capt. Vidal, R.N., who made a careful survey of all these islands in 1844, to be 1,880 feet high on the western side.

At the bottom are two lakes, separated by a narrow neck of land, and remarkable for the striking contrast of the colour of their waters. Seen from above, the larger one, or Lagoa Grande, is of a bright emerald, and the smaller one, or Lagoa Azul, of a deep cerulean hue. They are 866 feet above the sea level, and their depth varies from 1 to 14 fathoms. On the northern side of the Lagoa Grande, however, there is a spot where the depth attains 58 fathoms, and was evidently one of the " funnels" through which the molten mass poured.

On the north-west side is a great gap in the cone, the walls of which are 1,620 and 1,770 feet high, down which a stream of lava flowed into the sea.

There is abundant and unmistakable evidence that, at a still more distant period, the eastern side of the island, at the spot now occupied by the valley of the Furnas, as well as other localities, must have been the scene of violent dislocations. Unfortunately, no means are afforded us of ascertaining the precise dates of these.

Shocks and eruptions subsequent to those of 1445 and 1522, occurring at irregular intervals of from ten to twenty years down to the present time, appear to have gradually lessened in intensity, as if the mighty agency which caused them were slowly dying out. The history of Vesuvius, however, and of the volcanoes of Iceland and South America, which, after even centuries of complete quiescence, have broken out afresh with devastating energy, warn us that the " Ides of March" are not yet passed here, and that the terrible forces, now apparently inert, may at any moment break out again with renewed fury.

In 1538, a submarine eruption occurred on a shoal off the extreme north-west point of S. Miguel, known as Ponta da Ferraria, where an islet was formed, measuring over three miles in circumference. It subsided, and altogether disappeared at the expiration of twenty-five days, leaving a bank at a depth of 490 feet, and at a distance of about three miles from the shore.

The year 1563 was rich in disaster. Owing to the lengthened period over which the various occurrences extended, some slight confusion has arisen as to the positive dates of each; but it is clear that, from the latter end of June to the beginning of August, a succession of intermittent and severe eruptions took place, during which no less than forty shocks of earthquake were recorded within a period of four hours.

A cone to the east of the present mountain of Serra d'Agoa de Pao (3,070 feet in height) shot forth immense quantities of lava, pumice-stone and ashes. The mass of lava, bifurcating into two streams, destroyed everything in its way, until, reaching the sea, which it drove before it, it filled up the foreshore opposite Agoa de Pao, forming a shallow and rugged bank.

The mountain was entirely destroyed, and its site is now indicated by a romantic and beautiful lake, about a mile-and-a-half in circumference, and 15 fathoms in depth, almost encircled by precipitous cliffs.

Another terrible outbreak occurred about the same time on the northern side of the island, not far from Ribeira Grande, the Pico do Sapateiro, a large hill which almost dominated the town, vanishing from view.

Ribeira Grande itself providentially escaped destruction from the lava overflow, which skirted it on its way to the coast. The fearful detonations, however, produced by the escaping gases, and the bursting lava bombs, as they shot up high in the air, and the numerous earthquakes, caused much damage, scarcely a house remaining standing.

A third eruption broke out in the valley of the Furnas, in the vicinity of a lake, now known as Lagoa Secca, the outpour of lava being accompanied by loud explosions, as the captive gases expanded beyond their limits.

The lava emitted by the Pico do Sapateiro was highly charged with metallic matter (probably oxide of iron), which causes it to resist for a greater length of time the disintegrating influences of the irriguous climate of the uplands on which it mostly fell.

This lava is less scoriaceous, and of greater specific gravity than most of the lavas met with in the island; hence the sterility of the ground it covers. The burning cinders from these volcanoes wrapped the island in total darkness, and covered the ground in several places to a depth of many feet. Thick masses of this pulverised matter, mixed with pumice-stone, were met with floating out at sea, at a distance of 250 miles from the shore, greatly impeding the progress of vessels. Cinders also fell in the north of Portugal, 800 miles away.

From the 26th July to the 12th of August, 1591, a succession of shocks occurred, during which Villa Franca was again almost entirely destroyed by the falling in of its houses. In the ruins of these many persons were killed. The sea opposite this coast was much agitated, the motions extending beneath its bed, in a westerly direction as far as Terceira and Fayal, where they were severely felt.

On the night of the 2nd of September, 1630, violent tremors lasted for four hours, the villages of Ponta da Garça and Povoação, and again Villa Franca, being in peril of general annihilation. Two hundred persons lost their lives in these places, and many herds of cattle perished. These convulsions were followed by eruptions from some neighbouring cones, from which a compact mass of lava flowed, forming a cliff on the shore some 100 yards in length, and of great depth.

The cone which, in the valley of the Furnas, had remained quiescent ever since 1563, again burst out, and entirely desiccated the lake at its foot. This lake, before the eruption, covered a space of three miles in circumference, having a depth of about 100 feet. It is now filled up with cinders, pumice-stone and scoriæ, and is known as the Lagoa Secca, or the dry lake. This eruption was chiefly remarkable for the volumes of ashes it sent forth, enveloping the island in an Egyptian darkness, greatly terrifying the inhabitants. The impalpable dust covered the land in many places to a depth of from 5 to 17 feet, destroying all vegetation for the time being, but adding fertility to the soil itself.

In Terceira the fall of ashes was so continuous and alarming, that the inhabitants record the year in their annals as " O anno da cinza," or, the ash year.

In July of 1638, almost on the very spot where, just 100 years before, an eruption had broken out, and three miles off the western coast, flames shot up, accompanied by quantities of broken lava and cinders, forming an islet which, at the expiration of twenty days, when the eruption ceased, fell in and disappeared. This outburst was, as usual, preceded by severe shocks of earthquake.

The 12th of September, 1652, was ushered in by serious convulsions, the whole island labouring violently until the 19th, when two large cones, known as Paio and João Ramos, on the southern coast, broke out, expelling much lava and volumes of tuff.

Tremors were again felt in the latter end of 1682, succeeded by another submarine eruption in the channel bed between S. Miguel and Terceira.

In the middle of November, 1713, shocks were felt on the north-west side of the island, concurrent with an overflow of lava, near the village of Ginetes, which did little damage. The earthquakes, however, destroyed many buildings in the villages of Ginetes, Candelaria and Mosteiros, but no loss of life was occasioned.

In 1719, the submarine crater, so active in 1538 and 1638, again broke out and formed an island ten miles in circumference, which shortly afterwards subsided.

On the night of the 8th of December, 1720, a violent

earthquake was simultaneously felt in St. Michael and Terceira, the channel between being shortly afterwards illumined by immense sheets of flame, proceeding from another submarine eruption. This upheaval raised an island which was gradually destroyed by the action of the waves. On the cessation of the eruption it began to subside, and three years afterwards nothing remained of it.

In 1755, shocks were again felt. The sea became visibly agitated, and, rising to an unusual degree, threatened an invasion of the low lands.

On the 26th of October, 1773, several serious earthquakes were followed by a terrible storm which uprooted trees and wrecked many houses.

In the year 1810 the Pico de Ginetes was again in action, numerous shocks being at the same time felt in various localities; but little damage followed its incandescent overflow.

The year 1811 was memorable for the occurrence of one of the most interesting phenomena, perhaps, ever recorded in the history of submarine volcanic eruptions in this archipelago. The restless crater to the west of the island, and about two miles off the Ponta da Ferraria, suddenly electrified the inhabitants on the 1st of January by a tremendous explosion, expelling huge stones to a height of 300 feet. This eruption gradually ceased, after forming a dangerous shoal. An earthquake now followed, which was felt all over the island, after which the eruption re-commenced with great vigour, breaking out, however, two and a half miles west of the first site, and at a distance of one mile from the shore opposite the Pico das Camarinhas (so named from the berry-producing shrub, *Corema alba*), until, on the 18th of June, the mouth of the crater was distinctly seen rising on the surface of the water, and attaining a height, two days later, of 250 feet. It continued to form until the 4th of July, when the overflow ceased, the islet having then attained an altitude of 410 feet, and more than 4,100 feet in circumference. Like all similar structures previously thrown up, and consisting chiefly of unconsolidated cinders and pumice stone, it subsided by degrees, until, on the 15th of October, nothing of it was visible, and only a shoal now remains to indicate the spot.

Ponta Delgada, and the country for twenty miles beyond, was covered with cinders. This erupted islet was known by the name of " Sabrina," from the British frigate of that name, commanded by Captain Tillard, which happened to arrive at S. Miguel at the time of the eruption. Captain Tillard gave a very graphic account of the occurrence in the " Philosophical Transactions " for 1812.

He landed at Ponta Delgada on the 14th of June, and at once made for the cliffs, rising to a height of 400 feet opposite to the volcano, and, in his narrative, says that the eruption occurred a short mile from the shore, throwing out thick columns of smoke, alternating with successive showers of the blackest cinders, ashes and stones, shot up in the form of spires at angles of 10° to 20° from a perpendicular line, attaining an altitude as much above the level of his eye as the sea was below it.

During these bursts vivid flashes of flame continually issued from the crater. In the dense masses of smoke were a number of waterspouts. The part of the sea where the volcano was situated was upwards of thirty fathoms deep, and, at the time of Captain Tillard's viewing it, the volcano was only four days old. Before he quitted the spot a complete crater was formed above the water, not less than 20 feet high, its diameter being apparently about 400 or 500 feet.

" On the 4th of July," continues Captain Tillard, " I was obliged to pass with the ship very close to the island, which was now completely formed by the volcano, being about eighty yards above the sea.

" At this time it was perfectly tranquil, which circumstance determined me to land and explore it more narrowly.

As we approached, we perceived that it was still smoking in many parts. We found a narrow beach of black ashes, from which the side of the island rose, in general, too steep to admit of our ascending; and where we could have clambered up, the mass of matter was much too hot to allow our proceeding more than a few yards in the ascent. The declivity below the surface of the sea was equally steep, having 7 fathoms of water scarce the boat's length from the shore; and at the distance of 20 or 30 yards we sounded 25 fathoms. From walking round it in about twelve minutes, I should judge that it was something less than a mile in circumference; but the most extraordinary part was the crater, the mouth of which, on the side facing St. Michael, was nearly level with the sea. It was filled with water, at that time boiling, and was emptying itself into the sea by a small stream, about 6 yards over, and by which I should suppose it was continuously filled again at high water. This stream, close to the edge of the sea, was so hot as only to admit the finger to be dipped suddenly in and taken out immediately.

Within the crater was found the complete skeleton of a guard fish, the bones of which, being perfectly burnt, fell to pieces upon attempting to take them up, and, by the account of the inhabitants on the coast of St. Michael, great numbers of fish had been destroyed during the early part of the eruption, as large quantities, probably suffocated or poisoned, were occasionally found drifted into the small inlets or bays. The island is composed principally of porous substances, and generally burnt to complete cinders, with occasional masses of stone."

Slight shocks were felt in the years 1849, '52, '53, '62, and '82; but comparatively little damage was done.

On the 22nd December, 1884, two very severe earthquakes, closely following each other, were felt in the island, the direction being west to east; but fortunately without serious effects. A few days later, Malaga and Granada, and other places on the Spanish littoral, were severely damaged by earthquakes, and the captain of the barque "Isabel," from Cadiz to New York, reported that on December 18th, in lat. 38° 51', and long. 29° 55', those on board felt a terrific earthquake, with thunderous submarine roaring of an appalling character.

The contrast beween the submarine eruptions and some of those which have occurred on land is remarkable; in the former no solid combination, such as lava, seems to have been emitted, which might have given permanency and consistency to the structures raised; but, on the contrary, volumes of pumice, ashes, and arenaceous trap, formed an incoherent mass, which, constantly acted upon by a choppy sea, soon became undermined and scattered.

The theory has often been propounded that St. Michael originally formed two separate islands long before its discovery, the division occurring in the centre, between Ponta Delgada and Capellas, and that the narrow space between was filled up by the eruptions of Serra Gorda and other volcanoes. The chief argument against this supposition probably lies in the fact, that this very portion of the island exhibits, perhaps, stronger evidence than any other, that the waters of a tumultuous sea once covered the land.

Along the road from the city to Capellas there are deep banks and extensive pockets of perfectly clean gravel, mixed here and there with rounded pebbles, differing both in character and placement from the *ejecta* of aerial eruptions.

The soil too, on either side of the road, is deep and free from the mantle of lava which the above theory would lead one to expect.

In Fayal, and most of the other islands, are also found immense masses of similar gravel, singularly free from ashes, pumice, and other volcanic products, and which could only have been washed and deposited in their present positions by the action of a violent sea.

F

From careful research amongst the records of volcanic eruptions in St. Michael from the earliest times, I have been unable to trace any clear evidence of land having been raised in the island during any of these convulsions, although Hooke mentions that this occurred in 1591; undoubtedly the breadth of the island has from time to time been increased by flows of lava into the sea, forming shoals and solidifying over them, and this has especially happened in the neighbourhood of Ribeira Grande on the north side, and at places between Povoação and Villa Franca on the south. In Terceira, however, the evidence as to a gradual but distinct upheaval is beyond question, for in 1581 the bay of Salga and that of Mós were sufficiently deep to admit several large "náos" or battle ships, from which were landed 400 Spaniards who sought to deliver the island to Philip II., and, at the second named place, Prince Antonio, in July of the following year, sailed into the port with several large ships of war, from which he landed 1,000 men—facts which prove that at that time these were commodious and spacious harbours, which now are so shallow as to barely admit small boats in fair and calm weather. On the other hand, Padre d'Andrade, in his "Topographia of Terceira," published in 1843, mentions some curious facts as to the subsidence of considerable portions of land near Villa da Praia. Terceira had been free from volcanic disturbance from its first discovery to the 17th April, 1761, when a serious overflow of lava occurred at a place near Pico da Bagacina. On the 24th May, 1614, however, a terrible earthquake had almost destroyed Villa da Praia; the foreshore subsided, the sea now covering the site of what were once cultivated fields, and on which stood many dwelling houses, the walls of which were then (1843) still discernable at low tide.

At another site, known as "O Paul do Cabo da Praia," the subsidence was also considerable, comprising cultivated lands and woods within the points of Santa Catherina and

Espirito Santo, on which were many edifices, the site of the old road leading to the Cabo da Praia was pointed out under the waves.

Villa da Praia was again destroyed by the earthquakes of 24th June, 1800, and 26th January, 1801, and lastly on the 15th June, 1841, when it was reduced to a mountain of ruins at a time when the town numbered over 3,000 inhabitants.

Before concluding this chapter it would be well to consider the Fauna and Flora of these islands in relation to their occurrence in other countries.

In analysing the various groups of Azorean animals and plants, excepting mammalia, reptilia, and amphibia, which are unrepresented, and excluding fresh-water fish, nocturnal lepidoptera, mosses, and hepaticæ, Mr. Godman thus numerically distributes them—

	Total number of Species.	Percentage of Species Common to the Azores and			Peculiar to the Azores.	
		Europe.	Madeira.	Canaries.		
Aves	53	91	75	57	2	1 American
Diurnal lepidoptera ..	8	87	..	..	0	1 American
Coleoptera	212	83	65	55	6	3 American
Land and fresh-water Mollusca ..	69	38	10	6	46	
Plants	480	83	62½	54	8¼	5 American and African.

Owing to the close relationship between the botany of the Azores and that of the south of Europe and north of Africa, many hypothetical speculations have been hazarded respecting the former connection of this archipelago and those of Madeira and the Canaries with the neighbouring continents. How far these islands, which (if we take the evidences presented by Santa Maria) probably belong to the Miocene age, received European contributions to their flora, of plants whose structure lend themselves to aerial or oceanic dispersion, or by means of wandering icebergs during the Glacial period—the only mode of plant distribution which would seem to explain the presence of certain allied species in distant and unaccountable localities—it is impossible to say; but the undoubted volcanic origin of these islands, the absence of any terrestrial mammalia or reptiles except those imported by man, and the knowledge gained as to the platform upon which they rest by the investigations of the " Challenger " expedition, coupled with their great distance from the nearest masses of land, and the depth of the intervening seas, would appear to suffice for dismissing the theory of a previous mainland connection, and that the Azores are essentially what Mr. Darwin calls " ocean islands." The soundings and observations taken by the expedition show that the Azores (the highest point of which, Pico, rises from the level of its ocean bed a height of 16,206 feet and 7,613 feet above sea level) including the Madeira group, Canaries, Cape Verd, &c., are the topmost cusps of a vast submerged mountain ridge extending from Greenland in the north, and intersecting the Atlantic into two abyssal depths to a distance south beyond the island of Tristan d'Acunha. This longitudinal chain has been compared to the Andes of South America, both in its elevation and volcanic character, and presents a connected range of gigantic volcanoes whose highest cones pierce the clouds from Iceland to Teneriffe.

Writing upon this subject, Sir Charles Lyell says: " The general abruptness of the cliffs of all the Atlantic islands, coupled with the rapid deepening of the sea outside the 100-fathom line, are characters which favour the opinion that each island was formed separately by igneous eruptions, and in a sea of great depth." More recent researches have confirmed that opinion.

" From the parallel of 55° N. latitude, at all events to the equator, we have on either side of the Atlantic a depression 600 or 700 miles in width, averaging 15,000 feet in depth. These two valleys are separated by the modern volcanic plateau of the Açores. It does not seem to us to be at all probable that any general oscillations have taken place in the northern hemisphere, sufficient either to form these immense abysses, or, once formed, to convert them into dry land."*

This expression, "modern volcanic plateau," must be understood as geologically recent, and not as implying that the islands were thrown up within historic times, for all surface evidence of the Glacial period has by no means been effaced, and their formation makes it certain that they existed æons prior to the Reign of Cold which geologists compute occurred some eighty millions of years ago—a lapse of time the mind can scarcely grasp.

---

*"Depths of the Sea," by Sir C. Wyville Thomson.

Chapter VIII.

> So sweet the air, so moderate the clime,
> None sickly lives, or dies before his time :
> Heaven sure has kept this spot of earth
> To show how all things were created first uncurst !
>
> *Waller.*

DATING from the first arrival of the colonists, Ponta Delgada remained subject to Villa Franca during some 50 years, but frequent disputes arising between the inhabitants for the supremacy of their respective places, those of Ponta Delgada petitioned the king for freedom, and, in 1499, obtained the coveted emancipation. Subsequently, when Villa Franca was destroyed by earthquakes, the seat of government was definitely centered in Ponta Delgada, the town being raised by John III. in 1546 to the dignity of city, and it has ever since remained the capital of the island, and now possesses a population of close upon 20,000. In 1582, Philip I. granted it the same privileges as enjoyed by Oporto, and it ranks as the third city of Portugal in point of importance. The success of her fortunate rival proved a lasting blow to the prosperity of Villa Franca, and for long afterwards much enmity rankled in the feelings of her inhabitants.

Built on a talus, or gently sloping plain, situated on the western end of a shallow bay on the south of the island, formed by Delgada Point on one side and Galera Point on the east, and set in a frame with a background of rich and

LIGHTHOUSE

ER IN COURSE OF CONSTRUCTION AT PONTA DELGADA. (Taken f

abounding vegetation, Ponta Delgada presents a remarkably picturesque appearance viewed from the sea, with its numerous churches, convents and white-washed buildings gleaming in the benison of a generous sunshine; it extends east and west for a distance of about two miles, covering a breadth of about a mile and a quarter.

The town is badly placed for purposes of commerce, its open roadstead affording little or no protection to vessels from the prevalent south-east and south-westerly gales. This drawback, however, is being rapidly remedied by the construction of a very commodious breakwater, which, when completed, will effectually make this the safest harbour of refuge in the Açores.

A decree of the Cortes of the 9th August, 1860, authorised the commencement of this important work, towards which the Government allowed 10 per cent. of the revenues of the Custom House of Ponta Delgada to be appropriated, and imposed a tax of 10d. upon every box of oranges exported, also 1½ per cent. *ad valorem* upon all imports or exports. From all of which, and the Government contributions, some £18,000 per annum was derived for some years, and expended upon the works every year.

As the tax of 10d. per box, which in good average seasons amounted to £12,460, weighed heavily upon the orange growers, it was reduced in 1878 to 3d., and the special *ad valorem* duty increased to 3 per cent. In 1879-80, owing to the diminished orange production, the tax was again reduced to 1¾d. per flat box, barely bringing in £1,068 per annum, but in June of 1884 the *ad valorem* duty was reduced to 1 per cent., and the tax on the export of oranges altogether abolished. In 1832 a decree was issued by the Lisbon Government, providing that the surplus income of the suppressed religious orders in the Açores, after defraying the trifling expenses of maintenance of the expelled members, who, from age or infirmities, were unable to support themselves, should be applied to the bettering of the various harbours of the three islands of S. Miguel, Terceira and Fayal. These amounts, which in the aggregate reached very considerable sums, would have very materially contributed to the improvement of the ports, without encroaching upon the pockets of the islanders, but the coffers of the Government being empty, this decree was, upon some pretext or another, set aside, and the Michaelenses forced to provide most of the money requisite for the construction of their breakwater, upon which over £450,000 has already been spent, and it is estimated that the work will cost £600,000 before completion.

The works were commenced on the 28th October, 1862, upon the plan originally designed by Mr. John Scott Tucker, C.E., but subsequently modified by the late Sir John Rennie. For some years past they have been under the entire direction of native engineers, controlled by a committee of management.

This important work consists of a mole formed of loose blocks of basalt, of which considerably over two million tons have already been employed; the length of this wall is now nearly 2,000 feet at low water, and it already shelters some 48,000 square yards of space against all winds, with varying depths of from 6 to 30 feet, within which about 46 vessels can at present be accommodated in lines, as follows:

LINES.	No. of Vessels.	Draught of Water.
First line, at entrance of Port ..	6	14 to 20 feet.
Second line	12	12 „ 18 „
Third line	12	10 „ 17 „
Fourth line	8	10 „ 14 „
Fifth line	5	6 „ 10 „
Sixth line	3	5 „ 8 „
Six lines	46	5 to 20 feet.

The entrance is E.S.E. and at present is 443 feet wide, and varies gradually in depth from north to south from 18 to 40 feet. When completed in its projected entirety, the breakwater-wall will extend for 2,800 feet, and will shelter some 95,000 yards of space, capable of accommodating 100 vessels of all dimensions and draught.

It is accessible at all times, except during a south-easterly gale, and is in lat. 37° 45' 10'', long. 25° 41' 30'' W. of Greenwich.

Loading and unloading is at present carried on by means of lighters, but vessels will presently be able to get alongside the quays now in course of construction, and which will have an extension of 1,640 feet, with varying depths of from 9 to 19 feet at low water.

The rise of tide is $7\frac{1}{8}$ feet.

The mooring and unmooring of ships is carried out by practised pilots, who receive their instructions from the captain of the port.

Within the breakwater is a wooden floating dock, capable of raising vessels of 1,200 tons, and there are also ample workshops where repairs requiring foundry and smiths' work can be well and expeditiously carried out. A body of trained divers also exists, and a steam tug for the service of vessels.

From 350 to 375 ships, of from 87,000 to 110,000 tons, annually frequent the port, and the number is increasing as its capabilities become better known.

Careful observations have shewn that, prior to the construction of this great work, there were 41 days of interruption of communication with the shore in the winter time, and nine in the summer; its existence, therefore, is an inestimable boon, not only to the island, but to shipping interests at large—as it has effectually done away with the *nom empesté* this and the other islands were known by.

On the breakwater wall stands a harbour light, visible at a considerable distance out at sea, which will ultimately be permanently placed at the head of the mole. The system adopted is to run out wooden scaffolding some 30 feet in length, through which huge blocks of stone, some of them weighing from six to eight tons each, are thrown into the sea, until the slope is in the proportion of six at the foundation to one in height, and the desired breadth and inclination has been attained.

These blocks are obtained from the quarries of Santa Clara, about a mile off, and conveyed by a narrow gauge railway, which runs from the quarries along the whole length of the mole. This basalt is extremely hard and has hitherto withstood the action of the heavy winter seas surprisingly well. It has been observed that the requisite inclination of the slope can only be properly attained by the action of the waves during stormy weather; of course, portions of the end work are every winter carried away, but where the incline has been established, the resistance is perfect. The power of each wave striking against the breakwater wall is estimated to represent a force in the roughest weather varying from one-and-a-half to two or even three tons to the square foot. As these waves recur several thousand times during the twenty-four hours, it is astonishing that greater damage is not sustained by the works in progress every winter.

The quantity of stone which will probably be absorbed in this great work will not fall far short of four million tons.

The progressive movement of the port may be better gathered from the following figures :—

In 1881, the entries of vessels possessing a tonnage of 14,168 numbered 150; 49 steamers of 51,396 tons; 76 ocean-going vessels of 20,746 tons, and 75 casual steamers of 77,501 tons.

In 1882, the entries of vessels with a tonnage of 12,511 numbered 148; 47 steamers of 49,425 tons; 83 ocean-going vessels of 25,274 tons; and 68 casual steamers of 68,691 tons.

In 1883, the entries of vessels with a tonnage of 10,864, numbered 134; 46 steamers of 49,013 tons; 72 ocean-going vessels of 22,572 tons, and 70 casual steamers of 83,316 tons.

The wreck returns show a very satisfactory decrease. In 1850-52, the number of vessels wrecked at S. Miguel amounted to 8; from 1853 to 1855, 2; from 1856 to 1858, 11; from 1859 to 1861, 9; from 1862 to 1864, 7; from 1865 to 1867, 8; from 1868 to 1870, 2; from that time to the present no disaster of the kind, arising from bad weather *alone*, has been recorded.

On the 1st October, 1880, during the first equinoctial gale which swept these isles from the S.W., three steamers that had put in for coals, the " Robinia," " Benalla," and " Stag," all closely and badly moored at the entrance of the breakwater, were wrecked; the cause, however, was attributed to defective mooring, the harbour pilot being held to blame. A sudden shift of wind coming on caused the first-named steamer to bump against the " Benalla," sinking her immediately; the same steamer then swung across the bows of the " Stag," which caused her to founder and the latter, riding up and down on the sunken wreck, became so damaged that her captain hauled her as far ashore as possible, when she settled. Of these, the "Benalla" was successfully raised by private enterprise, and now trades between Portugal and the United States; the other two were broken up.

The harbour works have been carried on in the face of considerable drawbacks; not only have large portions been carried away by heavy seas every successive winter, but the decadence of the productions and trade of the island has of recent years thrown the onus of construction and expenditure almost entirely upon the Lisbon Government. The Portuguese, therefore, who are accused of being the only people who build ruins, deserve no slight meed of praise for their patient persistence in a work almost beyond their powers, and it is to be hoped that in course of time, when the prejudice against the port has been dispelled and its security fully recognised, they may be amply rewarded.

Unhappily, the submarine cable, that greatest of civilising agencies, has not yet linked these islands with the Old and New World. When this shall have been effected, these will become important points of call for both homeward and outward-bound vessels.

Owing to the small area they occupy, the commerce of these islands must necessarily be restricted; nevertheless, until the oïdium destroyed the vines, and the orange blight threatened the staple export, it was both remunerative and progressive.

The custom-house returns show that 284 ships entered the harbour in 1883: of these 120 were steamers, the rest sailing vessels. 146 were Portuguese, 99 English and the rest other nationalities. A few sailing vesssels and three steamers of 1,000 tons burden, chiefly engaged in the fruit trade, are owned in the island, as are also in great part the two mail steamers running to and fro from Lisbon. Efforts have been made of late to divert some of the trade to Germany and the United States; New York and Boston, trying hard to supplant Manchester and Sheffield in the supply of cottons and hardware, but hitherto with but slight success, and the chief exports of the island, must, from a variety of circumstances, continue to be divided between Portugal and Great Britain, to which countries exports were, but a few years back made to the annual value of from £144,000 to £160,000; the imports being far in excess of these figures and ranging from £182,000 to £224,000.

The imports consist chiefly of manufactured cotton and woollen goods, silks, colonial produce, salt, iron, coal, timber, hardware, &c.; the exports, of some 45,000 quarters of corn, maize, beans, and haricots, tobacco, pozzolana, oranges, pineapples, spirits, &c., &c. The customs revenue for the twelve years from 1860-61 to 1883-84, averaged £48,890. Although, as we have seen, the mother country and England divide between them the produce of this archipelago, it was only in May of 1882 that Great Britain, in the matter of duties, was allowed to import her manufactures "on the most favored nation" tariff, France having, ever since 1866 enjoyed much greater immunity in this respect. This concession was only wrung from Portugal at the expense of the abrogation of the Treaty of 1842, which exempted from taxation British subjects resident in the country. It was but in 1885 that the law of cabotage was modified in favour of foreign vessels, which may now (with the exception of the ports of Angola and Cape de Verd) convey every kind of merchandise throughout the Portuguese Colonial possessions, and between them and the mother country.

In 1876-77 there commenced that general failure of crops, which has recurred every year with more or less intensity to the present time, causing a complete stagnation in trade, and reducing numbers of families dependent upon the produce of their lands to considerable straits. How serious this diminuation of crops has been upon the general trade of the island, may be gathered from the following figures:—

The total exports for the years 1861-62 to 1875-76 amounted to £2,508,476, the imports for the same period to £2,261,912, showing an annual excess of exports over imports of £16,437.

From 1876-77 to 1878-79 the total exports amounted to £330,466, and the respective imports to £472,930, showing an excess of imports over exports of £142,464 during that period. At the present time, these figures are reduced to little more than half; the imports, however, being far in excess of exports.

The average receipts on account of imposts and taxes of the district of Ponta Delgada for the 13 years from 1870-71 to 1882-83, amounted to £88,288, and the average expenses for the same period of administration, &c., to £67,640, leaving an average annual surplus of £20,648.

Small as this amount was, it, however, paid an income tax or *contribuicāo predial* to the Government of £23,928 ; the total annual average sum paid into the coffers of the State by the island of St. Michael alone amounts to £84,567, or nearly half the public revenue of the island, which latter reaches in the average £182,000 per annum.

In 1864 the total revenue of landed property in the island for purposes of assessment was estimated at £205,590, on which a tax of £16,376 was imposed.

In 1871 we find this valuation reduced to £194,376, and the tax to £15,842.

In 1877 the rateable value was again assessed at £169,278 and the tax further reduced to £13,350.

Since then the decrease in the value of property has been even more sensible, and estates, if put up at auction, barely realise one-fourth of what they did five years ago.

St. Michael presents an area of 224 square miles, or 143,360 acres, of which 100,000 consist of forest lands, lakes, dwellings, &c. The immense fertility of the soil may, therefore, be gathered from the fact that from the remaining 43,360 acres are produced the large quantities of oranges and some 84,000 quarters of grain and pulse of all kinds annually raised. This inexhaustible fertility is probably due to the phosphoric acid, potash and other fertilising properties held in a state of tenuity favourable for assimilation, contained in the volcanic sands and detritus, which are for ever being transported by ærial and pluvial agency over the land.

In the good old times the yearly rental of the land amounted to £150,000, but the present estimate barely reaches half that figure.

One of the most favourite systems of land tenure in Portugal, and consequently in these islands, was—and in some parts still is—that known as the *Emprazamento*, *aforamento*, or more commonly, the *emphyteutic*, or perpetual leasehold. The rent may either be paid in kind at the end of each successive crop, or in cash at the end of each determined year; this rent is fixed and unalterable.

These leases, or *prazos*, are hereditary, but the property, however extensive, must be held by one single tenant, unless the owner of the fee-simple previously consents to its being sub-divided.

These leaseholds may be bought and sold, or even mortgaged, but in the former case the senhorio or freeholder has always the right or option of redeeming the lease, and the tenant, on the other hand, of buying the senhorio, should the freeholder wish to sell. On the sale of one of these *aforamentos* the vendor pays to his senhorio a tax of five per cent on the amount of sale.

The prosperity of the Minho Province in Portugal has been attributed by Mr. Consul Crawford to land being parcelled out among small tenants on the above system and therefore carefully cultivated.

Other land tenures there are, such as the allodial or freehold, the censo or limited leasehold, the quinhão or part interest in the produce only of any indivisible estate vested in one of several co-proprietors, the direito de compascuo or communal right of property belonging to divers proprietors or parishes. This last has proved a fruitful source of litigation in the neighbouring island of Terceira, where serious disturbances periodically arise through the peasantry imagining their communal rights to be infringed.

In the early days of orange culture in S. Michael's, the majority of gardens were transferred on the emphyteutic system, to tenants who agreed to pay from 6$000 (£1. 1s. 6d.) to 8$000 (£1. 8s. 7d.) and 9$000 or £1. 12s. 2d. per alqueire* of

---

* In describing the extent of a field or quinta, the Portuguese use the term alqueire, 60 of which make a moyo, 5·16 alqueires being equal to one English acre. The alqueire is also a dry measure, and holds one peck, three quarts, and one pint. 60 of these alqueires equal a moyo of grain.

orange-planted land. In those days each alqueire produced on an average 10 large boxes of oranges, each containing 800 oranges, and which returned the grower an average of 3$000 (10s. 9d.); now, however, so depreciated has both produce and value become, that his alqueire of land only yields him 5 large boxes, and his average net profit is barely 1$400 (5s.) per large box, or 7$000 (£1. 5s.) per alqueire, leaving him a dead loss on his rental from which he cannot free himself, of from 1$000 (3s. 7d.) to 2$000 (7s. 3d.) per alqueire. Verily, Portugal is much in need of a new Land Act.

If the cultivation of the orange is no longer remunerative, it is a satisfaction to find that the profits derived from cereal growing will return the farmer from 45 to 50 per cent. on the capital employed in good average seasons, notwithstanding the high rent paid. The Azorean farmer would appear from this to be the happiest of mortals, but the passion of these islanders for agricultural pursuits makes them keen competitors for any scrap of land that may be offered, and it is seldom that a man can get hold of more than from 3 to 12 alqueires at a time, yet from the produce of such patches as these he will maintain a numerous family.

Cost of cultivating one alqueire of land at 6$000 yearly rental :—

Receipts, 30 alqueires maize at 400 Rs. 12.000
        Fodder for animals   800
                                        ——— 12.800
Expenses, manure and cost of lupin .. Rs. 2.500
        Seed   360
        Ploughing, sowing, gathering   1.800
                                        ——— 4.660

        Amount left after paying expenses ..   8.140
        Rent 6.000
                                        ———
                Profit   ..   .. Rs. 2.140

The productiveness of this volcanic soil is truly astonishing. One alqueire of land will return regularly 20 alqueires of wheat, 30 of maize, and 50 of broad beans; in some instances even 62 of the latter, after which they get another late crop of maize. Wheat is hardly ever cultivated now, owing to the uncertainty of the seasons, and tendency to degenerate of the seed. Haricots, which a few years back, were one of the chief articles of food of the poor, are not now much grown, owing to the aphis blight, which of late years has attacked the plant.

Maize is what the islanders chiefly turn their attention to, and is cultivated sufficiently for home consumption and export.

Commercial intercourse between the Açores and Great Britain dates from a remote period, for we find English vessels coming here in the middle of the 17th century for cargoes of a blue granulated dye, made of the woad or pastel plant (*Isatis tinctoria.* Linn.) This trade, of great importance to the islands at that time, gradually died away, being unable to compete with the cheaper East Indian indigo produce, which contains 30 times as much indigo blue as the woad, not a single plant of which is now to be found on any of the islands.

In 1747 four boxes of lemons shipped to England seem to have proved a happy venture, for these were followed by 130 boxes two years later; the trade steadily increased during the following 50 years, until five to seven thousand boxes were annually exported; but shipments ceased entirely in 1838, owing to more regular supplies from other countries.

The first exports of oranges were made in 1751, when four boxes were sent in a sailing vessel to Cork. From this period the cultivation of the orange tree seems to have been systematically carried on, for in 1802 nearly 40,000 boxes of oranges were shipped to London alone.

Until about eight years ago, an average of 500,000 boxes,

each containing from 350 to 400 oranges, was annually sent to the English markets from S. Miguel alone, and represented the staple export of the island. The present shipments, however, barely reach one quarter of the former production, and the islanders are anxiously asking themselves whether the enormous and increasing quantities which pour into the English markets from the Mediterranean ports of Spain, Sicily, and Portugal, will not, as in the case of Terceira and Fayal, altogether extinguish their trade. The St. Michael orange, however (of first quality) has no European rival, and must ever be pre-eminent for the fineness of its quality, and surpassing sapidity.

"The gardens of the Hesperides, with the golden apples, were believed to exist in some island in the ocean, or, as it was sometimes thought, in the islands of the north or west coast of Africa. As to the origin of these precious golden apples, there is a myth which says that among the deities who attended the marriage ceremony of Zeus and Hera, bringing various presents with them, was Titœa, a goddess of the earth, whose gift consisted in her causing a tree to spring up with golden apples on it. The care of this tree, which highly pleased the newly-wedded pair, was entrusted to the Hesperides, but as they could not resist the temptation to pluck and eat its fruit, it became necessary to place the serpent Ladon to watch it. Hercules, among his other adventures, slew this serpent and carried off some of the apples."*

The Hesperides were seven beautiful sisters, daughters of Atlas, who bore the world on his shoulders, and Hesperis a personification of the "region of the west." In this legend is supposed to occur the first mention of the orange tree, and if its existence in the islands of the blest more than three thousand years ago can be reasonably accepted, then its introduction at a very early period into northern Africa and

---

* "Manual of Mythology." Murray.

south-eastern Europe, thence even to the East, its supposed habitat, can be readily accounted for.

The chronicler of Vasco da Gama's famous voyage, in 1498, says that the ship S. Raphael, running aground to the south of Mombaça on the east coast of Africa, was surrounded by many natives in boats, who brought a great quantity of oranges for barter, " much better than those of Portugal," showing that a variety of the fruit already existed in the country prior to 1498.

The earliest mention of oranges in the Azores is made in the will of one João Corrêa, who died at Agualva in Terceira, in December, 1524, wherein he leaves to each of his four children "three orange trees in his orchard of Agualva."

Fructuoso, who died in 1591, mentions in a garden at Rosto de Cão 107 orange trees, many of which existed as late as 1830, when they were killed by the "lagrima" disease. The first orange tree from China was brought into Portugal about 1635 by D. Francisco de Mascarenhas, who sent it, viâ Goa, to his garden of Xabregas, near Lisbon. So great was the desire amongst cultivators, both in Portugal and abroad, to obtain plants from this tree, that a special decree, dated 30th January, 1671, prohibited the export from the country of plants from this parent tree under penalty of 100 cruzados, captains of vessels being fined in a like sum if found conveying such trees out of the country.

In course of time the China variety entirely superseded the old orange of Portugal, which could not, however, have been so very inferior, for Camöens thus sings its praises:—

> The orange, here, exhales a perfume rare,
> And boasts the golden hue of Daphne's hair,
> Near to the ground each spreading bough descends;
> Beneath her yellow load the citron bends.
> The fragrant lemon scents the shady grove,
> Fair as when, ripening for the days of love,
> The virgin's breasts the gentle sigh avow;
> So the twin fruitage swell on every bough.

Pico, which at one time was densely covered with timber of large size, and supplied the other islands with valuable wood, also boasted of a very fine variety of orange, which Linschoten (writing about 1589) thus describes:— "It (Pico) hath the pleasantest and savorest oranges that are throughout all Portugal, so that they are brought into Terceira for a present, as being there very much esteemed, and in my judgment they are the best that ever I tasted in any place."

From the aurantiaceæ family spring the various species known as the common orange (*Citrus aurantium*), the bitter or Seville orange (*C. bigaradea*), the bergamot, so famous in perfumery (*C. bergamia*); the lemon (*Citrus limonium*); the citron (*C. medica* Lin., *C. cidra gallesis*); the shaddock (*C. decumana*); the lime, of which there are sweet and bitter varieties (*C. limetta*); to which we may add the tangerine, a variety of the mandarin orange (*C. nobilis Loureiro*).

The orange is subdivided into an infinity of varieties too numerous to specify, the result of climatic and other conditions.

According to Lindlay, however, there are 15 distinct species with a few varieties; Steudel enumerating 25, besides numberless varieties; and Risso, in his work on the orange, gives 43 species and varieties of the sweet orange, 32 of the bitter, 59 bergamots, 8 of limes, 6 of shaddocks, 46 of lemons, and 17 of citrons. All these belong to one genus, the *Citrus* of Linnæus.

The orange appears to have been well known to the Romans, for on the walls of a room in an excavated villa, near the Porta del Popolo, was found the painting of a grove of orange trees, in excellent preservation.

In England the tree was apparently first introduced by a member of the Carew family, who for more than a century continued its cultivation at Beddington, in Surrey.

Nothing can exceed the luxuriant growth of the tree in

these latitudes, although in every one of the islands there is a perceptible difference in quality and appearance of the fruit. This is the more remarkable, as they all present the same apparent conditions of soil and temperature. It has been observed that the orange tree will only properly thrive on a coast zone within reach of the saline particles with which the air in such localities is charged; a volcanic soil too, would seem to change the character of the fruit, imparting to it a more delicate flavour. The Valencia orange, which differs so much both in appearance and flavour from that of St. Michael, loses its characteristics when transplanted to this soil, and in course of time becomes identical with the island fruit.

Formerly the St. Michael orange was grown entirely from " pips," and took about 15 years to attain maturity. The fruit of these trees was luscious in the extreme, with rinds no thicker than a wafer, and not the vestige of a seed, but the high prices obtained for it in England induced the owners of " quintas " to graft on a large scale; so that from one of these seed-grown trees twenty others were obtained, the fruit of which was never comparable to that of the parent tree.

There are several modes of propagating the tree in the Açores, the most favourite of which are the following :—

A likely branch for a future tree having been found, a truss of straw two feet long is securely tied round it, the branch is then barked for about an inch high all round and sifted earth carefully filled in below and above the wounded part until the truss assumes the shape and size of a large pine-apple, the straw is then fastened at the top and the operation is complete; in three weeks' time the barked portion commences to throw out rootlets and in seven months the branch, now fully rooted, can be sawn off and planted out; in a year or two it will commence to bear fruit.

Another system is to peg down the lower branches of

the tree and graft in the ordinary way, these trees also fruit in a short time.

Large numbers of trees may be obtained by budding seedlings, but these take longer before fruiting. All the *Citrus* varieties are periodically assailed by blights and parasites which seem peculiar to them, and which have brought destruction upon many a flourishing plantation.

When the Spaniards, in 1512, made Florida one of their colonies (which they held for two centuries and a half) they introduced the orange tree from Spain, and the country, bathed by the moist and temperate breezes of the Atlantic on one side and the Gulf of Mexico on the other, favoured its development in a high degree; it spread far and wide until attacked in course of time by the *Aspidiota conchiformis*, a minute grey-coloured parasite of the *Coccus* family, which, appearing in myriads, soon sapped its life, withering thousands of trees.

An American gentleman, who had settled in S. Miguel about the beginning of the century, and who was conspicuous for his love of horticulture, introduced a few trees of the far-famed Florida orange into the island in 1835, and with them, unhappily, the then quite unknown insect. In a few years its ravages became so serious that many of the old trees were destroyed, and as it adheres to the bark by the whole of its ventral surface, it was only by persistently scraping and whitewashing the trunks and branches, and uprooting the trees specially affected, that an ascendancy was obtained over the pest. It is impossible, however, to extirpate it entirely, and in 1842 it was also discovered at Fayal, and soon spread to the other islands. I have often found it in apple orchards in England, where it has been introduced from the St. Michael oranges imported into the country; but the severe cold in winter prevents its increasing to any extent. This insect is also common in the whole of South America. Another scourge of the orange tree, now common in some parts of the Mediterranean board, appeared in S. Miguel some 40 years ago in the form of a disease supposed to have its seat in the roots of the tree. The ba a would crack and emit a reddish and glutinous exudation which the Portuguese call " lagrimas," or tears.

In a short time the tree was weakened and dried, but not before imparting its disease to the neighbouring ones. Energetic steps were at once adopted to stamp out the evil, and in 1840 nearly one-third of the trees in the island were rooted up, fortunately with signal success, for the blight, although never entirely disappearing, ceased in a great measure.

An apparently identical disease has recently attacked the chestnut (*Castanea vesca*) and the pine tree (*Pinus maritima*), resisting all attempts at suppression. The late Mr. James Hinton, the eminent surgeon, had recently visited the island and taken this matter up in his usual energetic manner; but his untimely death unhappily deprived the islanders of the benefit of his scientific researches.

In North Carolina huge tracts of pine forest were, 20 or 30 years ago, entirely destroyed by an insect plague, but here no visible cause for the decay of the tree is discerned.

The fig trees, which here attain immense proportions, have of recent years been attacked by a fine longicorn beetle (*Tœniotes sealaris* or *farinosus*) common to Brazil, whence it is supposed to have been accidently introduced.

The larva of this insect completely honeycombs the trunk of the tree, which in course of time ceases to bear fruit. This beetle is now established all over St. Michael's, and, I believe, the other islands as well.

These islands have seldom been visited by insect plagues other than those already mentioned, and the *Sphinx convolvulis* or potato insect, and the ordinary apis blights; but it is on record that on the 16th November, 1884, vast swarms of the red locust (*Acrydium migratorium*) were driven by a gale of wind from off the African coast on to the islands of St.

the nael's, Terceira, Fayal, San Jorge, Graciosa and Madeira, in a the astonishment and dismay of their inhabitants.

After resting for a while and apparently doing little se amage—for the crops had not yet begun to show above ground—the invading hosts, as if with one accord, left the islands.

In 1877 a formidable disease, hitherto entirely unknown, appeared amongst the orange trees in certain parts of the island, more especially in the south, and in the quintas around Ponta Delgada. The trees will present every promise of an abundant harvest, but just as the fruit is about to turn it falls to the ground upon the slightest breeze in alarming quantities, and, if shipped to England, the first pickings especially will, with difficulty, withstand the voyage; a curious brown decay spreading in a ring from the stem to the centre of the sphere, destroying a large proportion of this evidently blighted, or as they call it in Pudding Lane, "blind" fruit.

There is no mildew, parasite or indication of any sort, beyond, after a time, a yellow and sere appearance of the tree, and occasionally a viscid secretion at the extremities to mark the presence of disease, and its origin is as yet obscure. Its true cause is probably to be found in some peculiar atmospheric condition, possibly in the absorption by the tree of an overplus of moisture, combined with the exhaustion of the soil after ages of culture.

A disease, having the same characteristics, first appeared in Portugal in 1853 and raged until 1860, destroying numerous plantations in the districts around Lisbon, Santarem, Coimbra, and S. Mamede de Riba-Tua, where the finest oranges were at that time produced.

The trees in Madeira, then an important orange-exporting country, were similarly attacked and ruined.

Bermudas, where the cultivated orange was once so plentiful, was attacked in 1854 by one of numerous coccidæ, the enemy, *par excellence*, of the orange. The symptoms of an attacked tree were very similar to those of trees in St. Michael's, afflicted by the mysterious "molestia," and in a few years every plantation in Bermudas was destroyed by its ravages; here, however, there is no insect, and the blight has every appearance of possessing a more permanent and intractable character.

It does not appear that the oranges here are ever infested with the maggots or larvæ of the orange fly (*Ceratatis citriperda*), so destructive to this fruit in Madeira and other places, but it is useless to grow peaches or apples unless grafted with English hardier and better kinds, owing to the ravages of other Tephritidan or allied Diptera.

The orange tree is known to attain a great age; we find them in the old Moorish gardens in Spain, said to be at least 500 years old, the grand old trunks still flourishing. At the Sabine convent in Rome, a tree is still pointed out, which is said to have been planted by St. Dominic in the year 1200, and not very long ago, there was still to be seen in the garden of the Dominicans in Fondi, near Naples, an orange tree which tradition said had been planted by St. Thomas Aquinas; if so, it must have been more than 500 years old. In France, Holland and England, many trees are to be found under glass, of stunted growth, but of ages varying from 200 to 350 years. In S. Miguel, most of the old trees have long since perished, few having been known to exceed 200 years.

The varieties of the orange tree are very numerous, and China, the proverbial land of oranges, has supplied some of the best kinds.

The tangerine, now so abundant in these islands, must have originally come from China, and is closely allied to the famous mandarin orange *(Citrus nobilis)*, perhaps the richest variety known.

The St. Michael's growers have of late years been untiring in their efforts to seek for the orange best suited for their soil and climate, and they now cultivate with considerable success, the following excellent varieties: comprida (long), prata (silver), selecta (selected), besides the old island " real St. Michael," so well known in the streets of London, and the delicious tangerine, with other kinds of lesser note. The " selecta " is a fine fruit, devoid of pips, and ripening only in April, which makes it all the more valuable.

It is strange to reflect upon the rise, temporary prosperity, and gradual decay of successive industries in the island. During the sixteenth century the sugar cane culture, introduced originally from Sicily into Madeira, extending thence to St. Michael's, St. Thomé and Brazil, was for some years carried on extensively in this island— notably at Villa Franca; but its rapid increase in the South American colony and West Indies, where sugar could be produced under much more favourable conditions and in much larger quantities, gave the death blow to its successful manufacture here.

In 1509, there were no less than 20,000 arrobas of sugar manufactured in these islands, and one of the conditions stipulated by the Crown in the lease of the Açores to Fco. Carducho and Fco. Pinhol was that during the period of their holding of the islands from 1502 to 1505, they were to pay the Crown, amongst other produce, 5,000 arrobas or 71 tons of sugar, or at the rate of nearly 24 tons per annum.

In the middle of the following century we find the pastel, or woad plant, largely cultivated, and the dye exported to Europe, until it met a fatal rival in indigo.

In 1591, the exports of this article reached the maximum of 60,000 quintals; in 1620 they had fallen to 36,840 quintals, in 1639, when the industry appears to have ceased, they amounted to 14,200 quintals. The impost derivable from this source alone during the period of its prosperity, amounted to 40,000 cruzados per annum. England, Holland and Seville were the chief markets for the article.

In the eighteenth century we find the vine and the orange the Alpha and the Omega of the island, the former alone producing more than 20,000 pipes, worth £71,420 per annum, before the visitation of the *oïdium tuckeri* in 1853 destroyed all the vines in the entire group, which, until then, produced 50,000 pipes of very good wine. At that time the orange crop was not considered an average one which did not produce at least 560,000 flat boxes, containing 400 oranges, each box valued at 3s. 6d., or nearly £100,000 for the entire production; often it exceeded this figure. Now one-third of such a crop is considered a satisfactory return. The actual number of flat boxes shipped to England during the year 1884-85, amounted to 131,341, and in the previous year 1883-1884, 156,227.

The pine-apple industry, which commenced in 1867-68 with an export of 427 pines, has now apparently reached its utmost limit of profitable expansion, close upon 130,000 pines having been shipped to England during the year 1883-84, giving the growers a net profit of £25,000.

The palmy days of St. Michael were those when oranges were almost as great luxuries in England as peaches and hot-house grapes are now in winter, and were prescribed by custom as the special refreshment for young ladies after dancing. Colonel Fergusson, in his entertaining life of Henry Erskine, relates an amusing anecdote regarding the etiquette of oranges about the beginning of the century.

A country youth at a ball, who was more at home in the compounding of certain festive beverages, thus addressed a young lady at the close of the dance. " Miss, wud ye tak' a leemon ?"

It frequently happened that a young lady, suddenly called upon to dance, would hand over to another, whose fate it was to " sit out," the refreshment upon which she had been engaged, with a caution against an undue consumption of the fruit she had temporarily relinquished.

During the five years from 1873-74 to 1877-78, there were shipped to England 2,322,512 flat boxes of oranges, or an average of 464,500 flat boxes per annum, which represented a total value of £124,600 for each year.

The 1882-83 crop only produced 144,280 flat boxes, and the 1883-84, 156,207 flat boxes ; but, owing to bad prices, and the tender condition of the fruit, these crops barely left sufficient to cover the heavy emphyteutic onus under which the gardens labour.

The decadence of the orange trade has been an irreparable loss to the islanders, for they calculate that it left to the growers and those engaged in it an average of £177,000 a year, during the height of its prosperity.

Owing to the position of these islands in mid ocean, subject as they are, during the winter months, to the gales which sweep the Atlantic, care has to be taken to shelter the orange trees from the violence of the winds ; they are therefore generally planted in rectangular plots enclosed by the tall and fast growing pittosporum or incenso (*Pittosporum undulatum Vent*), a tree introduced forty years ago from Australia, but now disseminated throughout the islands to their very hill tops. It is not without a certain beauty, its small white blossom loading the air with a delicious pungency, but its immense lateral roots exhaust the soil, and as its fast-spreading branches shut off the sun and air, so necessary for the proper maturity and keeping qualities of the fruit, it is being gradually replaced by the *Faya myrica*, an endemic tree of slower growth, but of greater durability, and free from the disadvantages of the pittosporum, indeed the leaves and berries of the faya are said to greatly enrich the soil, an important consideration in a country where artificial manures are expensive and difficult to obtain. The pittosporum is native of New South Wales and Victoria ; the wood attracted some attention at the International Exhibition in 1862, and was found well adapted to certain kinds of wood engraving, and regarded as a possible substitute for box in this industry; it is light and even grained, but exceedingly tough, and inferior to that of *Pittosporum bicolor*, Hook. The *tabira* variety resists the sea breezes better than the two already named, and is therefore found in orange gardens bordering the coast in this island.

Almost the only manure ever put into the land here is the lupin plant (*Lupinus termis*), which is sown broadcast and then dug in, when it attains a height of two feet, strengthening the soil to a remarkable extent.

The secret of its fertilizing quality lies in the plant possessing when nearly matured, and especially in its seeds, large quantities of azotic, or nitrogenous elements, which, combined with what it receives from the soil, makes it act as one of the best earth stimulants.

The practice of fertilising the land by means of the lupin plant, now so universal in the islands, commenced in St. Michael in 1550, the first seeds having been sent for from Tolosa, in Spain, by the then donatary and governor of the island, D. Rodrigo. The value of the plant for this purpose was well known to the Romans, who probably introduced it into Spain.

Although the surface of this light volcanic soil readily transmits the pluvial waters, the lava rock itself seems to attract moisture in no small degree, and is supposed to condense it within its vesicles, for pieces of it taken from below the immediate surface, when broken, are often found to hold water. This peculiarity, doubtless, accounts for the luxuriant growth of the vine and orange tree on rocky or biscouto ground, and especially when planted within the singular circular pits dug out for their reception in stony sites four or five feet deep and five to six in width, which are often observed in such localities, where otherwise nothing would grow. The buried and water-laden lava is known to be more friable and permeable to the delicate roots of plants than that on the surface; thus, with little else besides loose scoria to cover their roots, the vine and orange grow wonderfully well in these sunken pits, sheltered in winter from the gales, and in summer their roots being kept moist by the surrounding wall, whilst the fruit, exposed to the full effects of the sun and the radiated heat of the stony ground, soon ripens to perfection.

They still cling in these islands to the ancient, though graceful, mode of cultivating the vine by training it round their tall abrigos; but these, not being pollards, and, as a rule, profuse of foliage, the grape gets little sun, and cannot properly ripen. As in the Minho district in Portugal, the "latada" or bower system is also here largely adopted, especially over road-side balconies where shade is required.

Some few growers, who wish to improve upon these modes of cultivation, plant the vines as in France and Estremadura, in rows, each plant being kept to the height of from three to four feet; but this is exceptional, as stony and "biscouto" localities, fit for little else, are generally reserved for the vine.

New stocks from the United States, and especially the scented Isabel variety, are gradually superseding the exhausted kinds so long cultivated here, and which are unable to resist the ravages of disease. One great disadvantage, however, presents itself in these American vines, for, though producing enormously, the grapes seldom even in this climate ripen simultaneously, producing on that account a wine too acid to be pleasant, but which is now generally consumed by all classes, and the quantity produced in the islands will, in a short time, rival that of olden days.

Besides this Isabel grape, the islanders would do well to try two other American and disease-resisting vines, the Jacquez and the wild Riparias, the latter for grafting the numerous varieties of acclimatised but exhausted vines, such as the Buäl, Verdelho and Malvasia, the latter one of the best wine-producing grapes, originally introduced from Candia. The Italians called this wine Malvasia, from the place Monemvasia, whence they chiefly obtained it, the French corrupting it to Malvoisie, and the English to Malmsey.

A curious arboreal habit of the black island rat *(M. rattus)* may be observed in these quintas, for those who pry closely into the higher branches of the shelter trees will occasionally find large nests built of twigs and lined with leaves, very like that of the rook, but a trifle smaller; these are the nests of rats. This singular trait of nidification on trees on the part of rats I do not remember to have seen mentioned before. Its only explanation is perhaps to be found in the fact of the common Norway or brown rat (*M. decumanus*) which has increased so alarmingly since its importation, waging inveterate warfare against his black confrère, the instinct of self-preservation driving the latter to seek safety for its young in the branches of the higher unfruitful trees, where the brown rat is not likely to follow; whatever the reason, the habit affords the young Azorean much excellent and exciting sport, for these creatures are particularly fond of ripe primes, scooping out the whole interior so cleverly as to leave nothing but a wafer-like hollow rind, destined in time to disappoint the orange picker when he comes round.

The first flush of blossom takes place in the middle of January, and continues to March, when the air is loaded with its delicious and almost overpowering perfume—oftentimes wafted out to sea for a distance of two or three miles. The fruit commences to turn about the beginning of November, and when in full hue, the sight of these gardens with their densely-loaded trees, is inconceivably beautiful; the transformation, however, is quick—once they are handed over to the ruthless bands of packers or *rancheiros*, who, mounting the trees with baskets, which they hook on to the branches, soon strip them of their golden freight. The fruit is then carried into sheds, where it is wrapped in the leaf of the maize cob, in boxes containing from 350 to 400 oranges.

The chiefs of these packers are called Cabeças, and so perfect is their training, that by a mere cursory look round they can tell to a nicety the number of boxes a quinta will produce. It was, and still is, by their aid, that the merchants purchase the garden crops on the system here known as " buying by the round," or so much for the whole crop, but which is fast being substituted by the less precarious plan of paying so much per box, thus saving the buyer his frequently heavy and even total loss by wind-falls.

The cost of a flat box of oranges placed on board here is about 3s. 10d. The orange is the most prolific of trees, 2,000 being a common number for a well-grown tree to produce; some have been known to bear as many as 8,000, but this is rather the exception. In the quinta of Sñ. Lacerda, in the Canada da Cruz, in the island of Terceira, may be seen a gigantic tree said to be considerably more than a century old, from which as late as May of 1864, there were gathered 9,000 oranges. During the fruit season, the ordinary quiet of the country gives place to busy scenes, everywhere sounds the incessant clanging of the packers' hammer, as if the whole population had been condemned by Vulcan to some expiating penance, and from all quarters beasts of burden are seen wending their way between two boxes of golden fruit to the far-off warehouse or quay, and this goes on from November to March.

The camellia thrives here in unrivalled beauty, and wherever this plant grows, the tea, itself a species of camellia, will do equally well.

Under the auspices of the " Society for Promoting Agriculture," composed of a body of intelligent island proprietors, two Chinamen versed in the cultivation and preparation of tea were brought here in 1878, and steps taken to give this industry a serious trial; the results already achieved have exceeded the most sanguine expectations, and may help perhaps, at no very distant date, to resuscitate to a certain extent the drooping fortunes, especially of Terceira and Fayal. The variety cultivated is the *Thea bohea*, *T. chinensis* (Sims) *Camellia theifora* (Griff.) A sample of which was analysed in 1879 by Mr. Schutzemberger, of Paris, with the following results :—

Cellulose resin .. ⎫	insoluble ..	64.3
Albumen, oily matter ⎭		
Theine or caffeine 4.2 ⎫		
Tannin .. .. 1.1 ⎬ soluble ..		35.8
Gummous matter 30.5 ⎭		——
		100.1

To the above is appended a rider to the effect that the analysis reveals qualities of an excellent tea, which was fully borne out by the flavour of the infusion.

It is curious to note, that on the east coast of Spain, and particularly in the province of Valencia, as well as in California, much attention is at present being paid to the systematic cultivation of this important plant. In the islands, as well as in St. Helena and Madeira, it thrives luxuriantly on the rampas, or steep stony inclines or sides of hills where nothing else but the pine-tree can be got to grow.

The cultivation for export to England of the pine-apple *(Ananassa sativa)* under glass has, as we have seen, attained considerable development, the capital employed in glass-houses not being far short of £100,000.

The pineries are well worth visiting; some contain as many as 4,000 plants under one single roof in all stages of growth.

The largest group of houses is owned by Dr. Botelho and the Pine Apple Company, in which from 6,000 to 8,000 pines are every year raised.

The cultivation of the pine-apple is by no means easy or free from considerable expense. Each plant requires 200 kilos of vegetable soil laboriously collected in the woods at two reis per kilo delivered at the pineries, or 1s. 5d. for each plant for soil alone; not to mention the expense of attendance, &c., which brings up the primary cost of the pine to close upon 2s., to which has to be added the outlay of wood for boxes, packing, freight, and worst of all, the sale expenses in England.

The varieties of the pine-apples are very numerous. Mr. D. Munro enumerates no less than 52 kinds which fruited some years ago in the Horticultural Society's Gardens at Chiswick. The variety cultivated here is almost exclusively that known as the smooth Cayenne, and when in perfection is quite equal in flavour to any English-grown fruit, which, by the way, they have completely driven from the London markets. When fully ripe these magnificent pines weigh from 5 to 8 lbs. each.

Vineyards in France are often protected from spring and autumn frosts; their growth retarded and insect life destroyed by the burning of piles of damp straw, the smoke of which burns over the plantations. Here volumes of smoke are sometimes generated in the pineries for the purpose of staying the too rapid growth of the plants, which, if unchecked, would prove unfruitful. Beyond arresting their quick development and accelerating their flowering, the plants do not appear to ultimately sustain any damage from this treatment and produce average-sized pines.

The fruit is timed to ripen in the winter months, when it is carefully packed in crates singly, or in boxes of 6 to 12, and exported to England. The cost of these pine-houses averages from 15s. to 20s. per set plant; and so remunerative were the prices realised during the first few years that one or two crops were sufficient to cover the primary outlay. Now, however, that the annual produce has reached over 150,000, the returns have proportionately decreased. Considerable care is expended upon these pineries, the smallest oversight being sufficient, at certain periods, to spoil the whole crop, and the leaves of the plants have to be periodically wiped to keep them free from blight.

In such a climate as is here enjoyed, no bottom or

artificial heat is necessary, thus enabling this cultivation to be carried on at a comparatively small outlay. Fresh and rapidly fermenting vegetable soil being always used for every successive crop, an accumulation of the old vegetable mould takes place around the glass houses, in which quantities of the finest strawberries are grown and sold in the spring in the streets of Ponta Delgada, at extremely low prices.

The pine-apple industry in St. Michael's has already in a great measure compensated the islanders for their deficient orange crops, for on the outlay expended in hot-houses they have been getting a return of from 10 to 15 per cent. Well may they exclaim—

> Thou blest anana! thou the pride
> Of vegetable life, beyond whate'er
> The poets imaged in the golden age.

To provide timber for making up the fruit boxes, very extensive tracts of country, which a few years ago were barren and valueless, have since been cleared and covered with trees of various kinds, amongst which we see *Pinus maritima, Austriaca nigra*, and *Insignis*, growing side by side with *Cryptomeria japonica*, the Australian *Eucalyptus* and *Acasia melanoxylon*, all having, apparently, found their native habitats here, and attaining arboresence with astonishing rapidity and sufficient girth at the end of 15 or 17 years to render them fit for felling. During the prosperity of the fruit trade, these trees were, at that age, worth from 12s. 6d. to £1 as they stood, and many proprietors who had turned miles of otherwise useless properties into forest lands, saw glimpses of large fortunes in the near future; but the attenuated orange crops of recent years have immensely depreciated the value of these woods, no longer in such demand.

A few months ago, 22 alqueires of pine forest, of above 20 years growth, and in splendid condition, were sold for 600$000, or rather less than £5 an alqueire. Some half-a-dozen years ago this same property would have realised at least £17 the alqueire. Such has been the frightful depreciation in the value of timber during the last few years.

It seems incredible how the pine-tree here thrives on what appears to be absolutely bare and naked rock, on which even thistles are sparse, and the ubiquitous *Pittosporum* cannot find a footing, but once plant it between the scoria crevices, and in a short time the moisture it attracts crumbles the easily disintegrated tufa, affording the young tree a shallow but rich soil whereon to thrive. It is a common and picturesque sight, when riding through the country, to see men at work in these woods felling and sawing great trunks; every now and then the ring of the woodman's axe, or the hideous sound of the steam saw, falling upon the ear and startling the stillness with its unearthly screech—lengthened by the echoing forest.

It is estimated that from six to seven hundred moios (thirty-six thousand to forty-two thousand alqueires) of land, have been planted with pine and other trees; the consumption of wood for orange and pine-apple boxes in average seasons not exceeding what two to two-and-a-half moios would produce; there is therefore abundance of timber to meet the requirements of the island for some considerable time to come.

It is true that since 1877, when the orange trees first began to show signs of the blight which has so much injured the yearly yield of fruit, the increased supply of timber over consumption has reduced the price of the flat box delivered at the purchaser's warehouse ready for nailing together, to one tostão or 5d., barely sufficient to cover the cost of felling, sawing, &c., but this state of things is probably transitory, and the price of timber will rise with increased orange crops and consumption.

Until the year 1832, the timber employed for the orange boxes had been imported from Figueira in Portugal; but the " War of the Brothers," which then broke out, stopped all further supplies. The exporters were therefore compelled to look to America and the north of Europe for their requirements, and forced to cut down every available tree they could procure in the island; thus it is that so few *old* trees are now found standing.

We have seen the terrible effects of the destruction of the woods in the islands of Malta, Cape de Verds, the West India group, and other places, where the lands have become deserts, and even circumscribed in area through denudation. Such was the danger which at one time threatened St. Michael's, until the exigencies of her orange trade fortunately averted a similar fate. Undoubtedly the increase of wooded surface, and the constant attraction of rain thereby induced, is slowly altering the climate of the island by lessening the summer droughts: but dangerously prolonging the wet seasons.

Many of these trees, such for instance, as the *Eucalyptus*, of which many tens of thousands have been planted, absorb ten times their own weight of water, which is returned to the atmosphere in the shape of vapour. To what extent in limited areas like these do such trees affect the climate?

The rainfalls in the Açores are capricious in the extreme, and it is a question how far the planting and subsequent felling of extensive tracts in the island of S. Miguel affects the regularity of the seasons; that these, more especially during recent times, have been much disturbed, there is no doubt, for climatic changes are now more frequent and violent, bringing about total failures of the crops, so that, with a genial climate and soil of unsurpassed fertility, the anomaly of gaunt famine amongst the poor classes is not an uncommon event here.

Occasionally too, these islands come within the influence of icebergs from Baffin's Bay, which pass a little to the westward of them, causing quick condensations of vapour in their track, and probably often accounting for those masses of cloud which canopy their mountain tops, and thus shut out the rays of the sun when most needed.

Perhaps, on this account, nowhere is one so charmed by the occasional glories of the rising and setting summer and autumn sun as in these islands. Dense cloud cumuli, massed together by the aerial currents, until they look like solid and gigantic battlements against a zenith of pure blue, offer splendid play for the rays of the great orb; these beautiful tints, reflected upon the prevailing deep green of the orange plantations, and gilding the tips of the distant pine-clad hills, present a combination of lights and shades of incomparable loveliness, calculated to drive an artist mad, in the impotency of his power to portray them.

A word for the Milho—the staff of life of these poor people—and to them what barley cakes were to the Roman gladiator. An introduction into Europe from America in the middle of the sixteenth century, the Indian corn *(Zea mays)* is perhaps the most useful of all the cereals to man, and is certainly in these islands made much of.

Von Tschudi mentions maize as having been found in Peru, in tombs apparently more ancient than the times of the Incas, and consumed by the Indian tribes in Mexico and the valley of the Mississippi; it was regularly cultivated, and their chief means of sustenance.

Recent travellers in China, moreover, state that the potato, corn, and both the white and yellow varieties of maize, have been cultivated in that country from time immemorial.

It is certain, too, that maize was known and cultivated by the ancient Egyptians in very remote ages, and it appears to have first been introduced into Portugal, not from America, but from African Guinea.

Nothing can exceed, during favourable seasons, its luxuriant development in this island.

When it attains full growth, and the panicle begins to appear, the tender top *(espiga)* is broken off a foot or so

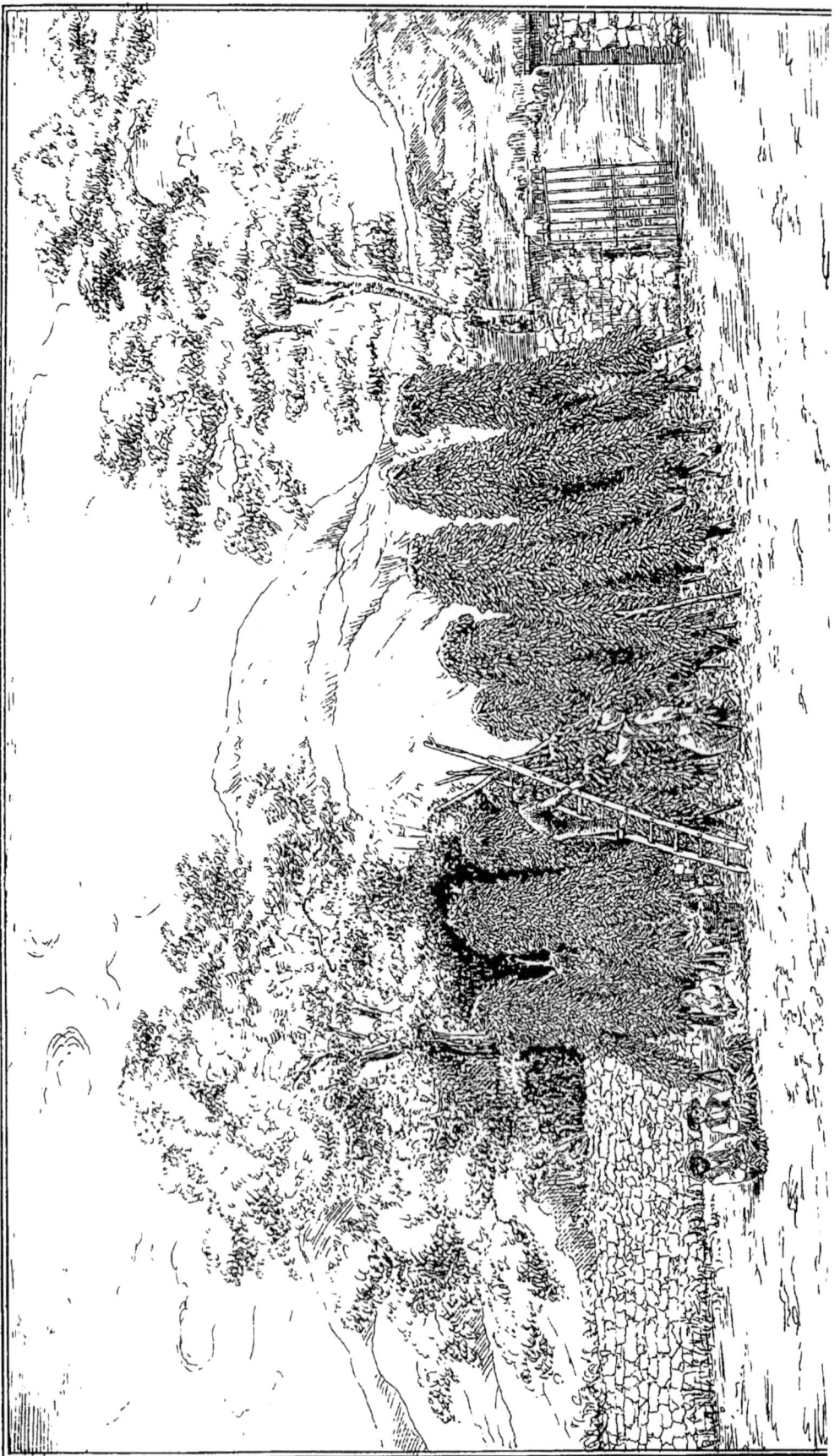

from the cob, and given as forage to cattle; the remaining leaves are then allowed to dry on the stalk, and presently gathered into bundles, are stored as winter fodder—gavella—for horses and cattle.

The dry cob leaves are split into ribands and used for stuffing mattresses—a material always clean and elastic and unattractive to insects.

This leaf is also used, as we have seen, for wrapping round the oranges—a mode of packing peculiar to these islands. Maize contains from 6 to 12 per cent. of oil, and its meal upwards of four times as much oleaginous matter as wheat flour—hence the shiny coats and sleek appearance of animals fed upon it.

To man, maize is just as sustaining as oatmeal, and possesses all the elements necessary for supporting the greatest physical exertion and giving considerable muscular strength. The soundness and whiteness of the teeth of the natives is attributed to their eating so much pão de milho, and children given the maize will be found to make bone and altogether thrive better on it than on wheaten bread. The stalk contains sufficient saccharine matter for the profitable production of sugar, and from the husk, after the grain has been extracted, Herr Holl, of Worms, has recently invented a process whereby alcohol equal to potato spirit can be obtained, the residue forming a pulp suitable for the food of various animals.

The Indian corn, when gathered in these islands, is stacked in a very effective and pleasing manner; the cobs, when ripe, are taken and stripped of their leafy covering, with the exception of two or three sufficient to tie them in bundles of twenty or more. These bundles are then threaded one above the other on tripod poles fixed in the ground sixteen or twenty feet high, thus exposed to the full hardening effects of the sun, and may we also add, to the depredations of the rats. These bright yellow pyramidal "toldas," occurring, as they do, in groups of a dozen or twenty, form an exceedingly picturesque and characteristic sight. When thoroughly dried, the maize is taken down and inned before the winter commences ; sometimes, however, the maize is stacked with its leafy covering, when it remains out during all the winter.

Like all mountainous countries, these islands are rather subject to sudden transitions from sunshine to rain: the high and frequently wooded summits of their hills attract passing currents, the cooler temperature condensing the moisture they contain, which falls in unseasonable showers. Over the country, too, is spread a fleecy canopy, through which oftentimes at critical harvest periods the sun cannot penetrate with full ripening force.

These oft recurring failures of the crops are aggravated by the whole land being held and owned by the rich to the utter exclusion of the labourer, who, unable to rise above his even precarious 10d. a day wage, is condemned to a lifetime of ill-paid labour, and when the maize crops, their staple article of food, fail, and grain has to be imported at high prices, the labourer and his numerous progeny have a bad time of it here.

Notwithstanding these occasional disadvantages, the climate of S. Miguel, as of the other islands forming the group, is mild, equable and balmy, no extremes of heat or cold occurring at any season of the year.

Homer's description of the Hesperides aptly applies to them—

> Stern Winter smiles on that auspicious clime,
> The fields are florid with unfading prime,
> From the bleak pole no winds inclement blow,
> Mould the round hail, or flake the fleecy snow ;
> But from the breezy deep the bless'd inhale
> The fragrant murmurs of the western gale.

In summer the prevailing winds are north-east and easterly. In winter, however, they are oftentimes visited by severe gales from the south, south-west, and more rarely, from the north-west and south-east, when the temperature falls to its lowest, especially during the prevalence of the latter, but, except on the higher mountain tops, frosts are quite unknown.

The temperature during the winter months shows a maximum of 75°, minimum of 48°, and mean of 61°. In summer a maximum of 82½°, minimum of 50°, and mean of 69.5°.

The rainfall, as we have seen, is very irregular, but has increased considerably of recent years, owing to the covering of the highlands with timber trees. Here the fall must considerably exceed 60 inches; but on the lower levels the average may be taken at 40 inches—the annual amount of evaporation showing a mean of 45 inches.

Volcanic soils are, as a rule, too light to retain water long, and especially is this the case here, where the land almost everywhere slopes gently to the sea, any excess of rain being quickly carried away; no inconvenience is therefore felt from persistent rainfalls, as in some of the heavier soils of England.

The absence of any annoying insects beyond mosquitos also conduces in no slight measure to the enjoyment of this pleasant climate; but, owing to the humid and enervating character of the sea-board air, it affords but temporary relief to pulmonary complaints, and patients suffering from phthisis, in search of a genial yet bracing change, cannot be too strongly warned against taking up their permanent residence here; let them rather seek Algiers or Southern California (Los Angeles or Sta. Barbara), where the air is drier and therefore more suited to that fell complaint. The unceasing evaporation from the surrounding ocean naturally contributes to the humidity of isolated oceanic islands in greater or less degree, according to the temperature of the air, absorption being, of course, greater in summer than in winter; it follows, therefore, that the air of these islands during hot, sultry weather is damp almost to saturation.

That the Gulf stream—that wondrous oceanic "warm river" issuing from the Gulf of Florida, with a breadth varying from thirty to sixty miles, possessing a depth of 2,200 feet, and a temperature of eighty-six degrees Fahrenheit—exercises, from the vicinity of its southern arm to the group, a very decided thermic influence upon the climate of these islands there can be no doubt, for we know that the northern deflection of the stream modifies and ameliorates, in no small degree, the climate of the shores of Britain and north-eastern and western Europe. To this heat-dispersing agent is doubtless due that humidity in the atmosphere of these islands, which, though not injurious to the healthy and strong, is yet fatal in its ultimate effects upon the consumptive; add to which, Ponta Delgada still lacks hotels* or pensions possessing the comforts which patients are accustomed to at home; the houses, too, are not, in the absence of fire-places and other conveniences, adapted as residences for invalids in the winter time.

Owing to this excess of humidity, it is difficult to keep grain of any kind for lengthened periods—a disadvantage which could be easily overcome by establishing the kiln-drying process.

The early inhabitants of these islands successfully preserved their corn by keeping it in pits or silos containing about twenty quarters each; almost every townsman had his silo, which was lined with straw, and so constructed that no rain could enter. The opening was just large enough to admit a man; and in this way grain kept the whole year.

Each pit was covered by a large stone with the owner's mark on it, and a certain quarter of the town was set apart expressly for the construction of these grain receptacles.

*English and American visitors will find the hotel kept by Mrs. Brown at Pinheiros, Ponta Delgada, comfortable, clean and moderate (about a dollar or 4s. 6d. a day). There are also two Portuguese hotels, one the 'Azorean,' kept by Snr. Manoel Corrêa, and the other, which is more of a boarding house, kept by Snr. Gil; both are fairly good and very reasonable, but the first named is specially recommended to visitors.

CHAPTER IX.

> Where in a smiling vale the mountains end,
> Form'd in a crystal lake the waters blend,
> Fring'd was the border with a woodland shade,
> In every leaf of various green array'd,
> Each yellow-tinged, each mingling tint between
> The dark ash-verdure and the silvery green.
>
> *Mickle's " Camöens."*

Emigration, generally clandestine, has of late years greatly relieved the necessitous condition of these poor islanders, but the difficulties in the way of the overplus population seeking their fortunes elsewhere have been increased by a law passed in the Cortes in 1880, compelling all males, on attaining the age of 14, to deposit £40 with the State, before being allowed to leave the country; this sum being kept in pawn with a view to providing a military substitute, should the emigrant not return when required to undergo the period of service in the army all Portuguese are liable to.

The stream of emigration from the three most eastern islands of S. Miguel, Santa Maria and Terceira, has through accidental circumstances generally proceeded steadily to Brazil, whereas that from the westernmost islands of Fayal, San Jorge and Flores is directed mainly to the United States, whilst Madeira, singularly enough, contributes a by no means insignificant quota to the Sandwich Islands, where the number of Portuguese (chiefly from

Madeira and the Açores) had in 1884 reached 9,000, as against 436 in 1879.

The total annual emigration from this archipelago fluctuates between two and three thousand of both sexes, but is continuous. Besides the English, German and Portuguese steamers which occasionally call at these islands for their living freights, there are three or four sailing vessels employed between them and Boston and New Bedford, U.S., carrying each about 170 passengers, and making five or six voyages in the year.

Brazil, however, is the El Dorado of these poor islanders; once there, they fondly imagine themselves for ever manumitted from the vexatious and hopeless drudgery they are subject to here. But how different the sequel in the majority of cases!

From 1870 to 1874 there landed in Brazil from Portugal and the Açores 46,828 emigrants, of whom 9,157 were minors.

The following emigration returns for the year 1879, taken from a Brazilian paper, speak volumes for the fate the majority of these unfortunate people meet with.

During the whole 12 months, 49,538 emigrants from Europe landed at the various Brazilian ports; of these, only 3,240 (3,127 being Portuguese) found employment, chiefly as agricultural labourers and miners; 15,237 were still seeking engagements at the end of the year; 16,661 died within the period from various diseases, consequent upon exposure and want, and 11,400 returned to Europe.

An official table of the emigration from St. Michael for the ten years, 1872 to 1882, shows the following:—

Years.			Emigrants.
1872–74	..	..	2,460
1875–77	..	..	2,232
1878–80	..	..	3,834
1881–82	..	..	6,947
			15,473

From the whole group of islands during the same period 22,794 persons emigrated.

Notwithstanding this constant flux of emigration, the population of the island would seem to be on the increase, for the census of 1864 showed that the number of inhabitants amounted to 106,000, whereas in the last census of 1878 they had increased to 120,000 approximately, distributed between thirty-five towns and villages.

The amounts remitted by successful emigrants to their friends in the islands are very considerable. The fortunes of Terceira have of recent years positively revived under this influence, and Fayal alone receives in some years as much as £20,000 of savings from the Western States. I have seen it stated in a generally well-informed native paper, that the sums remitted to these islands by absent colonists have occasionally amounted to 300 contos or £53,600, but this must be an exaggerated or very exceptional estimate.

The emigrants from the Açores ever retain an affectionate remembrance of their former homes, and unless prevented by family ties, return, sometimes with considerable fortunes, to end their days here. I once met a man on board the " Açor," who had been away in one of the Western States for twenty-five years and was visiting Fayal to see his friends. He had forgotten every word of Portuguese except " Saudades," * for his native place, which he felt must be satisfied at any cost.

Every steamer from Lisbon carries as passengers to the islands, one or more of these fortunate emigrants returning home with their " little pile," after an absence of many years in the United States or Brazil.

These islanders, on returning from Brazil, are known as " Brazileiros " ; if from the United States, as " Americanos."

A Lisbon paper, the *Commercio de Portugal*, commenting

---

* Almeida-Garrett, one of Portugal's most gifted writers, thus describes this expression of tender longing. The word "Saudade" is perhaps the sweetest, most

recently upon the respective influences exercised by these emigrants, draws so exact a picture of their different types as to be worth reproduction.

"The 'Americano' is a man strengthened in frame, with a mind braced by the grand intuitive feelings of goodness and sympathy. He possesses extreme application for work; his modest capital is consecrated to the honest transactions of industry and commerce. He understands the word family, educates his sons, is sober, intelligent, and extremely liberal. His house is elegant, bathed by fresh air and light; it possesses that solid yet economical furniture which is characteristic of American habitations. Within resides a family, the members of which are beloved of one another, and who work. The 'Americano' in the Azores is a patriot. He is proud of having lived in the United States, and he nourishes the hope that those good and generous lands will one day be as free as those of the Great Republic. There are many people who regard the emancipation of the Açores as an Utopian idea, or at most as a threat to the metropolis. They are mistaken. Emancipation is a fact which is being prepared for by education in social institutions and by a

---

expressive, and delicate expression in our language. The idea and sentiment it conveys is certainly felt in all countries, but I do not know of any special term in any other language to designate it, except in Portuguese.

Oh Saudade !

Magico numen que transportas a alma,
Do amigo ausente ao solitario amigo,
Do vago amante á amada inconsolavel,
E até ao triste, ao infeliz proscripto
—Dos entes o miserrimo na terra—
Ao regaço da patria em sonhos levas.

(Oh Saudade !

Soul-transporting, magic word ! whose influence sweet
Knits with far-reaching links the hearts of absent friends,
To maid disconsolate draws the fickle lover's thought,
And to the outlaw sad, a gleam of comfort lends
—Of all earth's beings, for pity the object meet—
Yet by you, in dreams, to his country's bosom brought.)

certain culture many possess from long residence in the
United States.

" The 'Brazileiro' in general is, *um anemico*, utterly devoid
of good instincts, and without social education. He does not
at first sight inspire great sympathies. He is the embodiment
of laziness. No sooner has he arrived than his capital is
employed in impudent stock-jobbing. His idea is enjoyment—the enjoyment tainted by the brutality of an evil
instinct. For him family has no charms nor sacred ties.
Libertinism to him is not a thing repugnant and vile. Without
any idea of religion, of country, or of family, the 'Brazileiro'
is an impious being. He speaks evil of all principles of
truth and justice, 'to give himself the airs' of a free-
thinker. From time to time he has the pretension to display
greatness; he indulges in charity for vanity's sake, and
bestows public alms upon the poor with great noise and
ostentation. In the poor villages the 'Brazileiro' is
appreciated and judged by the amount of alms he bestows
on the day of his 'festa.' Contrasted with the 'Americano'
the 'Brazileiro' has only one pre-occupying thought—the
usurious and profitable employment of his capital.

" The 'Americano' is ever employed in the great initiatives
of work; he introduces new machines, he seeks to make
American products known, and, so to speak, to naturalize
them. Not so the 'Brazileiro'; he is all routine. He
arrives, and the small glebe of land which belonged to him
by patrimony continues to be scratched by the old useless
plough; the agricultural processes continue to be the ones
followed by the old forefathers. Nothing of innovations,
nothing of studies, and nothing of work. We positively
affirm that morally the influence of the 'Brazileiro' has
been as unfortunate to Azorean civilization as the moral
and material influence of the 'Americano' has been useful
and profitable."

The Azorean islander flies from the recruiting sergeant
as he would from the Evil One, and, to escape service, will

run any risks—not that he fears soldiering and its vicissitudes, but because to him it means banishment from the country, and friends he dearly loves, and the lost chance of a possible competency in the autumn of life. He will, however, cheerfully submit to an exile of many years, if only, at the end, it holds out the possibility of a return, with means sufficient to keep off "chill penury." This is the hope he ever harps upon when absent, and to him the words of the poet aptly apply—

> Land of my sires, what mortal hand
> Can e'er untie the filial band
> That knits me to thy rugged strand?

By law of 7th April, 1873, monetary payment in substitution of enlistment was abolished, and the unhappy emigrant was still liable to be called upon to serve, if he returned prior to attaining his 36th year. Thus, if he wished to escape service, he was forced to expatriate himself during the youngest and happiest period of his existence. This decree was, however, abrogated in 1883, and substitutes allowed, upon payment of £40 for each military or naval recruit.

The number contributed for the two services by the entire Azorean group is on an average 712, of which the district of S. Miguel furnishes 341. The Açores form the 5th Military Division of Portugal, the headquarters and *place d'armes* being permanently established at Angra, Terceira.

The entire garrison of the island of S. Miguel, consists of a battalion of the 11th Caçadores, and a company of artillery.

The fort of S. Braz, already mentioned, derives its name from a chapel which formerly stood upon the site. It was commenced in 1552, and completed at a cost of £6,500— a large sum for those days. Its chief purpose was to repel the attacks of corsairs and roving marauders, who made happy hunting grounds of these seas, lying in wait for the fleets of richly-laden náos, or Portuguese East Indiamen, which, during the zenith and brief hey-day of Portugal's colonial empire (the glamour and memory of which every true Portuguese still fondly cherishes), regularly made for the Açores to provision on their long voyages home from India, China and Africa; or making prizes of the ponderous Spanish galleons returning from the Antilles.

During the reign of Emanuel (Dom Manoel), and for at least twenty years of his reign, an average of thirteen naós arrived annually at Lisbon from the Portuguese Indian possessions, laden with spices and other valuable commodities, and bringing quantities of gold and precious stones—and for the sixty years ending 1756, Portugal received from Brazil alone upwards of 100 millions sterling of specie, excluding precious stones and the fortunes accumulated by colonists and others. At present, except in the famous diamonds belonging to the Braganza family, scarcely a vestige remains in the country of this vast wealth, unless it be in the numerous palatial (but now ruinous) residences, built in those prosperous times, which are to be met with throughout Portugal—alas! mere shadows of their original grandeur.

These rovers appear to have held the Azorean defences of little account; for we find a governor of S. Miguel in 1572 complaining to the king of a French privateer, carrying twenty guns, and a motley crew of 300 men running defiantly under the very guns of the fort, and carrying off the peaceful caravels at anchor there, even within shot of his arquebusiers. The "Castle" sweeps the bay of Ponta Delgada, at the head of which it stands, but, as in former times, is utterly useless as a means of defence. No objection is made to the curious visitor prying into the mysteries of its arcana, and he may be interested in the examination of some few obsolete and even ancient 40-pounders, which arm its parapets—harmless, except to the braves who occasionally on Saints' days venture to discharge them.

I

In none of these islands is a single Armstrong or Krupp gun to be found; the government, apparently, being of opinion that the gates of Janus are to be for ever closed in these remote and peaceful islands, forgetting that quite within the memory of man such playful accidents as the sinking of a friendly nation's vessel by the guns of another friendly flag, have happened under the very walls of some of these Azorean castles.

One would have thought that during the struggle between the Northern and Southern States of America, and more recently, during that between France and Germany, when war vessels of these nations played at hide and seek amongst these islands, the government would have seen the necessity of placing these crumbling forts in a position to at least command respect—for the smallest hostile sloop of war, if armed with modern artillery, could at any time defy them with impunity.

In former times, every foreigner arriving here was at once escorted to the "Castle," where his papers were examined and, even if found in order, he had subsequently to obtain permission from the chief magistrate to remain in the island; needless to say, that all these formalities have been done away with, and passengers are free to come and go without even the necessity of a passport.

The basilica of S. Miguel is the church of Saint Sebastian, better known as the Matriz; it owed its origin to a plague which broke out in 1523, and lasting eight years, carried off many victims.

As a propitiatory offering that the pest might be stayed, contributions were raised amongst the terrified community, and with the proceeds the finest religious edifice in the island was erected and dedicated to the martyr Saint Sebastian.

Like all the Azorean churches, it is rigidly plain, its rectilineal outlines being utterly devoid of architectural beauty. The style of these Portuguese churches is probably an imitation of those of Lombardy and Upper Italy, without the elegant rose windows which distinguished them. The freedom in ecclesiastical architecture which in 1589 to 1680 superseded the more austere style so long under the influence of the priesthood in many parts of Europe, never penetrated permanently into Portugal, where we find the clerical in-

MATRIZ CHURCH, PONTA DELGADA.

fluence too powerful for any innovation or improvement in the outward building of their churches, and this influence continued even after the expulsion of the Jesuits in 1760 from Portugal and her dependencies. All their efforts at embellishment seem to have been expended upon the interior, especially in the brilliant colouring and painting of the ceilings and walls, fine examples of which may be seen in the Estrella and other churches in Lisbon, and Sé at Terceira.

Several writers on Portuguese church architecture, and notably Mr. Crawfurd, have very aptly classified this as the Jesuit style.

The western and southern entrances are ornamented with some passable marble carvings and bas-reliefs, executed and brought from Lisbon; on the facia over the latter are carved busts of Dom Manuel and his queen. The interior is divided by two rows of massive pillars into a handsome nave and aisles; there is some good work on the capitals of these columns, which, in a measure, relieves their heaviness. The altar is very elegant. On high festivals an excellent organ makes the edifice resound with "music's melting, mystic lay." Very good vocal music may also be heard on these occasions, the choir being highly trained, and some of the voices really very fine. Some processions and celebrations are held within its walls, amongst others an interesting one, yclept "a festa da Pombinha," at Easter time, to commemorate certain miraculous events which happened thus:—The comet of 1672, observed by several astronomers in Europe, became conspicuously visible in these islands in March of that year, and as these mysterious bodies were at that time looked upon as presaging dire calamities, and as the visible signs of divine wrath, the superstitious inhabitants were filled with fear, and by fastings and prayer strove to ward off the threatened evil. It so happened that a few days after the appearance of this comet a choleraic epidemic broke out in Ponta Delgada, the daily mortality being so great that the cemeteries could no longer afford room for interments. At this juncture, many processions were resorted to, and a religious and charitable confraternity established, known as "a irmandáde da misericordia," who commenced their ministrations by a solemn procession within the precincts of the town, beating a large drum, that its sounds might expel and drive away the malignant fevers. This belief in the efficacy of sound to drive away "wycked spirytes" seems to have been pretty general at the time, for on

the authority of Brand, bells were rung in England to "drive away divils and tempests." The old Portuguese chronicler goes on to say that no sooner had this procession issued from the church than the sickness ceased ; a special service of thanksgiving was thereupon held at the Matriz, attended by thousands of the inhabitants. The service had scarcely commenced when a dove was seen to fly into the crowded edifice, and after fluttering about for some time, alighted on the chief altar piece. The preacher, being equal to the occasion, hailed the bird as the harbinger of peace, assured the multitude that their prayers had been heard, and that the Divine wrath had been appeased. Every year this festival is held on Easter Monday—the anniversary of this occasion—the same miraculous dove always putting in an appearance.

Another famous ceremonial is the "Imperio do Espirito Santo" or, as it is sometimes called, "Imperio dos nobres," from its aristocratic associations, which had its origin in remote times, and was surrounded by many quaint rites. It was evidently intended to symbolize the Trinity, and was first instituted by the charitable Queen Isabella (of saintly memory) in 1300, at the small town of Alemquer, in Estremadura. The queen's biographer, Bishop Lacerda, and other writers of the time, thus describe this singular festival : " Having erected in Alemquer a church dedicated to the Holy Ghost, the queen resolved upon instituting the festival of the "Coronation of the Emperor," for which purpose she invited all the members of the neighbouring hierarchies to attend. Seated on a throne under the canopy was the individual called " the emperor," supported by two others, one on either side, whom they called " kings," and attending these were three pages bearing each a crown, that of the emperor, sometimes carried by the Prince Royal of Portugal, being extremely handsome, and presented for the purpose by the queen. Having placed the crown for a few moments on the altar, a priest in full canonicals then crowned the three typical monarchs, who, attended by all the nobles and a great concourse of people, carrying green boughs in their hands, and accompanied by the playing of bagpipes, proceeded in procession through the principal streets of the town, on their way to the parish church of S. Francisco. Here they were received by the prebendary, who handed bouquets of flowers to the nobles, some of whom then danced with three young maidens selected for their beauty and virtues, and who had attended the putative monarchs in the capacity of queens. The ceremony was ended by the bestowal upon these maidens of their marriage portions, contributed by the community at large; after which, the procession, reforming, returned in the same order to the Church of the Espirito Santo, where the crowns were deposited. Following this came the distribution of bread, meat, and wine to the poor.

This serio-comic ceremonial soon extended throughout all Portugal, but its accessories have been much modified. Preceding the customary procession, bands of fantastically dressed men, called Foliões, may still be seen going about the streets of these island towns, begging contributions from house to house for the coming festival, and uttering as they go wail-like and excessively nasal chants—veritable fugues of invocation—to the accompaniment of the guitar and other instruments. The name Folião is evidently derived from folle (gaita de folle), a bagpipe, which, in Portugal, was always used in folias or dances. The Portuguese appear to have been very partial to this instrument, and a treatise exists on the art of playing the bagpipe, by André de Escobar, organist to the Cathedral of Coimbra, who lived a century ago, and is said to have played the most difficult compositions on it.

In the chief thoroughfare of every village in these islands, however insignificant, is to be seen a small square stone building—generally ten feet by eight, and open in front and at the sides—called by the natives " o theatro," where the " emperor " is enthroned and holds his mimic court. He has it all to himself now, for his two rivals, the kings (with much of the ancient splendour of this ceremonial), have been, long since done away with. He is elected by " universal suffrage," belongs as a rule to the plebeian class ; and the age of the juvenile candidate varies from eight to twelve.

At Whitsuntide and on Trinity Sunday these little votive temples (for such they are) present a pleasing and animated appearance, being gaily decorated with flowers and flags, in anticipation of the imperial coronation which then takes place. Tables having been laid out on one side of the road-way in close proximity to the " imperio," joints of raw meat, bread and fruits, the gifts of the charitable, are set out on them, amid bright coloured flowers and bouquets ; the footway being strewn with highly scented blossoms and aromatic leaves (a relic of plague-stricken ages, when less regard was given to hygiene, and such perfumes were supposed to ward off disease).* The parish priest then proceeds to bless these good things, when they are at once distributed in equal shares to the poor of the district, all previously provided with the necessary ticket entitling him or her to the portion. After this ceremony lots are drawn by ballot for appointing the " imperador " for the ensuing year, and his various office-bearers, especially the mordomo do fogo, a personage of great importance, whose duty it is to provide and let off rockets and fireworks. At nightfall the " imperador " returns home in state, accompanied by the fanfare of martial music, his crown being carried before him on a silver salver.

---

* On these occasions, you tread on perfect carpets of the beautiful blue lily (*Agapanthus umbellatus*), masses of which adorn many a neglected road-side patch, mingled here and there with the scarlet spike of the *Tritoma uvaria* or " red-hot-poker."

Marshalled by four " foliões," in their peculiar garb, one of whom carries a red damask banner with the imperial crown worked in the centre, over which flutters a white dove, the procession with lighted torches moves in two wings at a slow pace, chanting portions of a hymn as they go along. Arrived at the house, or rather cottage, of the imperador the crown is reverently deposited on a high altar, on which, amongst masses of flowers, burn innumerable lights; the banner is laid by its side, a short hymn of praise is sung, and without more ado, the " balho " commences, and is kept up until morning. This description of an " imperio " admits of variation according to locality and the means of the people. So anxious are these poor folks to figure in these proceedings, that families have been known to beggar themselves in order to keep up the "imperio" with becoming splendour.

Sometimes its *éclat* is enhanced by the addition of two columns of little girls dressed in white, in whose centre majestically walks the " empress," preceded by her crown and standard bearer, and followed by her dames of honour.

Strange as these mock-dignities and quasi-religious ceremonies may appear, we are yet reminded by the elder D'Israeli, that in England in the middle ages we had our boy-bishops, and on St. Nicholas' day—a saint who was the special patron of children—the boy-bishop with his "mitra parva " and a long crozier, attended by his schoolmates as his diminutive prebendaries, assumed the title and state of a bishop. This child-bishop preached a sermon and afterwards, accompanied by his attendants, went along singing and collecting his pence.

Before the "imperios " were introduced into Portugal they had the "folias do Bispo Innocente," also common in France, and especially at S. Martin de Tours; but these dances, leading to contempt of religion, were suppressed in 1260, and afterwards substituted, as we have seen, by the

" Imperios do Espirito Santo " by Queen Isabel and D. Diniz.

In Siam also, there has existed from time immemorial, a kindred festival occurring every year in January, during which the sovereign of the country names a " three-days' king " from amongst his favorite mandarins, and nominally abdicates in his favor. The object, however, appears to be purely that of a carnival jollification, as no element of charity enters into the arrangement.

Many natures are shocked at witnessing ceremonies and processions such as these, which they look upon as akin to idolatry, forgetting that the lower orders, for whom these priestly mummeries were instituted, are yet so benighted as to be unable to understand the true nature of the Deity, and without some such ceremonies as these, which have existed from time immemorial, religion, to these poor people, would be a blank, unmeaning thing.

Another singular procession, now happily suppressed, was one called " a processão dos terçeiros," which issued from the chapel of " Nossa Senhora das Dores." In it were carried the life-size figures of Saint Francis, representative of this saint's various sufferings, and followed by a number of supposed penitents dressed in tight-fitting blouses of sackcloth with hoods completely covering their faces, only small apertures being left for the eyes and mouth. Each carried on his shoulder a huge cross, and in his hand a whip-cord; every now and then, the procession stopped that these penitent " Maroccos," as they were nick-named, might flagellate themselves. This procession appears to have first been introduced in Rome in 1260, and Jaques Boileau tells us that Saint Dominic redeemed his own and the sins of the people, by administering to himself in the space of ten days, 300,000 strokes with a scourge; that the saint was in earnest may be inferred from the fact of the skin of his back becoming perfectly blackened and impervious to the slightest sensibility.

Clement VI. suppressed these abominable practices within his dominions, but they still lingered in these islands until 1864.

A procession which every year attracts large gatherings of country people is one held on the fifth Sunday after Easter, and issues from the church of Esperança.

The figure of the Saviour, borne usually by Michaelense notabilities, was a gift from one of the early popes to the first nuns who inhabited the adjoining convent. In its left hand is placed a staff set all over with gems, said to have cost £6,700. Covering the image, as if to hide its execrable workmanship, are innumerable jewels of all kinds, the superstitious offerings of hope or fear from devotees in Portugal, Brazil and the colonies. It is difficult to realise that this jewelry represents a value of £90,000; but such is the estimated worth by competent authorities. These accumulated offerings have always been in the keeping of the nuns of the Esperança Convent, who must have experienced sore temptations anent this charge when the Government in 1832, under the plea of cleansing these Augean stables, confiscated the conventual property and abolished for the future all similar institutions. Permission was given to those of the sisterhood who wished to retire to their homes, and pensions (which were often never paid) granted to those who elected to remain in the nearly empty buildings. In some instances the secularisation of these vast properties was stayed during the lifetime of the inmates, but such concessions were exceptional.

This figure of the Christ is endowed by the priests with most miraculous powers. One one occasion, it is reputed to have descended from its elevated niche, and located itself behind a door to prevent the entry of some thieves who contemplated a midnight burglary and robbery of his valuables. On another, he is credited with having induced a most violent colic in a lady devotee who was a little behind with her donations, to compel her to present the church with a silver candelabra.

A considerable and lucrative trade in relics is carried on in this extinct convent; one of the most miraculously gifted articles being a ribbon called the " Medida do Santo Christo," or measure of the blessed Christ, one of which is possessed and religiously preserved by almost every family in case of serious illness, when they tie the ribbon round their persons, and thus hope to escape the clutches of death. Almost every night, numbers of women may be seen laboriously mounting on their knees, the stone steps leading to the church where this "Santo Christo dos Milagres" reposes. Multitudes of people come from all parts of the island to attend the annual procession of this image, which is borne on the shoulders of the most notable inhabitants, and under the bier or stand on which it rests, oftentimes walk lady penitents, members of the best families, in fulfilment of some vow. When a maiden is desirous to know what sort of news she will receive from her absent lover, she proceeds on foot at night, silently praying to the church where this famous figure is located, accompanied by a female friend who walks some little distance behind, the better to catch the remarks which may fall upon their ears, uttered by other perambulators in the streets, or inhabitants of the houses they may pass by. On their return home, they string together what they have heard, and thence deduce the nature of the communication from the absent one.

The convent of Esperança was founded in 1541, and contained 102 nuns and 57 novitiates and servants.

The convent of S. Francisco was the finest in the island; it was commenced in 1709, and cost more than 120,000 crusados, an immense sum at that time; its revenue, like that of Esperança, was very large.

Within the precincts of Ponta Delgada are still to be seen the now deserted three convents and four monasteries, besides three " recolhimentos," to which ladies might retire who did not care to take the veil; also no less than twenty-eight churches—all these religious institutions being richly endowed and supporting at the time of their prosperity 9460 nuns, monks and priests—veritable drones, who maintained themselves on their neighbours' industry.

The orders of friars established in these islands were confined to the Mendicant, Dominicans, Franciscans and Capucins—a most useless fraternity, regular Friar Tucks, who lived upon the community, and did little or no good. They amassed immense wealth, and their huge establishments stud the most fertile parts of the country.

The convents, if useless and pernicious, had at least the merit of purveying the public and visitors with exquisitely-made feather flowers, scarcely comparable to those made by the Mexicans and Brazilians, but still close imitations of nature. They also turned out perfect phenomenal productions, in the way of numerous kinds of preserves and sweetmeats, the ordering of which cunningly-made confections served very often as excuses for naughty flirtations with pretty nuns, who could only openly be interviewed, ensconced behind massive iron gratings. It was whispered, however, that Cupid was gate-keeper, and could gain admittance into the " sacred penetralia," and there would seem to be too good foundation for the taunt. Here, as elsewhere, we find that " love laughs at locksmiths." On procession days a vast consumption of confetti goes on, the convents formerly supplying the best; the streets on these occasions ring with the cries of vendors of " confeitos e amendoas," for which these black-eyed Azoreans have a passionate fondness, paying the penalty in attacks of indigestion and the ruin of beautiful teeth.

As in the Levant, a great feature on gala days in these islands are the deafening rockets sent up in showers, and without which no ceremony of this kind is considered complete. These rockets are manufactured in the outskirts of the city; the " sticks " are formed from the young reeds of the *Arundo donax*, enveloping at the upper end a fuse of the same cane, to which are attached five small twine-covered bombs, very ingeniously made, and which go off with the report of a musket; fortunately the great height to which they ascend lessens their effect. The careless manner in which huge bundles of these rockets are handled and carried about, frequently leads to personal injury. Not very long ago, a mass of them fastened underneath a country cart loaded with gavela—the leaf of the maize, used here as hay —accidentally ignited and flew in all directions, seriously wounding the drover and his oxen, and setting the contents of the cart on fire. It is common to see a mule laden with these mischievous engines pass along, with the driver on top, placidly smoking his cigarette.

Other active agents in all these festivities are the church bells, which peal loud and discordant changes, maddening to weak and sensitive nerves, and which are unhappily becoming so much the fashion in our own densely populated cities at home. Surely Moses never contemplated this state of things when he ordered the more tremulous harmony of silver trumpets to be sounded at the time of sacrifice. From these must, however, be excepted the Trindádes chime, pealing out the knell of parting day, and sending forth the evening benison, at the sound of which it is pleasant to see bands of labourers journeying home from their days' work, doff their caps, and devoutly repeat their " Ave Marias," showing that these poor sons of toil, neglected as they are, and without the slightest religious instruction from their pastors, yet possess much innate reverential feeling. Would that it could be fully worked upon !

How different this from the embruted and ruffianly language heard any evening in our crowded English streets, profaning the air and rendering it impossible for decent ears to escape being shocked.

The " Collegio," or College of the Jesuits, is well worth visiting on account of the excellent wood-carving in the interior. The building stands on the site of an old church, erected in 1592; the present structure, however, dates from 1625, and the stone ornamentation of its façade is remarkable.

In the extinct Augustine monastery, now known as the Graça, a spacious building erected in 1606, a very interesting natural history collection is being formed, which will prove invaluable to future students of Azorean fauna, &c. It already possesses some rare ornithological specimens found in this and neighbouring islands, and examples of fossil marine mullusca from Santa Maria. Here are to be seen the rare *Sylvia atricapilla* (touto vinagreiro), *Pyrrhula murina* (priolo), *Oriolus galbula* (papa figos), *Plectrophanes nivalis* (frigueiraõ), *Qtus vulgaris* (mocho), and interesting examples of migratory and stray birds from the African or American continents, occasionally shot in the little frequented lakes in the interior during winter time, and which must not be confounded with the local and permanent avifauna. Shells of the nautilus (*N. pompilius* and *Ocythœ tuberculatus*), occasionally picked up on the shore, are shown, but it is seldom that these beautiful objects are found entire on this iron-bound coast.

The chief curator is Dr. Carlos Machado, to whom the honor is due of the inception of this useful institution. Aided entirely by private donations, and with the enthusiastic aid of his assistant, Sñr. A. de Vasconcellos, he has succeeded in collecting, preserving, and classifying in a more than creditable manner the finest assemblage of Azorean birds and natural history objects ever yet brought together. Duplicates of these will be readily exchanged for examples from other countries, the limited means at the disposal of the curator preventing acquisitions by purchase.

Under the same roof is the Lyceo or Alma Mater, where the Ponta Delgada youth of the more necessitous middle class receive free instruction.

In the entire archipelago there are only 125 elementary schools, of which S. Miguel possesses 41; but in respect of educational matters, very little progress has been made amongst the working class during the past 30 years.

Here also is the public library, open on all days of the week, except Saint days. It was formed in 1843 with 5,000 volumes, taken from the extinct convents, other 5,000 volumes, chiefly theological, from the same source being added a few years later. Contributions have subsequently been made by private donors and purchases, chief among the former being Snr. José do Canto, who has presented the library with several thousand books—many being rare works upon the history of the islands.

The obliging custodian, Dr. Francisco da Silva Cabral, is ever ready to afford information to visitors seeking it.

In another part of the same building a well appointed meteorological observatory has for some time been established, where important data has been collected.

Ponta Delgada possesses a capital theatre (Theatro Esperança), completed in 1865 at a cost of £5,000, for which a company was formed, the shares being readily subscribed by the patriotic and pleasure-loving community; it is capable of comfortably accommodating 700 persons. Now and then a speculative operatic or dramatic company will come over from Lisbon, and electrify the unaccustomed Michaelenses with the splendour of their (mediocre) performances, achieving scenic triumphs which repay them well for their trouble. Occasionally, too, amateur concerts, reflecting the greatest credit on the performers, are held on its boards, to assist some charitable purpose. The Portuguese are very proficient and clever musicians, evincing considerable taste and execution. As part of these programmes, original poetical recitations sometimes enter, the authors showing no mean talent, and delivering their compositions with much grace and verve, and in the true lyric lilt.

As in the case of the streets and many public and private buildings, the theatre is lighted up by gas.

The shire of Ponta Delgada comprises four comarcas or

districts, *i.e.*, Ponta Delgada, with a conselho or township of the same name; Ribeira Grande with two townships, Ribeira Grande and Villa do Nordeste; Villa Franca with four townships, Agua do Páo, Lagôa, Villa da Povoacáo and Villa Franca do Campo. Included in this district or shire of Ponta Delgada is Villa do Porto, in the neighbouring island of St. Mary, with only one township of the same name.

The city of Ponta Delgada is divided into three freguezias or parishes.

The appearance of some of the principal streets, and the comfort of the dwelling-houses in them, is much impaired by many of the latter having their *rez de chaussée* occupied by unattractive shops, not always possessing the choicest of articles in stock; of course in the outskirts of the town, where most of the few English people here reside, this drawback does not occur.

The houses themselves, although in the bare and cold Tuscan style which characterises and disfigures Portuguese architecture in general, are solidly built of basaltic stone, with well-proportioned and lofty rooms.

The old Arabesque habit of narrowing the streets for shade, though possessing undeniable advantages in excessively hot climates, is altogether out of place in this temperate zone, and it is satisfactory to observe that, wherever possible, the islanders are substituting for these broad and handsome streets. The favorite old custom of securing to every house extensive gardens, even now tenaciously clung to, must have greatly impeded the planning of the city, and it is surprising how regularly laid out it is, comparing very favourably, both in this respect and in its cleanliness, with any town of similar dimensions in Portugal or any other European state.

The town is amply supplied with stores, where most of the necessaries and many of the luxuries of life can be purchased.

For the sale of cottons, woollens and clothing there are

at present 23 shops; haberdashery 18; apothecaries send groceries and liquids 139; bakers 10; leather dealers fruit goldsmiths 1 (besides 3 working gold and silversmiths) ironmongers 8; limekilns 4; nail cutters 1; soap-makers 1; tobacco manufacturers 4 (besides 7 shops for the sale of tobacco); distilleries 5; butchers 12; hat shop 1 (exclusively), but hats are also sold in other goods stores; bootmakers, 15; tailors, 8; besides numerous other smaller establishments.

One of the most praiseworthy institutions in the island is the hospital " da Misericordia "—a huge pile, once a Franciscan monastery, but since greatly enlarged and made capable of receiving nearly 400 in-door patients. It is a noble building, which would be a credit to any continental town. The infirmaries are spacious and lofty and the hygienic arrangements bear favourable comparison with the best of similar establishments in Portugal. The income is derived from investments in landed and other property in the island, bequeathed to the hospital at various times.

In the year 1882–83, notwithstanding the decline in the prosperity of the island, this revenue amounted to £6,136, and the expenditure to £5,500. The number of patients treated was 2,905, the death rate amounting to 3·25 per cent.

The establishment, as the above figures testify, affords a great deal of out-door relief and mainly supports the island prisoners.

It also maintains a convalescent branch at the Furnas, where, on an average, 150 cases, mostly rheumatic, are yearly sent for the thermal baths there.

Besides this hospital, but altogether disconnected with it, are some half-dozen almonries or irmandades for succouring the poor and sick. These are supported entirely by voluntary contributions, in spite of which, however, the number of loathsome beggars haunting the streets is comparatively large, the absence of mendicity control of any

K

distrior asylums to harbour the halt and blind, causes them of *eset every passer-by with reiterated cries of " Oh senhor, Ena esmolinha."

Nowhere is Belisarius a pleasant sight, but here least of all, where in contrast with a bountiful nature, his abject and filthy appearance shocks and saddens.

A very useful law existed in Portugal as far back as 1544, whereby all beggars were compelled to learn and ply some fitting trade, that reserved for the blind being the working of bellows at blacksmiths' forges. This salutary law, however, dropped out of custom and was never revived, and the beggars have it all their own way now. Custom would appear to have made the Portuguese callous about the remains of their dead. In the Cemiterio dos Prazeres in Lisbon, a medical student may easily pick up an anatomical specimen lying about after an old grave has been opened. This arises from the habit of burying twenty or more bodies of those too poor to pay for private interment, in a deep " valla," as these pits are called, which, after a period of at most five years, are re-opened, the contents burned in a heap and the hideous grave again used for fresh bodies. It is also customary for the wealthier classes in Portugal to exhume the remains of their relatives after a lapse of two or three years, breaking the limbs up at the joints and placing them in small boxes or children's coffins, which ultimately rest on shelves in the family vault.

Surely the advocates of cremation have a powerful argument in these reprehensible practices, which are fortunately seldom witnessed in the islands ; still, there is much room for improvement in the manner in which the poor here are consigned to their last resting place.

The sympathetic nature of the Portuguese was quick to adopt an exquisitely kind and interesting custom which obtains in Hindustan. On the occurrence of a death, the family not only preserve a strict seclusion for a few days, but the entire household abstains from work ; no cooking even being done; the neighbours and friends therefore send in trays generously laden with cooked meats and fruit to supply the household wants.

Until the time of Dom Manoel (1495), white was worn as mourning throughout Portugal, and down to 1521 (the reign of John III.) women known as Pranteadeiras or mourners were hired to wail over the dead.

The average Azorean padre, belonging as a rule to the bourgeois class, is a good-natured fellow enough, with no superabundance of piety or pretence to morality, and has never been accused of intellectual superiority. The following perfectly true story will, however, show that he is not devoid of rude, common sense. The argument turning upon the infallibility of the Pope, his reverence, who should have maintained this fundamental dogma of his church, openly and strongly expressed an opposite opinion, and clenched his adversary's argument by exclaiming, "Oh senhor, um homem com tripas, infallivel!" (Oh sir, a man possessing the bowels of poor humanity, infallible!) Only a decade ago, it was customary for the wealthier families to retain the services of a priest, who, besides officiating in the adjoining chapel, was expected, when the weather was cold and damp, to occupy the master's bed for a short time prior to the latter retiring there with his lady, so that it might be warmed for them.

Warming pans are things unknown in this country, but Azorean padres are generally verging upon obesity.

Madame Rattazzi in her inimitable "Portugal à vol-d'oiseau," exactly and amusingly delineates the character of the Portuguese padre, when she says—"Dans les rues, il se promène en bourgeois; il fréquente les théâtres, fume, va dans le monde, cause, ne s'exclut pas de la société; en un mot, il se fait même quelque-fois tout doucement et tout discrètement une famille, s'il habite la campagne."

Caves are now recognised as a common feature in volcanic countries, and are present in a marked degree in these islands. The theory, as Sir Charles Lyell tell us, is that they have been produced by the hardening of the lava during the escape of great volumes of elastic fluids, which are often discharged for many days in succession after the crisis of the eruption is over. There are some very extensive galleries which would rejoice the heart of any "marchand de champignons," in a field in the Rua Formosa, the entrance to which is close to the road and easy of access. Opening out from the sides of a wide circular space are three large vaulted orifices leading into as many separate galleries, one extending in a northerly, the other two running almost parellel in a southerly direction for a considerable distance, presumably to the coast. They are difficult of exploration for more than a few hundred yards, the ground being covered with variously-sized masses of broken lava, most of which, disintegrated by the constant damp, have fallen from above. Hanging from the roof are seen pointed lava knobs of all dimensions, looking as if a sudden icy blast had cooled the molten and falling drops; on every side the torches, absolutely indispensable, light up the silvery particles of selenite, making them sparkle like brilliants. Close to the entrance, the northern cave is quite twenty feet high and thirty feet broad, with a perfectly level floor, and if properly explored, would in all probability be found to join another gallery, the entrance to which is in a garden, recently belonging to Mrs. Brander, in the Forral do Carvão, and if so, would extend for several miles inland. The two southern caves apparently communicate with two corresponding ones, the openings of which are to be found in a field on the opposite side of the road, but are almost blocked up with fallen earth; from what can be seen of them, they apparently run down to the shore at Santa Clara. It is said that some of these caves, easily accessible from the coast, were formerly the resort of bands of smugglers, and that many an island fortune owes its origin to the nefarious trade they carried on.

Perhaps the most recent instance on record of the formation of similar galleries is mentioned by Miss Bird, in her work on the Sandwich Islands, where she met European settlers, who told her they had traced a river of lava burrowing its way 1,500 feet below the surface in the island of Hilo, and seen it emerge, break over a precipice and fall hissing into the ocean. In the same island, the ground south of Hilo burst open with a crash and roar. The molten river, after travelling underground for twenty miles, emerged through a fissure with a tremendous force and volume; it was in a pastoral region supposed to be at rest for ever. Along the south-western shore of St. Michael, there are several of these underground openings through which the lava from the volcano of Sete Cidades flowed into the sea.

Ponta Delgada has its baracão, or fish market, where, in early morning, a variety of the finny tribe may be seen, comprising the cherne, bicuda, garoupa, bezugo, tainha, john dory, bonito, sardine, pilchard, red mullet, cray fish, conger eel (whose size makes one no longer doubt the existence of the sea serpent), and other kinds of fish, to which the natives give peculiar names. The bonito (*pelamys sarda*) if much indulged in, produces a kind of nettle-rash; in Madeira, even leprosy is attributed to the too great indulgence in this coarse food by the poor. Sometimes the appearance in these waters of some huge basking shark or other monster of the deep scares away all small fish, and the baracão becomes deserted. The fishermen then apply themselves to the capture of bodos, toninhas, and other oil-giving fish.

The polvo, or *Octopus vulgaris*, is very common amongst the rocks, but generally of small size. At night, its highly phosphorescent trail may be seen flashing across the pools. The flesh is by no means despised here.

The delicious edible, or green turtle (*Chelone viridis*) is occasionally caught, but more often the hawk's-bill (*C. imbricata*), which, though not so good for eating, supplies the tortoise-shell of commerce. I believe the islanders must be unaware of its value, for they always throw away the carapace.

Notwithstanding the wealth of fish, a great deal of salt cod—the famous bacalháo—almost exclusively Newfoundland, is yearly imported from England. The history of this cod fishery is very curious. In 1353 a treaty to hold good for 50 years was entered into between Dom Affonso IV. (the Bold), of Portugal, and Edward III. of England, whereby Portuguese fishermen " puissent venir et pêcher fraunchement et sauvement en les portz d'Engleterre et de Bretagne, et en toux les autres lieux et portz, où ils vourront, paiantz les droits et les custumes à les seignurz du pays." The fish caught was chiefly cod, which the Portuguese salted, and so successful were they, that not only did they supply their own country, but England and other states as well. This trade with Great Britain died away about 1590, when the process of salt-making became more generally known, and the English fishermen commenced to salt their own fish. To the Portuguese, however, remains the credit of first establishing the Newfoundland fisheries,* definitely dis-

---

* Previous to the voyage of the Brothers Varciro, Cabot had caught sight, on ths 24th June, 1497, of a headland, to which he gave the name of Bonavista, and which proved to be a part of the island of Newfoundland. According to another account " Newfoundland was next visited by Cotorial, a Portuguese, and Cartier, a French navigator. Its value as a fishing station being ascertained by them, they gave to it a name (Bacalao) which signifies in the Indian language, a cod-fish ; and its banks soon became a favourite resort during the summer months of fishermen from all nations."—(Gleig.) That Gaspar Corte-Real, son of João Vaz Corte-Real, the Captain-Donatary of the islands of Terceira and St. George, visited Newfoundland in 1500, there can be no doubt; sailing from Lisbon in the summer of that year, he reached, after several month's wanderings in a westerly direction, a land which appeared to him so fresh and green, that he bestowed upon it the name "Terra Verde," which subsequently appeared on the maps of that period as "Terra dos Corte-Reaes." Many examples of the natural productions of this "Terra Nova" were brought to Lisbon, and on the 15th May of 1501, Gaspar Corte-Real sailed again from the Tagus with a fully equipped expedition, to more fully explore and settle his new found land ; but from this second voyage he never returned. Miguel Corte-Real, anxious to learn his brother's fate, fitted out two

covered in the beginning of the sixteenth century by the expedition which sailed from Aveiro under the command of the Brothers Vareiro, and named by them the Terra Nova. The cod fisheries off the coast were soon after established, and for a century continued to give employment to large fleets of vessels which annually repaired to the banks from the Tagus, until Newfoundland passed into the hands of the English. At the present time the tables have completely turned, and Portugal ever since the loss of that colony has imported salt cod to the average value of, in recent times, a quarter of a million sterling every year.

There is also a cattle market held on Sundays not far from the English church, where pigs, too, form a conspicuous commodity.

Of markets for vegetables and general produce, there are two; Corpo Santo and Graça, the latter being the most frequented; it is planted with acacia trees, and round its three sides are covered booths and stalls, where meat, bread and various articles are sold. Amongst the res mercatoria offered on Fridays and Sundays—the regular market days— may be noticed in their proper seasons, baskets full of the golden nespera or loquot, piles of the violet elliptic-shaped maracuja or granadilla (*Passiflora edulis*), the capucho or Cape gooseberry (*Physalis pubescens*), with its delicate gauze-like covering, the fruit, *par excellence*, for preserves ; baskets of sweetly perfumed mountain strawberries, vieing with the handsomer, but less tasty, cultivated ones, grown round the estufas. Here may be seen perfect mountains of melons (*Cucumis melo*), and water melons (*Cucurbita citrillus*). The araça, (*Psidium littorale*) and araçazão, of the Brazilian and China species (a fruiting shrub of the myrtle family) ;

naós, and set sail for the west on the 10th May, 1502, but was never again heard of. D. Manuel, the king, who greatly esteemed the Corte-Reaes, sent out two other ships in search of them in 1503, but of these also no tidings ever reached Portugal.

grapes, generally of the American scented or Isabel variety; oranges of the choicest kinds for which sometimes two vintens each are unblushingly asked in this land of the citrus; huge bunches of bananas (*Musa paradisiaca*), which, from having the sign of the cross at the apex, is held by Catholics to be the fruit with which Eve tempted the weak Adam— delicious as only you can have them in their native clime; apples and pears, peaches and plums, in variety too numerous to mention; apricots from Pico, brought over in open boats by the intrepid sons of old Christiano; and indiscriminately mixed up with all these may be seen the splendid red pimentão,* beloved of the Portuguese, and many varieties of chillies and peppers (*Capsicum frutescens*). The curious marrow-flavoured caiota, delicious in stews when freshly gathered and young; artichokes, the egg plant, so useful for entrées; immense bogangos (*Cucurbita pepo*) and abobaras (pumpkins); also calabashes and bottle gourds (*C. lagenaria*), much used for preserving; huge sweet potatoes, tomatoes, both red and yellow and of all sizes; and yams from the Furnas. Here and there are sacks full of bright yellow tramoço cortido, the pickled lupin bean of which all classes here and in Portugal are so fond. To foreigners it is unpalatable, but to judge from the quantities the natives eat, it must be perfectly wholesome and digestible.

There are also poultry of all kinds, brought from distant parts of the country, hung by the legs to poles slung across men's shoulders in a manner which would give our Society for the Suppression of Cruelty to Animals, much useful occupation. Besides the various fruits above enumerated, they grow the annona or custard apple (*A. reticulata*); guava (*Psidium pyriferum* or *Cattleianum*); jambro or rose

---

* Almost all the varieties of chillies (*Capsicum annuum*, Lin. and *C. fastigiatum*, Blume) are to be found here; in the large Pimentão the acrid resin (*capsicine*) being almost entirely absent, allows of their being largely eaten in stews, and plainly boiled.

apple (*Jambosa vulgaris*), the blossom of which is so beautiful, and a considerable variety of the green and black Turkey figs (*Ficus carica*). The pomegranate, emblem of Hymen, also thrives well.

A beautiful tree which grows in all these islands with remarkable luxuriance, producing a delicious sub-acid fruit, already mentioned, is the nespera or *Eriobotrya Japonica*, common all over China (where it is known as the pi-pa) and native to Japan. It grows well in India and southern Europe; and even in the botanical gardens at Kew it may be seen growing against a sheltered wall out of doors, but never fruits there; the loquot, by which it is known in India and England, was the name originally given it in Canton.

The caiota referred to above is the chayote (*Sechium edule* and *Chayotis edulis*, Jacq.), a climbing plant of the cucurbit family; it is very prolific, a single plant yielding in the first year from 80 to 100 pear-shaped pints. It is said to have been a favourite vegetable with the Aztecs, who cultivated it extensively, calling it chayotti: the root tubercles contain 20 per cent. of starch, but this valuable rhizome is never utilised in the islands.

The Portuguese are extremely fond of flowers, and in such a climate as this, everything thrives with tropical luxuriance. Ponta Delgada can therefore boast of some of the most beautiful gardens in the world. The difficulty is not how to preserve and rear plants of temperate and even tropical climes, but to keep them from growing beyond all bounds. A Portuguese garden would be incomplete without its alecrim (*Lantana mecrophylla*, Martius), or scented heath shrub, which the ladies here dub " sempre noiva " (ever a bride), from the profusion and permanence of its small white blossom. The cottagers, too, seem passionately fond of the bonina or boliana (*Calendula suffruticosa*) or common marigold, for its deep yellow flowers are everywhere seen. The fragrant rosa de Alexandria, double red and striped

York and Lancaster rose, too, has always a corner reserved for it in the peasant's garden; its powerful perfume giving rise to the saying—"onde está logo penetra"; and, greater favourite perhaps than any, the mangericão (*Ocymum basilicum*) or sweet-scented basil of which the peasant facetiously sings:—

> A flor do mangericão
>   Naõ abre senaõ de noute,
> Para nãu dar a saber
>   Os seus amores a outrem.

> (The sweet "gentle basil" flower
>   Opens not, except at night;
> Fearing, lest others her loves
>   May view in the garish light.)

Unquestionably, the finest of these gardens are those of Sñr. José do Canto, and the late Sñr. Antonio Borges, in the laying out of which, and introducing new plants and trees, many thousands of pounds sterling have been expended. In Sñr. José do Canto's collection alone some 5,000 species new to the island have been introduced, but the close proximity in which the outdoor portions of these were originally planted has, in a measure, prevented their proper development, and only by going in among the dense shrubbery can the botanical wealth collected there be fully appreciated.

At the Furnas, on a plantation bordering the lake, the same gentleman has formed a perfectly unique arboretum, embracing examples of forest and ornamental trees from almost every country in the world, and these, being less thickly planted, have attained extraordinary proportions— trees from North America and equally cold climes vieing with those of Australia, India, Japan and China, as to which shall outstrip the other.

The system adopted by Sñr. Antonio Borges, if more elaborate and in greater taste, has given better results. Removing and collecting together the rocky mantle which here and there covered his grounds, he formed with this *débris* picturesque nooks and grottoes where New Zealand

and other arborescent ferns seem to have found their habitats and thrive to perfection.

The deep alluvial soil of the cleared lands, rich in volcanic detritus, gives an additional impetus to whatever is therein planted, and being judiciously distanced to allow freedom of growth, many varieties of palms and trees from temperate and sub-tropical zones are here to be seen growing in unrestrained luxuriance. Towering conspicuous above their congeners, in all these gardens are the araucarias (*Excelsa*), rearing their graceful heads a hundred feet high, and in twenty years time rivalling forest trees in the girth of their boles. Now and then one of these giants is seen decapitated, telling of the severe winter gales. Less majestic, but equally beautiful, grows the species *imbricata* or *brasiliensis*. Examples may here be seen of the graceful cedros de Busaco *(Cupressus lusitanica, l'Heritier, and C. glame* of Lamark), from the famous avenue leading to the old Carmelite Convent of Busaco, propagated from trees said to have been brought there originally from the high mountains near Goa in Portuguese India in the sixteenth century. There is no evidence, however, that this was so, and I believe that no similar tree is to be found in that part of India, although we know the white cedar has its habitat in China and Cochin China, and Thunberg describes a species of cypress as common to Japan. Goa being, then, the junction for the richly-freighted East-India fleets when homeward bound, many plants really native of China or Japan (where Francis Xavier had already penetrated) were doubtless regarded on their arrival in Europe as coming from Hindostan, to the subsequent confusion of botanists. The natives also have a habit of applying the generic term " Cedro " to many coniferous trees, the juniper varieties being thus misnamed, and even trees in no way related to the coniferæ.

It reflects creditably upon the bare-footed fraternity, who were strongly represented in these islands as well as

Portugal's eastern colonies, that two valuable trees like this cypress and the (China) orange should have appeared simultaneously and for the first time in Portugal at the head-quarters of the order at Busaco. A suggestion made to me by Sir Joseph Hooker, and much more likely to be correct, is that the " cedro de Busaco " was found growing in the Azores by these Carmelite monks when the islands were first colonized, and by them acclimatised on account of its beauty in their grounds at Busaco; from thence it spread to Coimbra, Alcobaça, and other central parts of Portugal. In the south it is quite unknown, and even round Lisbon it does not thrive, a proof that it could never have thriven in the climate of Goa. It would be singular indeed, if it could be authenticated that this Azorean cedar, once so common, but extirpated by the early settlers, had been accidentally preserved in the mother country, and thence re-introduced after the lapse of four centuries into its native soil.

Although numerous trunks of this tree have been occasionally found in the islands, its identity has never been properly established, but I believe it to be akin to, and to closely resemble the *Juniperus oxycedrus* still to be found in the almost inaccessible mountain fastnesses of Madeira, where it once greatly abounded. In the pathetic tale of Robert Machim and Anna d'Arfet, we read that Zarco, in 1419, ordered the stately cedar tree, beneath which this devoted but unhappy couple perished, to be cut down for the construction of a small church to their memory, for which purpose the wood supplied by this one specimen amply sufficed.

Besides these, there are other gardens, the owners of which readily allow visitors to go over them. Amongst them may be mentioned those belonging to Snr. José Jacomo Corrêa and the Viscount das Laranjeiras; in the latter are some fine specimens of the eucalyptus and a palm tree 30 feet high, with a trunk thirteen feet in girth—not at its base, but some four feet from the ground. In the garden of Botelho, a pleasant half-hour's drive in the outskirts of the town, are two splendid magnolias of immense size and some fine Australian banksias.

In a wood opposite this property is a crypt containing a rudely-carved recumbent figure in stone, representing "Nossa Senhora da Lapa"—our Lady of the Grotto. Far back, tradition says that a poor woman who lived very unhappily with her husband, fled into the neighbouring woods to lead a life of sanctity. No one knew her whereabouts, until a hunter, whilst out in quest of coneys, stumbled across the dead body of Nossa Senhora, and being of a devout disposition, and shocked at the saint's neglected plight, determined to give her Christian burial in his own village.

This was no sooner effected, however, than, as in the case of Buddha's tooth, signs were apparent of an unmistakable resurrection, and search being made, the Senhora was found in the same identical place where first discovered. Again she was carried to the grave, but her soul found no rest therein, for three times she returned to the cherished spot, where, at length, a shrine was erected over her, and she has remained there ever since. To this, on the 28th September every year, a "romaria," or pilgrimage of her devotees, takes place, when, many young people from the neighbouring villages being present, the quiet locality is made lively with their boisterous mirth. Not far from Botelho, at a place called Maricas, in a garden which belonged to the late Sñr. A. J. Botelho, is a magnificent avenue of camellia trees nearly 50 years old, and probably the largest to be seen in the island. Close by is a pine-apple house, where 2,000 pines are yearly grown under the same roof.

In most of these gardens are clumps of bamboos (*Bambusa arundinacea*), tree ferns, pinnated, fan (*Chamaerops humilis*) and other palms and exotic growths in endless variety, which —with such flowering plants as the shrubby mallow from Syria (*Hibiscus syriacus*), *Stephanotis floribunda*, the exquisite white lily (*Crinum asiaticum*), a native of tropical Asia, the beautiful varieties of the Ceylon *Malastoma malabathrica* and numerous others—lend a character expected only in more southern lands. In a garden in the Rua da Louça may be seen a clump of majestic palm trees (*Phœnix reclinata*) seemingly quite at home in this congenial climate, their spreading hemispherical crowns forming conspicuous objects from almost every point of view. These palm trees commemorate a thrilling story of ninety years ago, which reads like a chapter out of the "Arabian Nights," and that my readers may view these unique specimens with sufficient interest, I will give the barest outlines of the romantic tale, as chronicled by Padre Souza, Arabic interpreter to the king of Portugal in 1793.

At the time when the French revolution was causing rivers of blood to flow in the streets of Paris, a similar agitation threatened to shake the empire of Morocco to its very foundations. When the emperor, Sidi Mahomed Ben Abdalà, died, leaving fourteen sons, he named as his successor a favourite younger son, by name Molei Abdessalam, who had performed a pilgrimage to Mecca. During his travels he had contracted a severe ophthalmic affection, which probably induced him to waive his claim to the throne in favour of an elder brother, Molei Eliazid, who caused himself to be proclaimed emperor, Abdessalam retiring to Tafilet, where he intended to live in peace. Another brother, however, Molei Haxem, appeared in the field to dispute the succession, and with such fury was the struggle carried on, that on one occasion the two brothers, who headed their respective partisans, met in personal combat, and so seriously wounded each other as to give rise to the report that both had perished in the battle; thereupon another of the late emperor's fourteen sons, Molei Salema, who was governor of Tangiers, proclaimed himself emperor and received the submission of the people of Fez. His two other brothers having meanwhile recovered from their wounds, again took the field, and the country became divided into three armed camps. Under these circumstances, Molei Abdessalam, with a numerous retinue and the whole of his family, retired for greater safety to the seaport of Agadir or Santa Cruz, situated in the extreme south of the province of Sús; from here he purposed transferring his family to the port of Rabât or Salé, and with this intention put them on board a small vessel which he had purchased at Santa Cruz, meaning to follow himself in another. The ship sailed on the 13th of April, 1793, having on board no less than 221 persons; among these were the princess Laila Amina, the chief wife of Abdessalam, three daughters and two sons of the prince, but by different mothers, nine of his lesser wives and four princesses of the blood royal, one of whom was Nana Rabú, the sultana of the late emperor. The ship, a brigantine, had however, barely put to sea, when a violent storm carried her entirely out of her course, and on the 19th of April she cast anchor in the Port of Funchal, in the island of Madeira. The governor, hearing of the distressed and crowded condition of the passengers, placed two other vessels at the disposal of the royal passengers, with abundance of provisions and water, of which they were greatly in need; they had not, however, proceeded far, when another storm drove them to the Azores, and on the 19th June the ships cast anchor off Ponta Delgada. After taking in provisions and water, they once more essayed their return voyage, but a south-westerly gale drove one of the vessels on shore, all lives being saved; the other one, after cruising about for some days, anchored again in the roads—this time to land the princess Amina and one of her attendants. Both were seriously ill, the latter dying a few days afterwards. Here these unfortunate people remained twenty-eight days, being hospitably entertained by the authorities. To commemorate their visit, the princess, accompanied by eighteen of her female attendants, all closely veiled, and by many of the chief ladies of

Ponta Delgada, proceeded to a small garden (now belonging to Senhora Berquó) adjoining the club house, and in the Rua da Louça, where the princess Amina with her own hands planted a young palm tree (*Phœnix reclinata*), which soon grew apace, its trunk attaining a height of 52½ feet and 39½ inches in circumference. Eighty-three years later, on the 29th November, 1876, this magnificent native of the desert was blown down by a gale of wind, leaving however a clump of seven younger trees around its site, and which now form quite a conspicuous feature in the landscape of Ponta Delgada as viewed from the sea. Sailing from St. Michael's in the beginning of July, our Moorish friends were compelled through stress of weather to put into Cascaes in the Tagus, where they arrived on the 13th of that month. Hearing of their sad adventures, and touched by the tale of their wanderings, the Portuguese royal family invited the princess Amina and her suite to visit them at the palace of Queluz, which they did, landing on the 30th July in the royal barges at Belem amidst great pomp and a salute of twenty-one guns, being subsequently entertained until their departure at the palace of Necessidades. On the 9th August, 1793, our wanderers again embarked on board the Portuguese ships supplied by the government, and, escorted by the man-of-war " Medusa," left the Tagus under another salute of twenty-one guns from the tower S. Julião, their destination being Tangiers, where, let us hope, they arrived in safety.

It is seldom that ordinary trees are ever met with in this island fifty years old, as, on attaining sufficient girth, they are at once cut down for boxwood and other purposes; if spared the woodman's axe, they grow to an unusual size. In a garden belonging to Senhora Berquó in the town, is a noble specimen of the laurel, and near it a glorious magnolia—the height and thickness of one of the full-grown oak trees in Richmond Park. Overshadowing the roadway may often be seen the Judas tree *(Cereis siliquastrum)*, which, in spring, is a mass of beautiful purple blossom.

Napoleon, at St. Helena, is said to have once exclaimed— "A l'odeur seule je devinerais la Corse, les yeux fermés." I feel equally sure that any native of St. Michael could, if suddenly transported thither, blind-fold, from the uttermost parts of the earth, divine his whereabouts by means of the indescribably delicious perfume of the incenso, orange, and other trees, which in the full flush of bloom permeate the air, in a manner surely unrivalled by "Araby the blest," and realising the idea of the "Sabean gales and scents of Paradise" poets love to sing about. The enjoyment, too, of these green aisles is much enhanced by the numerous birds of song, especially that of the green canary, which Bory de Saint Vincent compared to the nightingale, and the touto negro (black cap), and many other "light-winged Dryads of the groves" who flood the air with their exquisite madrigals.

Long after St. Michael was first colonized, the green canary was so plentiful and so appreciated in Portugal for his song, that every year two vessels came to the island expressly to carry back these little passengers to Lisbon, their cargoes consisting of sweet potatoes.

These delightful songsters are unfortunately accused of considerable destruction to the grain crops, and, with others of their tribe, have long been proscribed by the Camara. An ancient municipal decree taxed each proprietor of arable land at the rate of five birds' heads per alqueire, and seven per alqueire of vineyard or orange grove ; but it was soon found more effective to offer a vintem or 20 réis per dozen beaks of the following birds: the canario *(Serinus canarius)*, the merlo *(Turdus merula)*, the priolo *(Pyrrhula murina)*, the vinagreira *(Motacilla rubecula)*, and the tintilhão *(Fringilla canariensis)*.

A close examination of the trees and shrubs in these gardens will often reveal the existence of numbers of the

L

brilliant-coloured larva of the death's-head moth (*Sphinx atropus*), but they appear to cause very little injury to the plants they feed upon.

Visitors cannot fail to observe, as dusk sets in, the presence of large numbers of a small but particularly lively bat (*Vespertilio Leisleri*), a species common to the north-west countries of Europe, and supposed to have been originally accidentally introduced by the Flemish colonists.

———

CHAPTER X.

> Yon cottager who weaves at her own door,
> Pillow and bobbins all her little store,
> Content, tho' mean—
> > *Cooper.*

CHARMING excursions in the immediate neighbourhood of
Ponta Delgada may be made to the summits of some hills
known as the Pico do Salamaõ, Pico Tosqueado, Pico do
Julio, and Pico da Castanheira, from all of which superb
views can be obtained of the surrounding country and coast—
the great Atlantic stretching away in illimitable distance
to the south, on which, in clear weather, the island of Santa
Maria in a south-easterly direction floats like a misty mass
some 44 miles away.

These rides or drives through the country are rendered
less interesting in consequence of the lofty walls with which
each villa or garden is jealously begirt; the thongs of cacti,
fuchsias and delicate creepers ablaze with blossom, toppling
over and garnishing these lava barriers in wild profusion,
seeming to tantalize those fresh from northern climes with
the hidden wealth of foliage and flora within.

Along many of the by-ways and less frequented lanes
may be seen the beautiful *Amaryllis belladona*, in full
bloom upon a heap of rubbish, cast there as a weed from
some garden close by. The traveller, if out across country,
when the "pearl gray of morn" begins to show, may see flocks
of large, light-coloured birds, especially on recently ploughed
fields; these are sea gulls, reduced through the scarcity of

fish to seek food on land, and apparently too much absorbed in their agricultural pursuits to readily observe the approach of the stranger. These harmless birds should never be molested, as they are simply on the hunt for grubs, and are the farmer's best friends. It is a favourite Sunday amusement with the island *gamin* to " fish " for these over-confiding but greedy birds from the rocks in the harbour, with hook and raw flesh bait, which they readily swallow, and are at once drawn in. The sport is both cruel and wanton.

Within the precincts of the town is a smaller hill, known as the Mae de Deos, which in former times was fortified, but long since dismantled. It is now crowned with the emblem of peace, a small chapel dedicated to the " Mother of God." From this monticule, a delightful stretch of country in the vicinity of the city, with its mixture of *urbs cum rure*, lies before you, and a good idea may be formed of the beauty of this part of the island and the varied richness of its cultivation. The sloping sides of this mound have been ornamentally laid out, and fine examples of the aloe (*Agave americana*) may generally be seen with their tall pyramidal flower stems rising ten or fifteen feet ; also the prickly pear or Indian fig (*Opuntia vulgaris*), fringed with its insipid but thirst-quenching fruit, and many other varieties of cacti, seemingly at home in this drier and poorer soil.

At the foot of this hill, on its northern side, stands the protestant church, a barn-like structure, erected in 1827, at a time when Portugal would not allow such buildings to assume the form of churches, or to use bells. During fifty years or so, the English community here enjoyed the benefit of a chaplain, who was paid by means of subscriptions amongst the British residents and vessels entering the port, the English government under the Consular Act paying an equivalent sum. This was done away with in 1877, and for many years no clergyman has officiated ; prayers are, however, read every Sunday morning by the consul, or in his absence, by one of the English residents, and the services are generally well attended.

The British colony in the island is fortunate in having as its present consular representative a gentleman who adds to no mean literary gifts the charm of affability and unrestrained hospitality.

Very fair island-bred horses and ponies can be occasionally purchased at prices ranging from £10 to £30. English horses have from time to time been introduced, but the defective stabling arrangements, the chief ventilation of which is through the ceiling into the apartments above, and the consequent high temperature, added to change of diet, bring on lung affections, and the animals soon sicken and die. You can never make a Portuguese understand that horses, like human beings, require abundance of fresh air. The poverty of fodder, and the difficulty of getting the associated grasses of England to grow in the island, make the want of a good and cheap substitute a strong necessity. Nothing could more readily supply this want than the pine fodder of Styria. In the hope that some of my friends may be induced to utilize a not unimportant industry ready to hand, I here transcribe the manner in which pine-cake may be made.

In the spring of the year, when the pine trees become covered with young tender pins, they should be thinned and trimmed, a process here known as " desbastar," and frequently rendered necessary in consequence of their exuberant and rapid growth.

The lopped branches are then hung or spread out in well ventilated barns until the pins fall off; these are then collected and thoroughly dried in ovens preparatory to grinding. To every 25 lbs. of the flour, 1 lb. of salt is added, and well mixed in, and the compound is then ready for use. It is generally given as an adjunct with chaff, is grateful to the animals, and is said to preserve them from lung affections. Here, where immense quantities of this nutritious food, at present utterly neglected, could be had for the mere gathering, farmers would do well to turn their attention to its use.

The ordinary means of locomotion in all these islands is on donkeys, fed upon little else than green-stuffs, the poverty of their owners preventing the luxury of grain. These sturdy animals will, nevertheless, travel with heavy loads twenty or thirty miles at a stretch with apparent ease. The pace, however, is trying to one accustomed to more rapid modes of transit, and a strong reflection of the quadruped's patience is needed to go through a day's journey. The roads all over the island are excellent, and the longer trips may be broken by driving part of the way in mule-drawn carriages, of which there are many on hire in Ponta Delgada.

Travellers in these islands cannot fail to notice numerous circular mounds of beaten earth at the roadside corners of fields. These are the " eiras," or threshing-floors of the country. The natives are extremely fond of assisting in the " trilhar," or treading operation. Two or three pairs of oxen (always unmuzzled, according to the command in Deuteronomy xxv., 4, " Thou shalt not muzzle the ox when he treadeth out the corn ") are yoked to a common farm sled, on which you and the driver sit or stand, as best you can, and the oxen are then driven rapidly round and round the eira, over the slippery straw, until the wheat has been trodden out. A novice will find it no easy matter to keep his hold on the inclined and quickly gliding plane, and many amusing but harmless accidents occur. Subsequently the winnowing of the grain is effected by erecting a raised platform in the centre of the eira, from whence the grain is flung down, the breeze carrying away the chaff.

Men may often be seen on these eiras threshing out beans and other pulse with the flail of ancient days.

Taking one of these carriages and driving in a westerly direction along the coast, past the villages of Relva and

Feiteiras with their mile of human sties,* within which the women may be seen grinding corn in their stone querns, or seated at the doors, distaff and spindle in hand, spinning as their sisters did in the days of the Cæsars, and inspiring a native bard to exclaim in ecstasy at the sight,

> Quem, me dera ser o linho
> Que vós, menina, fiaes,
> Que vos, dera tanto beijo
> Como vós, no linho daes;

which a feeble imitation may thus render—

> Oh! were I the flax
> That thou spinnest, sweet girl,
> I'd kiss thee as oft
> As the threads your lips twine.

or with a child's head in their laps, occupied in the less interesting but more absorbing occupation of hunting for small game, that disgusting " 120th part of an inch," the abundance of which induced the wise Ynca Huayna Caapac of Peru to impose a tribute " in kind " upon the inhabitants of the province of Pastu, who were not remarkable for cleanliness. Whether at these or more arduous tasks, the island women often break out into song, for how true it is that

> Song sweetens toil, how rude soe'er the sound,
>   All at her wheel the village maiden sings,
> And as she turns the giddy circle round,
>   Revolves the sad vicissitude of things.

Here and there we pass splendid little bits of scenery, whose faithful reproduction on canvas would make the fortune of any aspiring R.A., until reaching the steep narrow path which leads up to the mountain; here (donkeys having been previously sent to await our arrival) we commence the slow and difficult climb over the flank of the vast truncated cone,

---

* Some of the villages in this island extend for nearly three miles in length, such as Arrifes, Bretanha, and Candelaria.

nearly five miles in circumference at its summit, within which is embosomed the lovely valley of the Sete Cidades or seven cities. The origin of the name is wrapped in some obscurity; the old writers attribute it to seven concavities which they say were observed after the great eruption already mentioned, but this derivation is probably imaginary. Possibly the fact of Lisbon being built, like Rome, "on her seven-hilled throne renowned," may account for the name, or perhaps some island sage of the 15th century, haunted by dreams of the Isla Antillia and its septem cidades (which in turn may have had its origin in the Saviour's seven resting places along the Via Dolorosa to Calvary, or the last seven words he uttered) sought thus to commemorate its mythical existence; or, again, the timorous explorers who first peered into the dark abyss may have realized Dante's dream of the seven infernos with the terrible mural inscription " Lasciate ogni speranza voi ch'entrate ! "

It will be remembered that when Cabral, on his first visit to S. Miguel, in 1444, left for Lisbon to prepare for its definite colonization, his pilot had noted this western mountain as his landmark, a probable indication that, prior to the great eruption which shortly afterwards caused its destruction, this was at that time the highest point in the island. An ascent of an hour and a half through wild but beautiful country, the surface of which shows how the lava welled in torrents over the crater brink, tearing up and eroding into deep impenetrable dikes and gorges the mountain sides, which

> ·Time but the impression stronger makes,
> As streams their channels deeper wear,

brings us to the edge of the cone, 1,800 feet above the sea. Here the view is really grand. In a vast hollow, 1,500 feet in depth, lies a beautiful valley, in shape like an ellipse, the most conspicuous feature in which are the two lakes already mentioned, occupying two-thirds of its area, and fringed on their western side by the white dot-like cottages of the

SETE CIDADES, ST. MICHAEL.

village, and on the north and east by the precipitous walls of the crater, rising out of the water on that side to a height of 2,700 feet. In all directions, on the inner and outer sides of this huge concavity, are numerous crateriform hills, looking at this distance insignificant, but really the shells of what must once have been large and terrible volcanoes. The absolute stillness around, the reflection of passing clouds gliding in quick succession over the waters, and the steep pine-covered banks, mirrored on the glass-like surface of the lakes, impart to the whole scene an unreal and ephemeral appearance, until a shrill "vamos para diante" from your donkey boy, whose soul is above such trifles as fine scenery, awakens you from your ecstasy and you reluctantly commence the tortuous descent into the valley below. In August last (1885) two carriages from Ponta Delgada succeeded for the first time in reaching this valley; the route they took was by the Lomba dos Mosteiros, past Ceara and the road of Romangos. Arrived at the bottom, you alight at a small, uncomfortable inn kept by one Travassos, where travellers are put up; but unless previous notice has been given him of the intended visit, they will fare but indifferently and feel inclined to parody the schoolboy's grace—

> Chicken hot, chicken cold,
> Chicken new, chicken old,
> Chicken tender, chicken tough,
> Of chicken we have had enough,—

for nothing is here obtainable but poultry, bread even having to be brought from town. Travassos, however, is a very willing and obliging fellow, and, proper attention being given to the commissariat, a week or ten days may be spent very pleasantly in exploring the lakes and surrounding heights, with their beautiful pine-glades, all full of interest and unexpected charms. A rickety boat owned by Travassos is at the service of visitors, but as sudden squalls often arise, and the larger lake especially becomes on these occasions flecked with restless and even angry wavelets, it is wise not to venture in uncertain weather far out in such an unsteady craft.

In these waters are to be found innumerable golden carp (*Cyprinus auratus*) introduced by the monks many years ago, and more recently by Sñr. José Maria Rapozo d'Amaral and his son—the Gillaroo trout (*Salmo stomachicus*), the brown trout (*S. fario*), and the char (*S. salvelinus*)—all from ova obtained from England or Germany. The size these fish have here attained, in spite of the apparent scarcity of food and grasses, is astonishing, and is certainly an inducement to other wealthy proprietors to stock the numerous lakes in the island with this valuable food supply. During the winter months, wild duck, snipe, storks, and other migratory grallatores, or waders, from colder climes, afford very good shooting to those who can stand the wet and damp of the valley at that time.

No signs are anywhere visible of volcanic activity in the valley, but near the village of Mosteiros and at Ponta Ferraria are two hot springs of alkaline sulphur water issuing on the shore below high water mark.

The soil hereabouts being much mixed with pumice, is of slight agricultural value, but the late Snr. Antonio Borges nevertheless managed to lay out a portion of his grounds here very tastefully. He formed beautiful avenues with geometric and artistic skill of the *Cryptomeria japonica* and other trees, of the former of which the largest in the island are to be found here; whilst azaleas, rhododendrons, camellias and similar shrubs thrive with astonishing vigour.

On a small islet opposite his house, called the " pico furado," Snr. Antonio Borges had a number of artificial caverns formed, the exploration of which is the delight of little folk. Hard by are some extensive beds of the beautiful white water lily *(Nymphea alba)*, growing as rank as weeds.

Charmingly situated on a height, and approached by a winding and stately avenue of cryptomerias, stands the country residence of Snr. Joaquim A. Cabral, overlooking the larger lake, and surrounded by tastefully laid out grounds, abounding in romantic spots, from which lovely inland and coast views may be enjoyed, especially under the willing guidance of the very hospitable proprietor and his accomplished lady, should the visitor be fortunate enough to find them at home.

A slight mount up the cliffs towards the north-west, where a gap occurs, leads to the high table-land above, the principal watershed district in the island, where herds of fine-looking cattle, of English stock, are seen nibbling the spare pasture, the tinkling of the bells fastened round their necks echoing strangely in these localities.

In this island the cattle may at all times be approached with perfect safety; not so, however, in the neighbouring Terceira, where it is absolutely dangerous to go near a herd feeding on the little-frequented uplands there, without considerable caution. The bulls of this semi-wild species often have desperate battles during the breeding season, when a whole herd will form a perfect ring round the combatants until the fight is over. I am not aware of this peculiarity being common to cattle generally, and it is remarkable how great an instinct it appears to be with the particular breed found in Terceira, for in none of the other islands have they exhibited this propensity.

Mr. Darwin, in his "Descent of Man," mentions the fact of bull-bisons in North America, on sudden danger arising, driving the cows and calves into the middle of the herd whilst they defend the outside, and that cows surround and stare intently on a dying or dead companion.

The Spaniards appear to have introduced the Terceira race from the banks of the Guadalquiver, and bull fights, during their occupancy of the island, were frequent; the cruel pastime being kept up long after they were expelled. Another introduction of the Spaniards into Terceira was the savage Cuba-mastiff.

In 1843 there were barely any sheep remaining in that

island, owing to the extraordinary number of these dogs owned by people who, unable to properly feed them, sent them abroad to forage for themselves. These animals assembled together in packs at night, and destroyed entire flocks of sheep.

The beautiful cabellinho fern (*Diksonia culcita*), sheltered under patches of heather, abounds in these higher situations: but the natives are doing their best to exterminate this handsomest of their ferns, for the sake of the silky down covering its fronds and roots, which they use for filling mattresses.

The ride round the eastern edge of the crater, along a rough bridle road, is one of the most charming in the island, for, until reaching its highest summit, the Pico do Ledo, the two lakes, several hundred feet below you on the one hand, and the Atlantic on the other, are kept fully in sight. From the Ladeira do Ledo, quite three parts of the island may be seen, with the ocean on either side, this view being only comparable to that from the top of the Pico do Fogo, on the opposite side, and is inexpressibly beautiful. Close by are several very perfect craters, the hollows of which are occupied with small but romantic lakes, and, like the larger ones below, teeming with gold and silver fish. Some of these are the size of an ordinary mackerel. In winter these lakes are the favourite resorts of wild fowl, where they can rest undisturbed. The largest of these tarns is the Lagôa do Carvão, which in winter time swells so as to join the Lagôa Empadada, divided from it in drier weather by a narrow ridge, and is well worth a visit. From one higher up the plateau, the water supply of Ponta Delgada is obtained, its immediate neighbourhood deriving the name of "Nove Janellas," from an aqueduct with nine arches having been constructed to convey the waters. The source, however, is precarious, and sometimes deficient. A scheme is under consideration for increasing the supply by conveying the purer spring waters rising at a place called "Janellas do

Inferno," in the mountains above Agua de Pau, and capable of furnishing 2,100 cubic metres a day. Facilities for a rest or pic-nic are afforded by a building, roofed, but open on all sides, about a quarter of a mile distant from the " Casa Branca," covering two immense stone slabs forming a table some eight to ten feet in length, by three to four feet in breadth, resting on stone supports, round which are benches also of rough stone. This structure is in close proximity to the famous " Agua Nova " spring, reputed the purest in the island, and during the hottest weather the spot is delightfully cool.

To the naturalist it may be interesting to know that under stones or overturned masses of sphagnum moss in this vicinity is to be found the rare little slug-like insect peculiar to these islands, the *Viquesnelia atlantica*, fossil specimens of which have been found in Roumelia and the Pyrenees; but only in India has a similar living species been met with.

Two routes are available from the " Seven Cities " to the north side of the island, but in either case it is absolutely necessary that the start from the village should be made not later than mid-day, as both present considerable difficulties after dark. The one offering the greatest advantages in every way is across the upland pastures, and skirting the aqueduct already mentioned. Should time permit, a rest and ramble along the shores of a very pretty lake, not far from the Casa das Aguas or Casa Branca (a white house where the custodian of the aqueduct lives) and the stone structure already mentioned, should not be neglected, as the descent from this point to Mato do Maranhão is rough and tedious in the highest degree; masses of loose scoria and ejected boulders strewing the ground in all directions.

> Nor tree, nor shrub, nor plant, or flower,
> Nor aught of vegetable power,
> The weary eye may ken.

The second alternative route is infinitely more difficult and less interesting, being nothing more than deeply encased mountain gulleys, the sides of which are so covered by over-hanging vegetation as to completely shut out the sun's rays. Down this steep incline the furious winter torrents have carried great rocks, which render the passage in places all but impracticable. Along such a way as this it was once my fate to descend from the Seven Cities with Mr. John (Rob Roy) Macgregor and General W. F. N——, both experienced travellers, but neither of whom had anywhere encountered anything so execrable in the way of mountain roads.

Starting on donkeys from the village at five in the afternoon, dusk soon overtook us at the entrance to the gully, and later a Cimmerian darkness prevented our seeing a yard before us. There was no remedy but to allow our brave little animals to follow their own sweet wills, and well did they carry us, jumping in the dark from boulder to boulder and getting over what seemed to be appalling ruts, without once stumbling. The absolute reliance of the donkey boys upon the sagacity of their animals was amusingly illustrated on this occasion. One of the party had for some time been engaged in an obstinate and hopeless struggle with his steed, the animal persistently wishing to take what looked like an impossible direction at a spot where the road bifurcated; the drivers, coming to the rescue, increased the difficulty by confessing their ignorance of the locality, but ruled that under the circumstances the donkey was the better guide. With many misgivings we accordingly "followed my leader" and were presently rewarded by emerging near the village of Stº. Antonio. The journey had been a trying one, for only at two in the morning did we reach our long wished-for bourn at Mato do Maranhão. From this point, an extensive and charming view of the valley of Capellas, with the villages of Rabo de Peixe, St. Vicente, Fenaes, and Ribeira Grande, girt by an irregular coast line, white with spray, can be enjoyed.

Capellas is famous for its tonic, salubrious air, and pretty dark-eyed brunettes; but it is only by employing a certain amount of stratagem that the last quality can be verified, for these Azorean maidens are coy, and hide, on seeing a stranger, as if he were a veritable Cossack. Nevertheless, under proper auspices—say the wife of a local resident, or, better still, the protecting ægis of that autocrat, the village padre—these damsels readily accept an invitation to a "balho," and go through their native dances with considerable spirit. These are mostly performed by from six to a dozen couples joining in a circle, and slowly moving round, each partner in opposite directions, and corkscrew fashion, the ladies keeping their partners in view by maintaining a backward movement, the gentlemen uttering in song the usual soft platitudes, which, if overheard, are generally expressive of his agonising admiration of his partner's coal-black eyes and merry lips; she, in response, sighing that men were gay deceivers ever, all in very appropriate and meaning attitudes, the voices being accompanied by the viola or island guitar, or violin playing of some of the men. The dance itself is graceless and monotonous, the interest centering in the impromptu compliments paid, and the replies given, or, as they term it, "cantar ao desafio," and to judge from the time the dance is kept up, and the unflagging spirit shown, they must consider themselves "Admirable Crichtons" in the Terpsichorean art, or else fully realise the idea that—

> Panting damsels, dancing for their lives,
> Are only maidens waltzing into wives.

Although much alike, there are many of these dances, such as the pezinho das caldeiras, bailarola, sapateia, fringlindin, &c., which, like the famous Santa Lucia of Italy, are the untiring and favourite accompaniments to some of the melodies of these people.

The working classes of St. Michael have occasionally furnished good voices for church singing, but, as a general rule, both men and women have harsh, unmelodious voices, which has earned for them, amongst the rest of the Azoreans, the epithet of " o povo mais bruto das ilhas," the roughest people of the islands ; but, in justice to them, this remark applies more especially to their mode of speech, which is harsh and inharmonious, and altogether unsuited for singing, their songs being delivered in the loudest possible key, and devoid of all sweetness as sung by them.

As national poetry is supposed, in a great measure, to mirror many of the general characteristics of a people, I select a few examples of the songs sung by these peasants at their " balhos," the rough translations of which give but a faint idea of the epigrammatic sarcasm occasionally exhibited in the vernacular.

Snr. Theophilo Braga, the eminent writer, and a native of St. Michael's, has done his countrymen good service by laboriously compiling a collection embracing several hundred island songs, but they are all much in the same strain as the specimens given.

[TRANSLATION.]

Quem me dera ser as contas
   D'esse teu lindo collar,
Para dormir em teu seio
   E nunca mais acordar.

Oh ! were I the beads
   On thy necklace strung o'er,
I'd sleep on your breast
   And awake nevermore.

Depois que os meus olhos virám
   A graça que os teus têm,
Nunca mais forám senhores
   De olhar para mais ninguem.

Since mine eyes have beheld
   The great beauty of thine,
They've never since gazed
   On a face so divine.

O sol não nega seus raios
   A quem d'elles necessita !
Porque me negas, ingrata,
   Os raios de tua vista?

The rays of the sun
   To all men are free,
Then why, cruel girl,
   Don't you smile upon me.

Até onde as nuvens girám
   Vão meus suspiros parar ;
E tu tão perto de mim,
   Sem me ouvires suspirar.

The clouds float afar
   And my sighs fill the air,
And you, altho' near,
   Neither heed me nor care.

Os vossos olhos, menina,
   São pharoes de mar e guerra,
Quando vão para o mar largo
   Deitám faiscas em terra.

Thine eyes, sweet maid,
   Are like two beacons bright
That flash o'er the sea,
   And the landscapes they light.

Não ha setta mais aguda,
   Nem penas tão penetrantes,
Como são as saudades
   Entre dois finos amantes.

No dart so keen,
   And no pain so acute,
As the torture of lovers
   Who long to salute.

M

There is much more melody in the "modinhas," or ballads of the islanders, than in the songs accompanying the popular dances; indeed, some of the airs are exceedingly pretty, but are now unfortunately seldom, if ever, heard, and as I foresee a time when these charming lays will be altogether lost, I have appended a selection at the end of this little work of a few of the prettiest of them.

Capellas is a favourite summer resort of the Azorean gentry, where they have many pretty villa residences and gardens. One of these, belonging to Snr. José Maria da Camara, is interesting for the numerous and beautiful varieties of camellias cultivated, presenting an exquisite sight when the trees are full of bloom. There is a small bay here, land-locked on three sides, completely sheltered by the high cliffs from the prevalent south-easterly gales. It was here that vessels and the Lisbon mail steamers took refuge, and received their cargoes, before the breakwater afforded protection. The great headland, known as the Morro das Capellas, presents many beautiful coast views from its heights; but its chief characteristics can only properly be seen from the sea, as on that side the base of the tufa cliffs have, in places, been worked by the continued action of the waves into perfect arches and deep recesses, into which the sea when rough dashes with great violence.

Higher up in the face of the cliffs are immense rents and clefts, in the topmost crevices of which large numbers of rock pigeons resort and afford excellent shooting. Their destruction is usually accomplished from boats procured at the little neighbouring fishing port, the grand scenery around adding enjoyment to the sport. There is no doubt that the name Capellas was derived from the quaint architectural appearance of the gothic-like arches, suggesting to the minds of the early inhabitants the entrances into chapels.

On the eastern margin of the "Morro" is a deep circular hollow—a wild forbidding spot, called by the people "a cova do morro," shut in on all sides by the land, but to which the sea has access by a subterranean passage. They tell a tender tale of how a poor girl—

> Whose bloom was like the springing flower
> That sips the silver dew,
> The rose was budded in her cheek,
> Just opening to the view—

disappeared at this place, where she was in the habit of coming every morning to bathe.

Hard by are the ruins of some buildings, which, in less watchful times, are said to have harboured smugglers and their contraband goods.

To the left of these ruined buildings, and at the base of the cliff, approached only by means of a boat, is the entrance to a vast cavern, of great length and height (the extent of which is but dimly discernible, owing to the faint rays of light which penetrate the narrow orifice), apparently traversing the entire morro from north to south.

During the months of June and July, it is an extraordinary sight to see large numbers of the huge cagarra (*Puffinus major*, of Faber, and *P. cinereus*, of Ch. Bonap.), sitting on their nests of two eggs, without a sound or motion as you approach, but fierce in the extreme, and even dangerous, if molested. The discordant note of this bird may be often heard overhead, in the dead of night, when they generally go abroad.

From Capellas, two capital roads lead, one across the island (at this part only nine miles broad) to Ponta Delgada; the other, past the villages of Nossa Senhora da Luz, Calheitas, and Rabo de Peixe, to the pretentious town of Ribeira Grande, so named from the stream on which it is built. This town is the second place of importance in the island, its population including Ribeirinha and Ribeira Secca, numbering some 11,800 souls. The people are of a different type and character to the other islanders, and share with the people of Arrifes the unenviable reputation of being disorderly and turbulent; conflicts with the military not infrequently occur over hotly-contested elections, on which occasions the use of the knife is not altogether unknown.

The ride past these places is varied by numerous bays and creeks indenting the broken and rugged coast; here, the sweet monotone of the gentle surf in some sheltered sandy cove—there the angry boom of the waves breaking over a rocky promontory—relieves the irksomeness of travel. The changes too, when the road turns inland, are equally enjoyable, for scoriaceous tracts alternate with patches of orange groves, and waving fields of wheat, maize, or tobacco, hedged, where the ground is highest, by the handsome *Arundo donax* reed, bending its plumed head to the slightest breeze; or by the elegant broom millet (*Sorghum dhurra*), from the beautiful panicles of which excellent brooms and brushes are made.

Tobacco grows here in surprising lankness. In 1864 a law was enacted, extinguishing the tobacco monopoly, and permitting its manufacture in the Açores and Madeira, where the receipts from the monopoly amounted to £15,500 per annum. In order to make up this amount, a direct tax of 200 reis per kilo on imported or locally manufactured tobacco was imposed. The result of this salutary measure was soon apparent, for so profitable did farmers find the cultivation of the plant, that its production in the district of Ponta Delgada alone rose from 5,110 kilos in 1865 to close upon 200,000 kilos at the present time. In 1885, this tax was reduced to 160 reis per kilo on all tobacco manufactured for consumption, the grower being also given the privilege of exporting his produce to Portugal. Unfortunately the plant impoverishes the soil to a great extent, and the difficulty and expense of obtaining artificial manures prevents its cultivation for any lengthened period.

There are no less than four tobacco factories in the

island, and the profits of this industry would be much greater if the proprietors of these (where all kinds of fancy tobacco and inferior cigars are made) had not, unfortunately, combined to pay the grower a fixed and uniform price for his produce, generally 6 tostoons per kilo for the coarse and a dollar for the fine leaf, of which, however, only a small proportion is obtained, and as the Government senselessly prohibits the export, unless the same duties are paid as on foreign tobacco, the Azorean grower has no alternative but to accept these terms, as the material loss in weight, which is soon apparent when it reaches the drier climate of Lisbon, places it at once at a disadvantage with tobacco imported there from other countries possessing less moisture.

The tobacco plant has been long acclimatized in these islands, for in a short description of Fayal, written in 1589 by Edward Wright, he mentions that it was then commonly found growing in every garden, " wherewith their women dye their faces reddish, to make them seem fresh and young "; this latter application of the leaf appears, however, in these days to be entirely discontinued. The loss sustained by the cultivation of tobacco can be recouped to the soil by alternating its growth with that of plants possessing fertilising properties. The cultivation of tea is found to exhaust the fertility of the soil, and the sau plant has been recommended as a remedy to Indian tea planters. Johnston, in his " Chemistry of Common Life," very truly says that " it is one of the triumphs of the chemistry of the present century that it has ascertained by what new management the ancient fertility of the land may be restored, and thus how new fortunes may be extracted from the same old soil." Tobacco growers in these islands are perfectly well aware of the fertilising properties of the " lupin," but even this surprising land " regenerator," like the too-willing horse, may fail them if persistently sown in the same soil, and an occasional interchange with the sau would probably prevent their having to lament over the loss of a profitable industry.

Through the praiseworthy efforts of my friend, Snr. Gm. Read Cabral, considerable attention has of recent years been devoted in this and some of the other islands to the cultivation of the *Phormium tenax,* or New Zealand flax, the fibre of which, when properly treated, can be worked up into the finest textile fabrics. Snr. Read Cabral's chief aim, however, is to produce paper pulp from the plant, and as nothing can be done in Portugal without protection, he obtained a patent from the Government which virtually concedes him the monopoly of this manufacture in the islands and Portugal for a term of 15 years. As it is alike profitable to manufacturer and grower, the plant thriving on any soil, however poor, its culture is likely in time to attain important proportions; if so, the credit of introducing this new industry is entirely due to the persistent endeavours and example of Snr. Read Cabral.

How this plant became common in all the islands is unknown; the oldest inhabitants remember it from childhood, and no one can throw any light as to how it first became introduced.

There are several Australian trees, such as the *eucalyptus, acacia, melanoxylon* and *pittosporum,* all of comparatively recent introduction, to be found in these islands, but botanists tell us that out of a total of 478 flowering plants in this archipelago, 400 are identical with European species. More than half of the European genera occurring in Australia are to be found also in these islands, no visible means, other than aerial transport of the seed across the vast expanse of ocean, being apparent to account for their introduction into these isolated isles ages ago. It is an interesting fact in connection with the recent cultivation of the Australian eucalyptus, all over temperate Europe, that its fruit was found by Dr. Ettinghausen in the Eocene beds of Sheppey.

The church of Nossa Senhora da Estrella, commenced as

far back as 1517, is a conspicuous edifice and passed through many vicissitudes when earthquakes were rife, having been more than once almost totally destroyed. The interior is spacious and imposing, and under the chief altar once reposed the remains of its old vicar, the erudite Father Fructuoso, who was born in S. Miguel in 1522, and died in 1591, after having been for forty years vicar of Ribeira Grande. His ashes were, some years ago, removed to the adjoining churchyard, where a handsome monument was by public subscription erected to his much venerated memory.

A far more lasting testimony to the worth of this old graduate of Salamanca, however, remains in his invaluable and voluminous MS. writings, of which four copies exist.

In these, are to be found a complete history of the genealogy of the families who came over from Portugal to people these islands, and of the chief occurrences which had taken place during his long residence here. His narratives, written in simple and ungarnished style, bear the impress of truth, and it is from them that the only reliable early history of these islands can be gathered. In addition to the tardy monument erected to the fame of unquestionably the greatest of their citizens, the Michaelenses should add the still more honourable one of printing his works.

The haughty ediles of Ribeira Grande have installed themselves in an imposing Casa da Camara, the ground floor of which, with low iron-grated windows facing the street, is used as a prison, a system formerly much in vogue in Portugal and which travellers even now may see at Cintra and other places.

Here the confined cut-throats, thieves and other desperadoes, can hold comfortable and unchecked converse with their friends, and perhaps mature plans for future misdeeds. I believe that motives of economy first prompted the authorities to introduce these open grates, which enabled them to cast the burden of maintaining the prisoners upon the latter's relatives and friends, and upon the compassionate passer-by. It is a wonder, and speaks volumes for this order-loving people, that under such a system crime should not be more frequent than it is, for under the humanitarian government of Portugal the worst penalty criminals of the deepest dye can expect to pay is transportation for life to Angola or some other West African "Cave of Adullam," where, after a year or two of idle and easy confinement, they are set at liberty with little or no surveillance, and attached as servants, or, if of the better class, as travellers and assistants to the traders, whose places they eventually occupy. Nearly the whole of the Portuguese colonial trade in Africa is in the hands of these men. The " degradados," as they are called for life, may not return to Portugal even on ticket-of-leave, but those who go for shorter periods come back completely purged of the stigma which attached to their deeds, and, if well-to-do, take their place as respectable members of society. I have often been told by African traders that they live in perfect harmony and confidence with these liberated convicts, of whose conduct they have seldom to complain. This goes far to prove that crime in Portugal is perhaps not so much the result of innate and confirmed rascality as the consequence of impulse; still it is melancholy to think that such are the men who by force of circumstances are the pioneers of Portuguese trade in West and East Africa, for they are sent by their employers far and wide into the interior to exchange goods for native produce. That they seldom lose their lives on these distant and sometimes dangerous expeditions, is a probable indication of their good conduct.

In 1867, as we have seen, the death penalty was abolished in Portugal, and penal servitude for life, or " degrado perpetuo," substituted in its stead.

The law punishes certain crimes with excessive severity,

but the juries invariably tend to leniency, and acquit 35 per cent. of the cases brought before them for trial. Out of a total of 9,267 crimes recorded in the criminal statistics of Portugal for the past year, 15 are included under the head of " want of respect for religion," including blasphemy. There were 24 trials, in all, of this class, resulting in 12 convictions, the offenders being in all cases subjected to light punishments.

The following extract from a recent Lisbon paper will give a fair idea of the disproportionate sentences to the crimes committed :—

" The prisoners mentioned below will shortly be sent to penal servitude ; Angelica Marques, maidservant, banished for 3 years, for the crime of theft ; Domingos Ferreira, man-servant, banished for 15 years for the crime of theft ; Francisco Braz, farmer, perpetual banishment for the crime of rape ; José Manais, shoemaker, perpetual banishment for the crime of homicide ; José Trusa, manservant, perpetual banishment for robbery ; Maria Dias, banished for 10 years for homicide ; Polycarpo Oliveira, miller, 4 years banishment for wounding ; João Noivo, labourer, perpetual banishment for the crime of homicide ; Antonio Fernandez, labourer, 5 years banishment for theft ; Antonio Felicio, labourer, 8 years banishment for theft."

Thirty years ago, prisoners were frequently seen with ankle-chains on, sweeping the streets of Ponta Delgada ; only the best behaved being allowed this privilege.

Passing through Ribeira Grande, as often happens in almost all these islands, one is strongly reminded of some Mauresque town, so eastern do the houses look, with their high-grated verandahs completely veiling the windows and impenetrable to the eye, but from behind which the fair occupant may be observed—

Peeping cautiously through,
Lest the neighbours should say
That she looked at the men.

These hideous "jalousie" blinds are said to have been originally instituted by the Moors, with the double object of shutting out the rays of the sun, as well as protecting the fair inmates—probably, like others of their sex, much addicted to the too serious study of street scenery—from the impious gaze of would-be conquistadores. But their adoption ruined the appearance of the dwellings and shut out all air; they had also a still more mischievous effect in inspiring the female population with a timidity and absurd fear of being seen, which condemned them to an altogether useless and unnatural life.

Perhaps the island cynic may, in a measure, be responsible for this feminine seclusion, when he penned the following warning to husbands :—

> Tendes a dama bonita,
> Não a ponhaes á janella ;
> Passam uns, e passam outros,
> Todos dizem :—quem m'a dera !

which may be thus construed—

> Who owns a fine wife
> Should in window not place her,
> Else passers by, seeing,
> Will long to embrace her.

These windows were also apparently used as substitutes for panes of glass; force of habit retaining their use in country villages to the present day.

Capt. Cook, who visited Fayal, and remained there six days, in July, 1775, to "find the rate of the watch, the better to enable us to fix with some degree of certainty the longitude of these islands," gives a short description of Horta, in the account of his second voyage, and incidentally remarks that "there is not a glass window in the place, except what are in the churches and in a country house which lately belonged to the English consul, all the others being latticed, which to an Englishman makes them look like prisons."

This exclusiveness appears to have been carried to an extreme by the earlier inhabitants of the island, for in such villages as Ginetes and Candelaria the older cottages may be seen, without even a door or window, opening out into the street, in the apartment facing which is located the kitchen and baking oven. At Arrifes, Bretanha, Ginetes and Feteiras, many of the cottages have their entrance at the back, or side yard, a small window only facing the street. In this yard lives the pig (who generally pays the rent), and whatever poultry the cottager possesses, making the access to the dwelling disagreeable, and the surroundings unhealthy. Hence, the chief diseases in these villages consist of gastric and typhoid fevers and small-pox.

In the Matriz Church of this town is a curious collection of small figures illustrative of various Scripture passages, the chief merit of which consists in their being the untaught handiwork of one of the nuns who resided here. It is uncertain what the plastic materials used consisted of, as this she kept a profound secret, but the inception and manner of depicting the chief events narrated in the Old and New Testaments are creditable, considering that the artist had nothing but her own instinct to guide her.

Ribeira Grande was always the centre of manufacturers in the island, and even now it is here that all the small iron agricultural implements are made. The stream flowing through the town also gives employment to many antiquated, but effective, corn mills, and a few looms for the coarser kinds of linen cloths worn by the peasantry are still kept at work.

The land around Ribeira Grande is very fertile, and this is the richest cereal-growing district in the island, which probably accounts for the extensive demesnes with their monasteries and convents formerly existing here, and then inhabited by numerous fat, lazy and unprofitable drones—but now, in their decay and emptiness, looking like " whited sepulchres." A very fair inland road leads to the picturesquely situate hamlet of Caldeiras, about three miles distant from Ribeira Grande, and built on heights about six or seven hundred feet above sea level—famous for its group of thermal springs, the second of importance in the island. A score or so of stone-built cottages (entirely deserted in the winter time), half hidden behind huge hydrangeas and arborescent fuchsias (*Gracilis*), dot the surrounding hillocks, and, although suggestive of damp and rheumatism they are much resorted to by health seekers in the summer months, who come to enjoy the baths and the pure restorative mountain air for which this place has always been celebrated. Those able to climb and stand moderate fatigue will find some charming excursions about the neighbourhood ; but on any lengthy trip it is well to start in ample time to return by daylight, as, in this broken and rugged country, night travelling is all but impossible.

The Ribeira Grande stream flows through a deep rocky gorge in the mountains, forming two beautiful cascades close to Caldeiras, known as the Salto do Cabrito, and the Salto de Luiz d'Aguiar ; the scenery hereabouts more than repaying the fatigue of descending into these steep fern-clothed glens. The walk to the dripping well of " Lagrimas," and, further still, to the foot of the Pico do Fogo mountains, reveals some of the grandest views in the island. At this latter place there is a cold spring of acidulated water rich in carbonic gas and containing carbonate and silicate of soda, carbonate of lime and magnesia, and oxyde of iron : its general characteristics are those of seltzer water, and it is no doubt of great medicinal value and very pleasant to drink.

Higher up the mountain, you reach the lip of the crater containing the beautiful lake known as " Lagôa do Fogo." This vast crater, already referred to, was the result of the eruption of the 25th June, 1563. The highest points around stand some 3,000 feet, or more, above sea level, and present a witching expanse of scenery as far as the eye can range, to those fortunate enough to have a cloudless day in which to enjoy it.

The shores of the lake itself are well worth exploring. It is here, and especially on the south-west side, that the beautiful cabellinho fern attains giant proportions, and immense beds of the remarkable moss (*Sphagnum cymbifolium*), holding water like a sponge, are found.

In this perfect solitude, the sea-gulls and other water-fowl build their nests undisturbed. On the south-east side of the lake the overhanging lava cliffs are magnificent, viewed from a boat below.

About a mile and a quarter to the east of Caldeiras, and on the rising banks of a mountain torrent, are to be found two springs of very strong iron water, welling up in considerable volume, and too hot to allow of the hand being dipped into them. The place is known as "o banho do Cabreiro," from a goat-herd having built himself a rude bath here which he used for chronic rheumatism, and the natives say he derived great benefit from the use of these waters.

Another very charming walk across country leads to the little village of Gramas de Cima, near which the Count da Silvã has a wood entirely of eucalyptus trees; by its side flows a brook, on the left margin of which, after crossing the stepping stones, another very curious spring of acidulated water—of less value, however, than that on the mountain side —rises in a sandy bed; it is very cold and free from gas, but pleasant to the taste.

Not far from Gramas is a noble forest property known as Lameiro, belonging to Snr. José Jacomo Corrêa, where you can ramble for hours through beautiful pine and eucalyptus woods, or drive along an avenue unequalled in the island for breadth and growth.

In another private property in this direction, is the " Ladeira da Velha " spring, rising out of the fissures of a large rock; it has a temperature of about 30 degrees Fah., and is rich in free carbonic acid gas; this makes it a delightful water to bathe in.

M. Fouqué obtained the following results from analysis :

Chloride of sodium	.120
Chlorohydric acid	.002
Sulphuric acid	traces
Silica .. ·	.021
	0.143

From the Pico das Freiras a very fine view of the town of Ribeira Grande may be had, as well as of the adjacent coast.

One of the most remarkable and enjoyable trips in this neighbourhood is to the Caldeira Velha, occupying about an hour and a half on donkey back. The road gradually ascends and crosses the Ribeira Grande stream several times, narrowing in places and winding through characteristic Azorean scenery, until it terminates in a *cul de sac*, at the very end of which, and at the immediate foot of a mountain spur, lies the Great Geyser, the second largest in the island, surrounded by a low circular stone parapet, containing a large volume of smoking acid water, which perpetually heaves and boils violently. The French savant, M. F. Fouqué, who visited the Açores at the special request of the Portuguese Government in 1872, for the purpose of analysing and reporting on the various mineral springs existing there, found the temperature of the water of the Caldeira Velha to be 97 degrees Fah., and an analysis gave the following results :—

Sulphate of soda	.155
Sulphate of peroxide of iron ..	.610
Silica	.350
Sulphuric acid	.680
Chlorohydric acid	.010
Sulphydric acid	.003
	1·808

A litre of evaporated water left a residue weighing 1·115 gramme.

M. Fouqué draws attention to the large proportion of free sulphuric acid (environ 5 décigrammes d'acide sulfurique libre par litre) and sulphate of iron which this well contains. Although there is a total absence of bathing accommodation, believers in the efficacy of this spring have been known to come from considerable distances, and by constructing rude huts, or cafuas, with boughs of brushwood, to use its waters with beneficial results in cases where the other mineral baths in the island had failed to relieve.

At first sight, the temperature of this water would be thought much higher than it really is, the perpetual rush of escaping gases agitating and working it up to the violently ebullient condition it presents. The natives cook their milho cobs and horse beans in the Caldeira, but its heat is scarcely sufficient to thoroughly boil harder vegetables, such as potatoes, yams, &c.

In the middle of the sixteenth century an alum factory appears to have been established here, but was soon abandoned, in consequence of its collection proving unremunerative. The article may still be found encrusted within the interstices and broken ground surrounding the geyser; here, also, are to be seen several mud-holes and lesser springs—all hissing and evolving hot gasses.

A few hundred yards on the way to this remarkable spot is the entrance to a very extensive tea plantation belonging to Snr. José do Canto, which is also well worth visiting. The shrubs are planted on a sheltered slope with a northern aspect, and grow to perfection. Tea is systematically made, and the quality is very good.

In 1885 there were upwards of 27,000 plants in this garden, flushing leaves five or six times a year. A plant four to five years old produces at each stripping 1 lb. of green leaves; and each 3 to 4 lbs. of leaves 1 lb. of manipulated tea. When we consider that the import duty on tea in Portugal is 3s. 6½d. per kilogramme, it is surprising that with such advantages of climate and soil, tea gardens

should not profitably replace the now exhausted orange
groves.

The pine woods around Caldeiras are very enjoyable, and
immense masses of dark blue *Hydrangea hortensis*, hedging
the paths in all directions, which are also rendered beautiful
in the autumn by long lines and clumps of the belladonna
lily, to be found here in incredible quantity.

The bathing establishment of Caldeiras is ancient and
primitive in the extreme, having been built in 1811,
and recently repaired by the Camara of Ribeira Grande.
The baths are deep stone troughs, dark looking and hardly
tempting to the over fastidious; but, properly cleansed,
are very enjoyable. The waters, which lack some of the
many virtues ascribed to the Furnas springs, owing to their
volume being increased by mixture with ordinary water,
are drawn off from a large reservoir protected by a
solid stone, completely enclosing the solfataras in which
they rise. Into this receptacle flows a constant stream
of cold spring water, which soon attains a heat of
95 degrees Fah. and becomes impregnated to a marked
degree with the mineral and gaseous properties of the wells.
There is no doubt that the fact of these repositories being
uncovered, and the adjunct of ordinary water, detract
from the value and efficacy of the baths; still they are
not only very pleasant, but of undoubted benefit in rheumatism and other kindred disorders.

Should these tanks not be frequently replenished, a
glairy, viscous substance (known as baregine) soon forms
and floats on the surface. A few yards to the east of
the larger reservoir is a smaller one, encircling some boiling
and hissing springs of iron water. A subterranean leakage,
however, appears to have been formed recently, and prevents
its holding any body of water, the volume of the iron source
itself being greatly attenuated.

A few yards to the west of these springs occurs another,
rising in a deep depression alongside the road; the water is

very hot, and being stronger in mineral properties than the others, is frequently conveyed in pitchers to the different dwellings, for use in sitz baths.

At the latter end of the sixteenth century, quite a large alum factory existed at Caldeiras, and a smaller one at the Furnas.

Dr. Gaspar Gonçalves, in 1553, noticing the presence of alum in large quantities around these solfataras, succeeded in extracting some three or four cwt., which he took to Lisbon. The queen, Catherine of Austria, became greatly interested in the new industry, and sent to Carthagena for experts to set up and conduct the necessary lixiviating works in the island. In 1564, some seventy people were already engaged at Caldeiras in the reduction works, and during the year some 438 cwts. of alum were manufactured. The industry seems to have flourished until 1590, when it completely died away; up to that time no less than 526 tons of good alum were exported to Lisbon.

The works at the Furnas, which were overwhelmed by the eruption of 1630, appear to have been of a purely tentative kind, for I can only trace some 690 cwt. of alum as having been manufactured, although the aluminous earth would seem to exist there in much larger quantities than at the Caldeiras. Here is a manufacture which, if properly and economically carried on, might be made highly remunerative, the cheapness of labour and abundance of water in the localities where the alum deposits occur offering special inducements for its development.

N

Chapter XI.

> The loud war-trumpet woke the morn,
> The quivering drum, the pealing horn;
> From rank to rank the cry is borne,
> "Arouse to death or victory!"
>
> *Hogg.*

LEAVING Caldeiras and its pleasant associations at daybreak, and following the coast road past Ribeirinha, we soon reach a place called Ladeira da Velha, where the road becomes exceedingly steep, dipping at an angle of 50° into what but a few years back was a deep ravine. This pass, and the neighbouring heights are celebrated in the annals of liberalism as the scene of as gallant a fight as ever took place for freedom. It seems, indeed, difficult to realise that these waving fields of corn to the right and left, and the wooded hills above them, should have once been soaked in human gore, and resounded with the fierce yells of war. We will presently revisit the spot, and describe what then took place.

The next village on our way is Porto Formoso—and, beyond, Maya—where a pretty waterfall, if the season be not too dry, can be seen in the grounds of Dona Hermelinda da Camara. From this point, the journey should be continued to Fanaes d'Ajuda, prudent travellers emptying their provaunt baskets here; after which, having sallied out in quest of a guide, we proceed a short way down the coast to inspect some singular basaltic reefs of columnar formation, which may justly be compared to those of Staffa. The locality is wild, and very interesting are these weather-battered prominences—

> Their bleak and visionary sides
> Containing the history of many a winter storm.

A little distance from the shore, and in deep water, stands a mass of basalt, in the form of a magnificent arch, through which the sea, in rough weather, dashes with furious violence; indeed, during all seasons of the year, the deep ululation of the waters characterises this spot. The lava rocks in this part of the island are highly crystalline.

To properly enjoy this beautiful coast scenery, beds for the night should be secured at the convent close by, once belonging to the Seraphic order of nuns, and built in 1681. This would allow of a boating excursion round these bold headlands, and of some good pigeon shooting.

A mile or two beyond, are the two villages of Achadinha and Achada, not far from which is a basaltic promontory called Pesqueiro da Achadinha, where the small liberating band, numbering 1,500 men, headed by Count Villa Flor (afterwards Duke of Terceira), landed on the 1st August, 1831. As a brief account of the struggle which ensued, and the circumstances which led up to it, may not be altogether uninteresting, I will here record what can be gathered on the subject from the most trustworthy sources.

When Junot, in November, 1807, was rapidly marching on Lisbon—in consequence of John the Sixth's refusal to ratify the decree of Berlin, by which the ports of the Peninsula were closed against England—the king, with the whole court and a large following, fled on the 29th November to the colony of Brazil, which he raised to a constitutional kingdom in 1818, leaving Portugal in the meantime to the government of a regency. Disgusted, however, with the court intrigues, and the unruly character of his new subjects, who had forced from him the constitution, King John determined to return to Portugal, and left for Lisbon in

July, 1821, leaving the new-born kingdom under the vice-royalty of his eldest son, the Prince Dom Pedro.

Envious of the distinction which had been conferred upon their South American settlement, the Lisbon court now influenced Dom João to withdraw the constitution he had granted them, and to reduce the government and country to a colony; but, once having tasted the sweets of self-government, the people replied to this ill-advised measure by immediately declaring their independence of the mother country, and proclaimed Dom Pedro their constitutional emperor in 1825. Besides Dom Pedro, King John had a second son, Dom Miguel—the favourite of his mother Dona Carlotta Joaquina, daughter of Charles IV. of Spain, a most bigoted woman, ruled completely by the priesthood, whose sole aim was the advancement of her cherished son Miguel to the throne; to accomplish which, the most unscrupulous means were resorted to.

The court now became divided into two camps—the liberals, who rallied round the king, clamouring for a constitution, and the absolutists, headed by Queen Carlotta and her son and the Marquis de Cháves. The assassination of the Marquis of Loulé, a staunch adherent and friend of the king, on the 29th February, 1824, and the discovery of a conspiracy to seize upon the person of the king himself, with a view to forcing him to abdicate the throne, drove Dom João on board the British man-of-war "Windsor Castle." Dom Miguel having been ordered by the king to join him on board the "Windsor Castle," was there severely reprimanded for his part in the conspiracy, and, having been transferred to the frigate "Perola," was banished the kingdom, many of his followers being also dispersed.

Portugal now enjoyed a short period of repose, but the death of Dom João in March, 1826, once more became the signal for fresh disturbances.

By his will, the crown of Portugal devolved upon his eldest son, Dom Pedro d'Alcantara, the Emperor of Brazil, who was at once proclaimed King of Portugal, but shortly afterwards abdicated his questionable rights in favour of his eldest daughter, the youthful princess, Dona Maria da Gloria, then only 8 years of age, under the regency of her aunt, the Infanta Isabel Maria. He also granted to Portugal, shortly before his death, the famous Carta da Constituição, or charter of constitution, which guaranteed legal equality, abolished the odious class distinctions, and conceded to the people suffrage rights, establishing the representative chambers, and many other privileges. Instigated by the old queen, the government of the regent now openly became absolutist, and sought to suppress, by every means in their power, the growing tendencies of constitutionalism. Encounters were frequent between the queen's troops and bands of liberals under the leaders, Saldanha and Villa Flor.

The queen-mother, having unfortunately successfully intrigued with the Emperor Dom Pedro for the return of her favourite son to Portugal, and his bethrothal to his niece, Dona Maria, Dom Miguel landed in Lisbon on the 22nd of February, 1828, after encountering at the mouth of the Tagus one of the most frightful tempests on record, which seemed to presage his own stormy administration.

Dom Miguel at once took the oath of allegiance, and assumed the reins of government as regent, swearing to defend and uphold the charter of the constitution. Twenty-one days afterwards this charter was abolished, and Dom Miguel had proclaimed himself king! The fierce struggle and fratricidal war of succession now broke out, which did not cease until July, 1833, when first the Duke of Terceira and subsequently Dom Pedro triumphantly entered Lisbon at the head of the liberating army. Some of the most brilliant acts of this lamentable war took place in the Azores, which at the time, though ripe for revolution, were yet, by reason of the strong Miguelite garrisons which held them, kept from openly pronouncing for the liberal cause.

Terceira had, during all these events, been in reality

more " Miguelista " than " Constitutional " ; but on the 21st August, 1826, the various municipalities of the island, owing chiefly to the earnest endeavours of Lord Stuart de Rothesay, who had been commissioned by Dom Pedro (who afterwards created him Marquis of Angra) to be the bearer of it to Portugal and the islands, gave a sullen adhesion to the constitutional charter, and to this date may be traced the dawn of liberalism in this "muito nobre e sempre leal cidade d'Angra." This submission of the Miguelistas was of short duration, for they once more occupied the public offices, and assayed to re-establish their master's rule. A revolt, however, initiated by some of the leading liberal citizens, and supported by the 5th battalion of Caçadores, under their commandant Quintino Dias, broke out at Terceira on the 22nd June, 1828, when the power of Miguel in the island was for ever overthrown, fortunately with little bloodshed. The malcontents, however, taking refuge in the more central and almost inaccessible parts of the island, and staunchly aided by the priesthood, were soon able to take the field, though with an undisciplined and badly-armed force, variously estimated at from 4,000 to 5,000 men, under the command of Captain João Moniz de Sá, a steadfast supporter of the "inauferiveis direitôs" of Dom Miguel I. They were strongly posted on well-chosen and hilly ground in the neighbourhood of Pico do Selleiro, where, on the 4th October of the same year, they were attacked and completely routed by that dashing cavalry officer, Colonel José Antonio da Silva Torres, afterwards created Barão do Pico Selleiro, for his splendid defence of the Serra Convent at Oporto. By this victory, Terceira henceforth became the focus and rallying point of constitutionalism; so enthusiastic became the inhabitants for the cause they had espoused, that they declared the very sun became "liberal," and shed in his rays the colours their party sported.

On the 22nd June, 1829, Count Villa Flor, who had been driven from Portugal and taken refuge in Terceira, was appointed, by Dom Pedro, Captain-General of the Açores, with instructions to regain the islands to the cause of Dona Maria. The Count now vowed that he would not again shave until he had freed Portugal from the tyrannical rule of Dom Miguel, and at once issued the following proclamation :—

Azoreans! The time has arrived for you to shake off the shameful and heavy yoke which has oppressed you so long. Your brothers, the brave Portuguese, who, after the most terrible catastrophes, and at the cost of every kind of risk and suffering, had the constancy never to despair of the salvation of the country, and knew how to maintain themselves firm and invincible in the island of Terceira, now come to break the irons with which an impious faction has bound your arms. Azoreans! We have not come to make war upon you; we know perfectly well that if violence can stifle the manifestation of your honour and loyalty, these sentiments yet exist in your hearts as pure as those that should ever animate Portuguese breasts.

The Regency, in the name of our gracious queen, Dona Maria II., sends us to free you from your oppressors, to plant among you the regimen of law, to unite you round a beneficent sceptre under the shade of which we enjoy all the benefits of a just and well-regulated liberty, and finally to vindicate the Portuguese nation from the eternal opprobrium with which all civilized countries would regard her, were she to remain any longer subject to the brutal tyranny which degrades her in the eyes of the entire world.

The sad experience of three years of tyranny and oppression have dissipated all those illusions which the perfidious authors of usurpation had succeeded in spreading. All now know that hyprocrisy clothed herself with the mantle of religion only to fill the dungeons with unhappy wretches, to people with victims the pestiferous deserts of Africa, and to shed on the scaffolds the generous blood of those who refused to violate their oaths. Perjury was discovered in virtue, fidelity was called treason, and thus were confounded all ideas of justice and injustice.

All the nations of Europe became horrified at sight of such crimes, and the indignant governments have ever refused to recognise the usurper of the Portuguese crown. Europe expects that the Portuguese will at length awake from the lethargy in which they have lain, and, spontaneously acclaiming the legitimate queen, will once more occupy that place amongst nations which always belonged to them.

Now, therefore, Azoreans! the moment has arrived which you and we have so ardently desired. Acclaim, with one accord, our Queen; re-establish the constitutional charter; enter once again into the enjoyment of the country's liberties, which our ancestors enjoyed, and which were restored to us by the august father and guardian of Her Majesty; and thus will you afford to all Portuguese a most glorious example. Viva the Senhora D. Maria II.! Viva the Constitutional Charter!

On the 11th August following, a powerful Miguelite fleet, consisting of 22 sail, under Admiral Roza Coelho, carrying some 350 guns, and having a large force on board, made an attempt to land 3,500 troops at Porto Praia on the east side of Terceira, but were beaten off with the loss of 1,000 men killed, amongst whom was their leader, Colonel Azevedo Lemos, although the defenders only numbered 1,300 bayonets, besides a small force of cavalry and artillery. The fleet also sustained considerable damage, and at once sailed for Lisbon.

The cause of Miguel suffered another irreparable loss by the death of his mother, D. Carlotta, on the 7th of January, 1830, and, in March following, by that of the Marquis Cháves. Nothing further occurred until May, 1831, when Count Villa Flor, after raising the queen's standard on the island of Pico, landed at St. George's, and after several sharp skirmishes overcame all opposition. From thence he crossed over to Fayal, which island at once pronounced for the queen, the garrison taking refuge on board the Miguelite corvette, "Isabel Maria," and an English schooner chartered for the purpose, which immediately sailed to strengthen the forces at St. Michael's, the other three small islands to the west having soon afterwards given in their adherence to the queen's government. St. Michael's now only remained to complete the conquest of the whole group. Owing to the crafty influence of the priesthood, this island had become the stronghold of absolutism; great efforts had therefore been made to set all the fortifications in order. They were defended by 100 guns and garrisoned by four regiments of the line and a strong force of militia; a man-of-war was also stationed here for the defence of the roads.

On the afternoon of the 30th July, 1831, a force of 1,500 men under Villa Flor sailed from Terceira on board two small ships of war and some smaller merchant vessels, and at daybreak on the 1st August came in sight of St. Michael's. Keeping to the north coast, the troops disembarked at the rocky spot already mentioned, called the Pisqueiro da Achadinha, where only one boat at a time could approach. Following the rugged shore for about three-quarters of a mile, over rocks and boulders, they arrived at the bed of a mountain stream, up which they ascended to the neighbouring heights, occupied by such defending forces as could be got together in time, whence a galling musketry fire was kept up, and immense stones were rolled down upon the invaders, who, nothing daunted, soon crowned the sides of the ravine, killing and dispersing the defenders.

The van of the invading force, which had now all landed, at once seized the road to Ribeira Grande and Ponta Delgada, the latter distant from this place about fifteen miles. They had not proceeded far, when, on the heights of Ponta da Ajuda, a strong detachment of the Miguelites which had been watching the movements of the little fleet, was met with, and at once attacked by Villa Flor, who put the enemy to flight with the loss of their captain, who was killed, a field-piece which proved of invaluable service to the invaders, and many prisoners. Another attack by a force of three hundred men, sent round over the mountains from the south with the object of falling upon the Count's rear, met with the same fate. At nightfall, the victorious liberals encamped at the Ribeira dos Moinhos, a mile and a half from the village of Maia. On the 2nd, they broke ground, and marched as far as Porto Formoso, without encountering the Miguelites; but, a little in advance of this place, they found them holding the pass of Ladeira da Velha, in force, estimated at 3,000 men, under General Touvar, with artillery posted on the surrounding heights—a splendid strategical position, covering both Ribeira Grande and the city—the occupying force having its flanks protected by an inaccessible coast and lofty cliffs on one side, and its front resting upon the sides of a precipitous ravine, the narrow bridle road across which had been cut and batteries erected for its defence.

As soon as the liberals approached, a heavy fire of musketry and artillery was opened upon them; the advanced positions were, however, soon abandoned, and occupied by Villa Flor, who now, uniting his forces—with the exception of a column of five hundred men which he detached to work round and turn the right of the Miguelites—advanced himself to deliver the direct assault. So rapid and determined was the charge of these gallant troops, combined with the now successful turning movement, that the enemy gave way on all sides, abandoning his artillery—of which the liberals were much in need, for they had been unable to land any—and losing many prisoners. The loss of the Miguelites in killed and wounded amounted to 350 men; that of the liberals being also severe. In this attack the brave Captain Borges of the Caçadores, a native of S. Miguel, who had greatly assisted the cause of Dom Pedro in Terceira with the 5th battalion, was killed.

On the 3rd August, the Count entered Ponta Delgada in triumph; the citizens, upon the news of the defeat, having proclaimed the queen and the " Carta Constitucional," disarmed the disheartened garrison, whose general, Touvar, with his staff, and Miguel's captain-general of the Açores, Admiral Prego, had fled on board the corvette " D. Isabel Maria," assisted in their flight by Mr. Read, the British consul.

On the news of the victory reaching Sta. Maria, that island at once espoused the rule of D. Maria II.; and thus ceased for ever, in the archipelago, the galling yoke—so long borne—of Miguel's government.

The spoils of war in all the islands, which fell into the hands of Villa Flor, now amounted to 250 guns, 5,500 muskets, 166 cwt. of gunpowder and much-needed ammunition, enabling the Pedroites to raise a loan in St. Michael's alone of £30,000.

Whilst the ordinary quiet of these peaceful islands was disturbed by these unusual events, the political condition of Brazil was approaching a climax. The wretched and inglorious war with Monte Video, and subsequently with the Argentine Confederation, into which Dom Pedro had plunged, together with continued and serious conflicts with the representative chambers, owing to the open protection extended by the emperor to Portuguese immigrants, induced the sovereign to abdicate the throne in favor of his son, the present enlightened emperor, Dom Pedro II., which he did on the 7th April, 1831. The ex-emperor then assumed the title of Duke of Braganza, and embarking for Europe with his wife on board the British man-of-war "La Volage," Captain Lord Colchester, arrived off Fayal on his way to Cherbourg on the 30th May, and continued his voyage after sending on shore through the British consul, Mr. Henry Walker, the following letter to Count Villa Flor :—

My dear Count and Friend,

Having, in consequence of a revolution of the troops and people, which took place in the empire of Brazil, abdicated in favour of my son, now D. Pedro II., the crown which the Brazilians had spontaneously offered me, and which I defended so long as honour and the constitution of that empire permitted me to do so, I resolved upon going to Europe, and am now on the way on board the English frigate " La Volage."

The forced circumstances of a voyage of sixty-days have brought me in sight of the harbour of the island of Fayal, and here the happy news reaches me, that your Excellency, ever animated by the purest sentiments of loyalty, love of country and the august person of Dona Maria II., my much loved daughter, has once more made the cause of justice and reason triumph, supplanting the usurping party in the islands of St. Jorge and Pico, wrenching them by virtue and courage from the claws of treachery and despotism. This liberal and noble act will magnify, if possible, your Excellency's memory, when the impartial pen of history shall indicate to a free people the names of the heroes, their defenders.

The Queen of Portugal, who left Rio de Janeiro on the same occasion as I, is now on her way to Brest in the frigate " La Seine," which the delegates of the French nation at that court placed at the disposal of the said august lady to convey her to that port.

As the natural guardian of my daughter, as a true constitutionalist, and an old affectionate friend of your Excellency, I take advantage of this happy opportunity to give you a proof of my respect for so much valour and constancy, and of my thanks for such heroic and sustained sentiments of honour and fidelity to the sovereign cause of unfettered law, and in the name of H. M. F. Majesty I authorise you to make known to all the brave defenders of her imperishable rights the high consideration in which the same august lady holds such high services. I can assure your Excellency, and all honourable Portuguese, that, unwearied with promoting in Europe the interests of my daughter, as her father and as a private individual, I shall devote myself with all my heart in favour of the cause of legitimacy and the constitution.

If I am unable to have the pleasure of showing your Excellency in some other way my satisfaction and esteem, let this letter serve as the more authentic proof of gratitude and friendship, which your Excellency will preserve as long as you live."

(Signed)   D. Pedro de Alcantara e Bourbon,
On board the frigate " La Volage."

30*th May*, 1831.

The fortunate fisherman into whose care this now interesting historical missive was entrusted, received at the ex-emperor's hands four gold pieces, together with a slip, on which were written these few words, probably intended as a proclamation :—

He who now speaks to you, and gives you these four pieces, is the father of your Queen. To arms, then, to arms, against usurpation! To arms, to arms! for the Count of Villa Flor is at Pico.

(Signed)   D. PEDRO.

From Cherbourg, Dom Pedro proceeded to London, and there several months were spent with the Duke of Palmella, and other champions of constitutionalism, in fitting out the expedition which was ultimately destined to restore Dona Maria II. to the throne. At this stage, the forces consisted of a few hundred Portuguese refugees, in France and England, but chiefly of French and British auxiliaries, the latter numbering some 500 bayonets, under Colonel Hodges—equipped under considerable difficulties in the teeth of our Foreign Enlistment Act. This is not the place to detail the deeds of this handful of brave Englishmen, swelled by subsequent reinforcements from England and Ireland; but the sequel shows that they bore the brunt of many a hard-contested fight, being ever in the thickest of the fray, and leaving more than one-half their number on the slopes of Oporto. The expeditionary fleet consisted of the "Rainha de Portugal," 46 guns; "D. Maria Amélie," 42; "Villa Flor," 16; "Terceira," 7; and "Fileira"; some other transports having been ordered in England to rendezvous at Terceira; and set sail from Belle Isle, in France, on the 10th February, 1832, with Dom Pedro, the Duke of Palmella, and other leaders of the movement, arriving at St. Michael's on the 22nd February, where they were received by the military commandant, Count D'Alva, with great ceremony. As Dom Pedro was the first royal personage who had ever visited the island, the people flocked from all parts, and exhibited more curiosity to see him than enthusiasm for his cause, and they apparently expected to witness in him some super-human being, for an amusing anecdote is related of a country woman in the crowd who, within earshot of the ex-emperor, loudly exclaimed on beholding him, in something akin to contemptuous tones, " Oh senhor, tem olhos, nariz, e boca, como o nosso Man'l ! " (Oh Lord, he's got eyes, nose, and mouth, just like our Tom !)

On the 2nd March the ships proceeded to Terceira, where Dom Pedro was received with great rejoicings and tokens of affection. Here he met his faithful adherents, the Counts de Villa-Real, and Rendufe, Candido Xavier, and others. On the 7th he declared himself generalissimo of the naval and military forces, appointing Vice-Admiral Sartorius,* an old Trafalgar hero, to the command of the former, and the Count Villa Flor to that of the latter. A month was here occupied in recruiting, and the following proclamation was issued to the Azoreans, and, as it reviews in emphatic and precise terms the condition of Portugal at the period of these occurrences, will well repay perusal :—

[PROCLAMATION.]

Called upon to succeed my august father to the throne of Portugal, as his first-born son, by the fundamental laws of the monarchy, mentioned in the charter of law and perpetual edict of the 13th November, 1826, I was formally recognised as King of Portugal by all the powers, and by the Portuguese nation, which sent to me at the court of Rio de Janeiro a deputation of the three estates ; and desirous, in spite of the greatest sacrifices, to secure the happiness of my loyal

---

* Sir George Rose Sartorius, G.C.B., died April 13th, 1885, at the great age of 95, having been born August 9th, 1790. He entered the navy as a cadet, at the early age of 11. During his long career Sir George Sartorius saw much service. Amongst other incidents in which he took part, he was present at the surrender of Napoleon I., in 1815, to the squadron under the command of Sir Frederick Maitland of the " Bellerophon "—he being captain of the " Slaney "—and he conveyed the news of the surrender to England. For the part he took, on behalf of the young queen of Portugal, against the usurper, Dom Miguel, he forfeited his rank as captain in the English navy. It was, however, some years afterwards, restored to him. For his services to Portugal he was made Viscount de Piedade, Count of Penhafirme, a Knight Grand Cross of the Order of St. Bento d'Avis, and was decorated with the Grand Cross of the Order of the Tower and the Sword.

subjects in both hemispheres, and not wishing that the reciprocal relations of friendship, so happily established between the two countries, by the independence of both, should possibly become compromised by the fortuitous union of the two crowns on one head, I decided upon abdicating the crown of Portugal in favour of my much esteemed and beloved daughter, D. Maria da Gloria, who was also recognised by all the powers and by the Portuguese nation. At the time of completing this abdication, my duties and sentiments towards the country which had given me birth, and to the noble Portuguese nation which had sworn fidelity to me, induced me to follow the example of my illustrious grandfather, Dom John IV., and, taking advantage of my short reign, to restore, as he had done, to the Portuguese nation the possession of its ancient rights and privileges, thus also fulfilling the promises of my august father, of glorious memory, announced in his proclamation of 31st May, 1823, and in the charter of 4th June, 1824.

With this object in view, I promulgated the Constitutional Charter of 29th April, 1826, in which is virtually reinstated the ancient form of Portuguese government, the constitution of the State; and that this charter should in reality be a confirmation and a sequel to the fundamental law of the monarchy, I guaranteed in the first place the most solemn protection and the most profound respect to the holy religion of our fathers.

I confirmed the law of succession with all the clauses relating to the chambers, as had previously been practised by D. Affonso V. and D. João III.

I recognised the two fundamental principles of the Portuguese government, that is, that the laws should only be framed by the Cortes, and that the contributions and administration of the public funds should only be discussed by them.

Finally, I determined that there should be gathered in one chamber the two arms of the clergy and nobility, composed of the great ones of the kingdom, ecclesiastics and laymen; for experience has shown the inconvenience resulting from the separate deliberations of these two branches.

I added some other provisions, all tending to establish the independence of the nation, the dignity and authority of the throne, and the liberty and prosperity of the people; and not wishing to subject these two to the risks and inconveniences of a minority, I thought that the only means of securing them would be to unite my august daughter to a Portuguese prince, who naturally, by conformity of religion and birth, would be more interested than anyone else in the complete realization of so many benefits which it is my intention to bestow upon the Portuguese nation; persuading myself also that the good example of my virtuous parent, the monarch at whose court he resided, would have rendered him worthy of appreciating the great confidence which a brother reposed in him, and who entrusted the destiny of his much loved daughter to his care. Such is the origin of the choice which I made of the Infante D. Miguel—a fatal choice which has caused me to deplore so many innocent victims, and which will mark one of the most disastrous epochs in Portuguese history.

The Infante D. Miguel after having sworn fealty to me as his natural sovereign, and to the constitutional charter, in the quality of a Portuguese subject; after having solicited from me the post of regent of the kingdom of Portugal, Algarves and its dependencies, which I in effect conferred upon him with the title of my representative, by decree of 3rd July, 1827; after having entered upon the exercise of such eminent functions, taken a free and voluntary oath to maintain the charter of constitution just as I had bestowed it upon the nation, and to deliver the crown to D. Maria II., as soon as she should become of age—he condescended to commit an attempt without example from the circumstances which attended it.

Under pretext of deciding a question which neither in fact nor by right was in dispute—violating the charter of constitution which he had just sworn to uphold—he convoked the three estates of the kingdom in the most illegal and illusory manner, thus abusing the authority which had been confided in him, and trampling under foot the respect due to all the soverigns of Europe, who had recognised as Queen of Portugal D. Maria II.; he caused the supposed mandatories who were assembled under his power and influence to declare that it was to him and not to me that the crown of Portugal should have devolved upon the death of D. João VI. In this manner the Infante D. Miguel usurped the throne which I had confided to his keeping.

The foreign powers stigmatised this as an act of rebellion, immediately retiring their representatives from the Court of Lisbon, and my ministers plenipotentiary, as Emperor of Brazil, at the courts of Vienna and London lodged the two solemn protests of 21st of May and 8th of August of 1828, against all and any violation of my hereditary rights and those of my daughter ; against the abolition of the institutions spontaneously granted by me and legally established in Portugal ; against the illegitimate and insidious convocation of the ancient Estates of that kingdom, which had ceased to exist by virtue of an old proscription ; against the precipitate decision of the assembled three Estates of the realm, and the arguments by which they supported it ; notably against the false interpretation of a law framed in the Cortes of Lamego, and another one passed on the 12th September, 1642, by D. João IV., at the request of the three Estates, and in confirmation of the above mentioned law of the General Cortes of Lamego.

All these protests were sealed with blood which has almost daily flown since then from so many thousands of victims of the purest fidelity ; and in truth this criminal usurpation, placing the Prince who perpetrated it on the highway of illegality and violence, has placed on the shoulders of the unfortunate Portuguese a weight of evils heavier than any they have yet supported.

In order to sustain a government which boasted of emanating from the national will, it was necessary to erect scaffolds on which were immolated a great number of those who tried to resist the atrocious yoke of usurpation ; all the prisons in the kingdom were filled with victims ; thus punishing, not crime, but loyalty and respect to sworn faith. Innumerable innocent victims were sent to the terrible deserts of Africa, others have ended their existence in horrible jails under the influence of anguish and torments ; and, finally, foreign countries became filled with Portuguese fugitives from their country, constrained to support in distant climes the bitterness of an unmerited exile ! Thus were unchained over the country where I was born all the horrors of which human perversity was capable.

The people, oppressed by the outrages which the governing authorities committed upon them ; the pages of Portuguese history stained by the outrageous satisfactions with which the fanatic government of usurpation has been compelled to expiate some acts of its thoughtless atrocity practised against foreign subjects in defiance of their governments ; diplomatic and commercial relations interrupted with the whole of Europe—in fact, tyranny defiling the throne, misery and oppression choking the noblest sentiments of the nation. This is the painful picture which Portugal has presented during the last four years.

o

My heart, afflicted by the existence of such horrible evils, consoles itself however by recognising the visible protection which God, the dispenser of thrones, grants to the noble and just cause which we defend.

When we contemplate that in spite of the greatest obstacles of all kinds, loyalty was able to preserve in the island of Terceira (the asylum and bulwark of Portuguese liberty, already displayed in other epochs of our own history) the scanty means with which its noble defenders have not only succeeded in bringing once more under the rule of my august daughter the other islands of the Açores, but also in gathering together the forces upon which we now depend, I cannot refrain from recognising the special protection of Divine Providence. Confident of his support, and the actual regency having represented to me in the name of H. M. F. Majesty, by means of a deputation which waited upon the said sovereign and upon me, the lively wishes which the inhabitants of the Açores, and the other faithful subjects of the Queen residing in the above-mentioned island, that I, taking upon myself the part which belongs to me in matters relating to Her Majesty, as chief of the house of Braganza, should employ at such a crisis as this such prompt and efficacious measures as circumstances imperiously demand; actuated finally by the duties which the fundamental laws of Portugal impose upon me, I resolved to abandon that repose which my actual circumstances would lead me to, and leaving on the continent the objects which are most dear to my heart, I came to join the Portuguese, who at the cost of the greatest sacrifices, have borne themselves by their heroic valour against all the efforts of usurpation.

After tendering thanks in all the isles of the Azores to the individuals who composed the regency which in my absence I appointed, for the patriotism with which they discharged their duties in face of so many difficulties, I shall resume, for the reasons already mentioned, the authority reposed in the said regency, and which I propose to retain until the legitimate government of my august daughter be established in Portugal, and the general Cortes of the nation, which I will immediately call together, declare whether it be convenient or not that I continue to exercise the said rights which are mentioned in Article 12 of the constitutional charter, and should this question be resolved in the affirmative, I shall take oath as the said charter enacts, for the exercise of the permanent regency. The time will then arrive when the oppressed Portuguese will see the end of the wrongs which for so long have afflicted them.

Fears should not be entertained for the vexations or revenge of their brothers who will be redeemed at the moment of being embraced ; those who have been so long exiled from their native soil will deplore with them the misfortunes through which they have passed, and promise to bury them in eternal oblivion.

As for the wretches whose culpable consciences fear the ruin of usurpation of which they were the abettors, they may rest assured that if the action of the law is able to punish them with the loss of those political rights which they so shamefully abused to the discredit of their country, none of them shall be deprived either of his life, of his civil rights, or his property, except the rights of the third estate (religious orders), as unfortunately happened to so many honourable men, whose crime was to defend the law of the country.

I shall publish a decree of amnesty, in which shall be laid down the limits of this exemption, and can only here declare that no ordinance whatever shall be enforced touching passed occurrences or opinions ; suitable measures being adopted so that no one may in future be disturbed for said reasons. Upon this basis shall I constantly occupy myself, with the most unswerving diligence for the furtherance of many other measures, not less acceptable to the honour and welfare of the Portuguese nation ; one of the first being the re-establishment of the political and commercial relations which existed between Portugal and the other states ; religiously respecting their rights and scrupulously avoiding all or any compromise in questions of foreign policy, which may disturb in future the allied and neighbouring nations. Portugal will profit by the advantages resulting from internal peace and from the consideration of strangers ; the public credit will become re-established by the acknowledgment of all the debts of the state, whether national or foreign, legally contracted, and on that account means will be found for their payment, which must without doubt influence public prosperity.

To that part of the Portuguese army which, at present deceived, supports usurpation, I tender an assurance of welcome—provided that, renouncing the defence of tyranny, it spontaneously joins the ranks of the liberating army, an army which will lend its strength to the maintenance of the laws and will become the firm support of the constitutional throne, and of the welfare of its fellow citizens.

I also assure those military men belonging to the reserve, and who did not take part in the defence of usurpation, that they shall not be inconvenienced, but will be immediately dispensed from the service, so that they may return to their families and domestic labours, from which they have so long been separated.

Not doubting but that these my frank expressions will penetrate into the hearts of all honorable Portuguese who love their country, and that they will not hesitate to unite themselves to me and to the loyal and brave compatriots who accompany me in the heroic task of the restoration to the constitutional throne of the most faithful queen, my august daughter, I declare that I am not going to carry to Portugal the horrors of civil war, but peace and reconciliation: hoisting over the walls of Lisbon the royal standard of the said sovereign, as the unanimous votes of all the cultured nations demand."

On board the frigate " Rainha de Portugal."

(Signed)　D. PEDRO, DUKE OF BRAGANZA.

12th February, 1832.

On the 7th April, Dom Pedro arrived at Fayal on board the " Superb," the first steamer that had ever ploughed the waters of that harbour, and was received by the inhabitants with every mark of respect, evinced by the most enthusiastic rejoicings; it was here, at a dinner given in his honor on the 10th by the British consul, that a celebrated toast was proposed, resulting in a slight disagreement between Dom Pedro and Admiral Sartorius, which afterwards opened into a wide breach. The gallant officer, in toasting " the ladies," invited the company to drink to " the empire of woman," which Dom Pedro erroneously interpreting as an intended slight to the cause of the queen, never forgave; needless to say, that a more unmerited charge was never brought against a brave and most courteous and loyal gentleman, but nothing could ever induce Dom Pedro to regard the words of the toast in any other light. On the 11th, Dom Pedro left Fayal for St. Michael's, calling at San Jorge and Terceira, where some time was spent in picking up recruits and organising the forces, which now numbered close upon eight thousand men of all arms. Never did the Bay of Ponta Delgada look so busy or to greater advantage than on this occasion, for nearly fifty vessels of various sizes, and altogether of 6,000 tons burden, were anchored in the roads for the purpose of conveying these troops in their descent upon the coast of Portugal.

Drilling was the order of the day, Dom Pedro being, himself, indefatigable in inspecting and parading the troops, in which he seemed to take great delight. He was active, besides, in framing and issuing decrees, amongst the most notable of which may be mentioned the abolition of all conventual and monastic institutions in the Açores. Their property was immediately securalised and incorporated with that of the state. By this decree, which was dated at Ponta Delgada, 17th May, 1832, eleven convents in the islands were suppressed, four only being maintained during the lives of the inmates who elected to remain in them; of the twenty-three monasteries belonging to various orders of friarhood, all but four were suppressed. A Portuguese writer, commenting upon these sweeping measures, worthy of a Pombal or Saldanha, quaintly remarks that the abolition of these institutions was not felt by the community at large to such an extent as might have been supposed, owing to the inmates having for some time past given themselves up more to the pleasures of things secular than was provided for by their statutes.

It is a question how far the sudden abolition of institutions which, although useless and even pernicious in their effects, yet dispensed with generous hand charity in a country where beggars abound, and where no poor relief establishments exist, was a politic step on the part of Dom Pedro.

The monasteries, in particular, when the decree of abolition took effect, poured out their inmates, who were counted by thousands, upon the world at large, penniless and utterly unfitted for work. Many of these men, driven to desperation, embraced with fierce energy the cause of

Miguel—the champion of Catholicism—and were found in the front ranks of his troops, cross in one hand, and sword in the other, urging their men on to death or victory, and, had it not been for this strong element of priestcraft diffused throughout Miguel's army, this hideous fratricidal war would never have lasted the time it did. The fate of the nuns was almost as hard, for the majority of these belonged to the wealthier classes, and on joining the sisterhood, whether voluntarily or not, had enriched its revenues with what would otherwise have been their marriage portions, which were all sequestrated on their eviction—no compensation being allowed them.

The priests everywhere preached the cause of Miguel, and swelled his ranks by threatening the peasantry with the terrors of excommunication on their failing to espouse his cause.

Another decree issued by Dom Pedro at S. Miguel, and which aimed at bettering the condition of the small farmers and tenants, related to the abolition of the " dizimo das miunças," or tithe, consisting of a tenth part of their cattle, asses, horses, poultry, fruits, milk, &c., which, with other burthens, impoverished the people. He also made many beneficial improvements touching the government of morgados, or entailed estates; many of which were on the verge of ruin, owing to the existing law forbidding the power of contracting loans by mortgage on the properties for necessary improvements, the owners being unable out of their revenues to do more than barely live, and pay their relatives the " alimentos," or annuities prescribed by law.

Educational rules were also formulated providing for the better elementary instruction of the labouring classes, and enactments were made limiting to a vast extent the, until now, all powerful influence of the priests. The revenues of the islands and public expenditure were reorganised, and the courts of justice remodelled on a healthier basis.

The astonished Azoreans, incapable of realising or appreciating the ultimate effect of these far-reaching measures, meekly acquiesced in them, and it was only by degrees that they began to comprehend the full force of their meaning, and how much they tended to emancipate them from the clutches of the hungry morgados* and rapacious priests who had, until then, ground them to the very dust.

The attitude which the British Government adopted with regard to this struggle was inconceivably hostile to the liberal cause and the constitution. The Duke of Wellington's unmistakable leaning at that time to absolute rule induced him to openly embrace the cause of Miguel, and pledge his government to a line of policy totally at variance with the principles of liberty which characterise the people of England. This was evidently the result of prejudice, and a mistaken estimate of the characters of the two brothers; and yet he had ample opportunity of gauging the disposition of Miguel.

Mr. Greville, in his Memoirs, relates a conversation he had with the Duke, on the 24th August, 1833 :—

"Talking of Miguel, the Duke related that he was at Strathfieldsaye with Palmella, where, in the library, they were settling the oath that Miguel should take. Miguel would pay no attention, and instead of going into the business and saying what oath he would consent to take" (the question was, whether he should swear fidelity to Pedro or to Maria), "he sat flirting with the Princess Thérèse Esterhazy. The Duke said to Palmella, 'This will never do; he must settle the terms of the oath; and if he is so careless in an affair of such moment, he will never do his duty.' The Duke added that the Government would be very foolish to interfere for Pedro, who was a ruffian, and for the constitution, which was odious."

Admiral Napier, who perhaps did more than any other man to firmly seat Dona Maria on the throne, thus writes

---

* The word "Morgado" was alike applied to the heir of an estate or to the entailed estate itself, the owners of such estates having, by courtsey and distinction, the title prefixed to their surnames.

of Dom Pedro, whose character he had many opportunities of studying. "He had the appearance of a savage-looking man, but that was not his character; on the contrary, he had no cruelty in his disposition. D. Pedro's name will go down to posterity as having freed the land of his birth from despotism, and restored the throne of his daughter, and without having anything personal in view except the desire of gaining glory. He was the most active man I ever saw; rose early, and looked into everything himself. He was a man of courage, but not of dash. He was frank, and I believe sincere, and hated both intriguing and lying."

On the 20th June the fleet set sail from St. Michael, arriving off the Bay of Mindello, ten miles to the north of Oporto, on the 8th July. A few hours sufficed to land every man, and so great was the panic which their unexpected approach created in the ranks of the Miguelites, that Santa Martha, their general, at once evacuated Oporto, and retreated across the Douro with 10,000 men. Thus was the first step taken towards liberating Portugal from that cruel despotism and tyranny which had already plunged a brave and generous people into untold miseries, and was gradually abandoning them to crass superstition and ignorance. To those interested in the ultimate result of this glorious struggle of a few half-disciplined patriots against 80,000 well-armed and drilled troops, and Dom Pedro's untimely end, I would refer them to the pages of Napier, Shaw, and Bollaert. Suffice it here to say that never in the history of nations was a change of government so fraught with momentous and beneficial results to its country as was that of D. Maria II.* to Portugal.

---

* Queen Maria II. died in 1853. As these pages are passing through the press, the announcement is made of the death (on the 15th December, 1885) of the titular King of Portugal, Dom Fernando, Duke of Saxe-Coburg and Gotha, who was married to Queen Maria on the 9th April, 1836. This prince possessed rare artistic taste and knowledge, and did much to foster archæological and kindred pursuits in his adopted country. He was universally respected, and even beloved, by all classes of Portuguese society.

Chapter XII.

> Through the rich greenery below
>   Were sprinkled quiet cots,
> Each fenced by bristling spires of maize.
>   Or yams in marshy plots;
> While mulberry, and quince and fig
>   Besprent the sunnier spots.
>
> > "*Charcoal Burners.*"

The valley of the Furnas being now the objective point, the road is retraced as far as Maia, a small uninteresting village, boasting a tobacco factory; the road gradually ascends, until we reach a level heathery plateau known as the "Achada das Furnas," where cattle are met browsing here and there, on the spare grasses the poor pumiceous soil affords them. For miles around nothing can be seen on this arid waste, but patches of the heath shrub (*Erica azorica*), queiró (*Calluna vulgaris, L.*) and broom (*Sida lanceolata*); every now and then, the rich bloom of bunches of the úva da serra, or wortleberry (*Vaccinium cylindraceum*) relieving the monotony of vegetation. A closer acquaintance with these sub-acid berries, excellent in tarts, will, if in the proper season, be subsequently made in the valley below, where baskets of them are, with wild strawberries, offered for a few coppers by children who have gathered them on these inhospitable hills. The long and eerie ride across this table-land, with nothing but distant hill-tops to break its uniformity, might strike a Ben Jonson "with all the gloom and monotony of Siberian solitude," but the climate it enjoys is certainly the most crisp and exhilarating of any in the island,

and during the hot summer months, those debilitated by prolonged residence on the coast would do well to pay frequent visits to the Achada and regain their vis and energy by breathing its pure and tonic air. The Count da Praia has been recently clearing and levelling extensive tracts of this land, with a view to growing wheat—with what success, it will be curious to see.

Following the capital carriage road which traverses this plateau, we presently reach a part where it abruptly descends, known as the Pedras do Gallego, and here a scene, likely to impress the dullest imagination, breaks upon our delighted view, for suddenly, hundreds of feet below, lies the "Cintra Michaelense," that Azorean "Vale of Tempe," the boast and pride of every islander—the Valley of the Furnas. Nestling amidst green trees and caracoling brooks,

> ———in which the willows dip
> Their pendent boughs, stooping as if to drink—

stand the white pigmy-looking village habitations of this cherished Baiæ. Right across, on the opposite broken edge of the crater—for this beautiful valley, like Rome, lies in the very bosom of a once fierce volcano—can be discerned the rising smoke of the ever-boiling geysers, their sulphurous and noxious fumes causing all vegetation in their vicinity to perish.

A broken but picturesque and cultivated country extends for some two miles W.S.W. to E.N.E., until it is lost, on the right, in another great depression now occupied by the lovely lake of the Furnas ; and along the side on which we stand is seen what remains of the north-east portion of the trunk of the once vast crater, forming, in places, a vertical and over-hanging semi-circle several hundred feet high. On our left winds the splendidly engineered road leading down into the valley, which—still lingering on this " vision of Paradise "—we leisurely descend.

However sultry and oppressive it may be in other parts of the island, here a sempiternal spring would seem to reign, and when, in the height of summer, vegetation in less favoured spots is dried and parched, with scarce a breath of air to bring relief, in this vernal vale, the gentle murmur and whispering of the tall poplar trees *(Populus nigra* and *angulata)*, like countless Æolian harps, and the welcome gurgle and ripple of rapid brooks, distilled on the surrounding wooded heights, may ever be heard.

> Forever sunny, forever blooming,
> Nor cloud nor frost can touch that spot,
> Where the happy people are ever roaming,
> The bitter pangs of the past forgot.

No wonder then, that during the hot summer months a great influx of visitors takes place, not only for the gain of several degrees in temperature, but for the sake of the celebrated baths which have made this valley so justly famous. For their accommodation, a very fair hotel has been constructed, and is kept by one Jeronimo, where visitors for a moderate charge are tolerably entertained, although Boniface, otherwise good natured and obliging enough, fails to sufficiently look after the cleanliness of his establishment. No Lucullus-like feasts of flamingoes' tongues and peacocks' brains await the Sybarite, but the limpit, conger-eel, and octopus enter largely into the domestic economy of mine host. Still the dishes are numerous, and there is always something eatable on the table; considering the small charge made, from 3s. 6d. to 4s. a-day, and the distance. many of the provisions have to come, it is astonishing how well Snr. Jeronimo caters. The Portuguese generally eschew the heavy nitrogenous food, which our dietetic mismanagement, and perhaps the climate of England, habituates us to—a diet so fatal to the consumptive, increasing, as it is said to do, the deposit of the tubercle; but, here, more regard is paid to the stew-pot, the " gizados " turned out by the native chef being delicious, light and inexpensive gastronomic productions. Unfortunately, the lazy, relaxing climate, though it makes existence to some a positive pleasure, kills all energy, and the native well-to-do,

foregoing all exercise, suffers horribly at middle-age from liver and indigestion; his "estomago," as he will pathetically tell you, being his greatest bane and enemy.

A dash of garlic—not altogether unpalatable to those who give it a fair trial—characterises Portuguese cookery; and the use of the dried carollas of the safflower (*Carthamus tinctorius*), for flavouring and colouring food, will recall to Anglo-Indians a culinary practice so much in vogue in the East. The delicious perfume arising from a patch of safflower in the flush of bloom is a thing to be remembered.

The hotel is situated in the very centre of the valley, and in all directions are charming lanes and narrow pathways, draped with greenest leaf.

The bird's-eye view of the lake having excited our curiosity, we cannot rest until we have explored its shores, and as the distance is about a mile and a half, and we shall have plenty of walking, the best way is to order donkeys to carry us there. Approached on this side, the most conspicuous object is a large white house on the opposite bank, on an estate known as Grená,* formerly the property of the late Mr. James Hinton, the celebrated London aurist, but now belonging to Mrs. Hayes, of Ponta Delgada. It is beautifully situated on a slight eminence overlooking the lake, every window in which presents charming views of the glinting waters and wooded hills around. Here, besides the cheery welcome of the kind hostess, if at home, visitors will find much to interest them, and I can conceive no fitter place than this for the temporary residence of those in quest of health, or anxious to escape for a time from the carking cares of life; the soft balsamic air, and dewy freshness, which always reigns here, contributing to make life without

---

* Fifty years ago, this estate was purchased by Mr. Harvey, a member of the Yacht Squadron, with the intention of erecting a mansion upon it, but circumstances preventing the carrying out of this idea, the property, in 1858, passed into the hands of Mr. Consul Vines, who built the present house. Mrs. Vines, a niece of Daniel O'Connell, named it Grená, from the family seat near Killarney.

its exciting amusements an absolute enjoyment. The estate, planted chiefly with pine and other timber trees, possesses also a considerable orange garden, and extensive pasture lands on the Achada above it, the whole comprising some four hundred English acres in extent. Here no horrid notices of "Trespassers will be prosecuted" offend the eye, but you may roam about as you list, through umbrageous paths or up the steep face of the hill behind, meeting at every step some fresh and pleasant point of interest.

In the grounds, and only a few minutes' walk from the house, an extremely pretty and lofty waterfall tumbles over the beetling cliff, with a single leap of one hundred feet, attaining in rainy seasons a considerable volume, draining as it does the extensive table-land above, and forming a bellowing and brawling stream, rushing to empty itself into the lake below, over masses of huge boulders and rocks, which make one wonder how they ever came there, forming pools of clear and icy-cold water very tempting to the bather.

Not far from this cascade, and at its foot, is a small deposit of lignite, which will be interesting to the geologist. It is about $3\frac{1}{2}$ inches thick, underlying a series of lava beds, the result of successive volcanic eruptions, extending over æons of time. The lake, some 865 feet above sea level, and covering an area of about three square miles, owes its origin, like all the others in the island, to igneous action, but differs from them in the softened beauty of its character. Perfect stillness reigns throughout this delightful region, the only sign of life consisting in the slow passage of some solitary gull, or the circling flight of a couple of buzzards; but at night this state of things alters, for there are thousands of frogs (*Rana esculenta*) in this lake. Until introduced in 1820, by the late Viscount da Praya, who brought some from Lisbon, frogs were quite unknown in the island; now, however, they swarm wherever there is water, and evening is rendered hideous by their unmelodious croaking, rivalled only by the unceasing barking of the numerous village curs, which, remarkable for nothing else, really seem to be the direct descendants of the three, or, according to some mythologists, fifty-throated dog of Erebus. The number of frogs in the lake must be prodigious, for it is said that, as in the case of the common cricket and other cicadæ, only the males utter these discordant love-calls, to charm and attract the opposite sex—a circumstance which made Xenarchus, the observant Greek poet, enviously exclaim,

Happy the cicadas live, since they all have voiceless wives!

The male mosquito is perfectly innocuous, the female only stinging and producing the maddening buzz.

As regards the frog, however, the thanks of humanity are due to this slimy inhabitant of the waters, if it be really a fact that the first dawn of the science of electricity arose from observations made on the muscular twitching of his little body.

There are none of those pretty lizards in S. Miguel, which lend such a charm to country life in Portugal and Madeira, but in the island of Graciosa I caught and preserved specimens of two distinct species, one being evidently *Lacerta viridis*, the commonest of the *lacertidæ*, the other, *L. dugesi*, peculiar to Madeira and Teneriffe. Graciosa is the only island in the archipelago where they are at present to be found. They were probably carried there accidentally from Madeira. Considering the ease with which the eggs of lizards can be transported amongst vegetables and plants to great distances, it really appears strange that they have not, long ere this, made their way to all the islands, for Ovington found them in large numbers in Madeira, as far back as 1689, when they were already very destructive to the grape and other fruit crops.

Before every height surrounding this lake became crested with the pine tree, evaporation went on at a great rate, sufficient in thirsty seasons to considerably narrow the limits of its waters ; now, however, when such an immense acreage absorbs and permanently retains 50 per cent. of whatever moisture the trees attract, this evaporation is being constantly returned and compensated, until fears are entertained about the low lying lands around.

For giving freshness and humidity to dry climates there is nothing like the pine tree, its alembic or distilling properties being enormous, but here, where the friendly Gulf Stream supplies this requisite, it is perhaps found to be " de trop."

The depth of the lake in its greatest depression is 50 feet; but of late years, as we have seen, its waters have sensibly risen. Like most of the others in the island, it abounds with gold and silver fish.

The Portuguese are said to have been the first to bring the gold fish from China to the Cape, and thence to Lisbon and the islands. M. Drouet asks how this fish, probably introduced into private tanks and ponds, is now found distributed over the islands, every lake or tarn, however remote, teeming with them; and he sees in this a natural propagation without the aid of man, attributing their spread to the agency of aquatic birds.

Several sailing boats are generally sent here from town in the summer, enabling its beauties to be fully explored and enjoyed, but like all deeply embosomed waters, with breaks and chines in their high banks, it is subject to sudden squalls of quite sufficient severity to make " turn turtle " a not infrequent occurrence to those unacquainted with its navigation.

On its north-east margin, and within a few hundred yards of Grená, is to be seen a dense column of smoke canopying a group of most interesting thermal springs; they occupy an area of about an acre and a quarter in extent, situated at the foot of the precipitous Pico do Ferro, the centre of the space being filled by a considerable natural basin containing a large volume of seething and boiling acidulated water, forming the largest and deepest geyser in the island. The mass of water, however, is adventitious, and was either left by the receding lake (which in very rainy seasons occasionally covers these springs) or has been fed by percolation from the brook close by. From this, it will be seen that both the temperature and mineral constituents of this source vary considerably. At the time of M. Fouqué's visit, the quantity of water appears to have been small, and the conditions favorable for analysis, which gave the following results :—

Sulphate of soda	.085
Sulphate of potash	.006
Chloride of sodium	.079
Sulphate of lime	.009
Oxide of iron	.004
Chlorohydric acid	.010
Silica	.095
	.288

A litre of this water on evaporation left a residue weighing 0.278 gramme. Surrounding this terrible-looking geyser are innumerable fumeroles evolving hot gases, which render the ground treacherously soft and spongy, and woe betide the unwary wight who neglects to carefully pick his way along this heated quagmire.

The natives tell us, with apparent glee, how that two "Inglezes," some time since, outstripping their donkeys and guides, and arriving for the first time at the spot, after darkness had set in, found themselves, much to their consternation, hopelessly bogged in the hot morass, from which they were only extricated some time later, with scalded calves and in gruesome plight.

Into many of these vapour-holes the water from the brook has filtered, forming pools of differing temperatures, some at boiling heat, others perfectly cold, others again furiously thirsty, emitting not a drop of water, but volumes of acid and scorching steam, which impart to most of these waters their acidulated characteristics ; one especially,

P

possessing in a high degree the same properties, though less intensified, as the famous " agua azeda " down in the valley.

A single glance around suffices to show that many pits and fissures, now cold and dry, were once the escape-holes of similar hot vapours, and the change they now present is very remarkable.

Mineral waters are generally divided into three classes—sulphureous, chalybeate or ferruginous and saline, acidulous or carbonated waters. These may again be subdivided into warm, thermal, and cold. Sir Charles Lyell, referring to the disturbance which sometimes takes place in their direction and temperature, says : " Notwithstanding the general persistency in character of mineral waters and hot springs ever since they were first known to us, we find on enquiry that some few of them, even in historical times, have been subject to great changes. These have happened during earthquakes which have been violent enough to disturb the subterranean drainage, and alter the shape of the fissures up which the waters ascend. Thus, during the great earthquake at Lisbon, in 1755, the temperature of the spring called La Source de la Reine, at Bagnères-de-Suchon, in the Pyrenees, was suddenly raised as much as 75° Fah., or changed from a cold spring to one of 122° Fah., a heat which it has since retained. It is also recorded that the hot springs at Bagnères-de-Bigorre, in the same mountain chain, became suddenly cold during a great earthquake, which in 1660 threw down several houses in that town." The numerous sulphur springs in the neighbourhood of Granada all ceased to flow on Christmas Day, 1884, at the time the first earthquake shocks took place, but upon the following day they burst out again with loud subterranean explosions, and discharges of hot vapour, and have since run as before. Here in the Azores several instances are mentioned, besides those noted above, of the sources of thermal springs drying up after a severe shock of earthquake, and of others coming into existence from the same cause, but these variations have generally occurred in remote times, no recent changes of the kind having been noticed.

The ride or walk along the eastern margin of the lake will not fail to reveal, in places, jets of gases escaping from holes in the lower banks, and innumerable bubbles are perpetually formed in the waters by large volumes of rising gases.

On the western shore, is a very pretty stone-built chapel in the Gothic style, erected by Snr. José do Canto and his wife, in fulfilment it is said, of a vow made by the latter. The design was obtained from M. Berton, the well-known architect, of Paris, and it is dedicated to " Our Lady of Victories." There is some very good oak carving on the altar and pulpit, the wood work, stained glass, candelabra, and other materials, having been imported from France. The windows, which are very handsome, represent the chief events in the life of Mary and Joseph, and were put up by a French workman, who came here for the purpose. They flood the edifice with a soft, delicious light. On the bell is the following inscription :—" Salve, Rainha ! mãe de miserecordia, vida, doçura, esperança nossa !" The edifice is highly creditable to those engaged in its construction, and is unique in its departure from the orthodox and hideous Jesuit style.

The above-named gentleman is the largest landed proprietor in the neighbourhood, and it is here, on the western and southern banks of the lake, that he has collected and acclimatised, at great expense, the surprising arboretum already mentioned, consisting of foreign and trans-oceanic forest trees. The grounds at the back of his very pretty châlet are exceedingly beautiful, the Valle dos Fétos especially presenting some magnificent growths of rare tree ferns and cryptomerias of giant proportions.

At another spot within these lovely woods are to be seen certain chinks or fissures in the earth like the " moffettas " of Switzerland, from whence issue vapours of strong sulphuretted hydrogen, acting as a perfect holocaust to the lower orders of animal creation, if one may judge by the numerous skeletons of small birds and insects which strew the site. As these emanations were very destructive to vegetable life as well, Sñr. José do Canto, some time since, tried the experiment of opening up the surface of the ground into deep furrows and ruts, and has since found that vegetation is no longer affected by the gases. It is here, in these charming glades and little frequented avenues, that the woodcock may still be seen, but he is sadly persecuted by the cruel sportsman.

A delightful walk or ride across this extensive property, through long aisles of sombre green, leads to a deep chasm, known as the " Gruta Cagarra," or " do Echo," where a fine echo can be heard. The depth must be considerable, for our guide, Antonio Rebicca, threw a stone weighing some 30lbs. over the brink, and it took 18 seconds to reach the bottom, making the welkin ring again. In the valley below, a dim streak marks the course of a running brook.

The views in this neighbourhood are of unsurpassed beauty, and the number of rides and drives endless. Excursions may also be made to the summit of the Pico do Ferro, Pico dos Cedros, Pico do Gafanhoto, and others, dominating the valley and the country beyond.

On the return ride from the Gruta Cagarra, a broad and now dried-up lacustrine bed, half-a-mile in diameter, is crossed, covered here and there with patches of wood and copse; but the soil is too much mixed with pumice and of too barren a nature to admit of cultivation.

It is said that the waters of this lake were lapped up by the fiery eruption of the 2nd September, 1630. Ashes and lapilli from this outbreak fell in the island of Terceira, and were thrown out in such quantities that 191 persons, who had taken refuge in the neighbouring hills around the Furnas, were suffocated by the fall.

A narrow ridge of loose volcanic débris, divides this

GRUTA DO ECHO, FURNAS.

desiccated bed from the Lake of Furnas, and the site is interesting as indicating where the third eruption of importance took place in this eminently volcanic region— subsequent to its first discovery by the Portuguese.

Fructuoso gives the following account of this great eruption :—On the 2nd September, 1630, between nine and ten at night, in calm weather and a clear sky, the earth commenced suddenly to tremble, and with such continuous and violent movement that the people fled terrified from their dwellings.

The shocks caused the clock at Ponta Delgada, in the tower in the Praça do Municipio, to strike so rapidly as to closely resemble the alarm bell, everyone fearing the tower would fall.

The shocks continued thus until two o'clock in the morning, when a furious eruption took place at the site of the now dried-up lake, destroying nearly the whole of the extensive woods around, as well as much cattle; many people, too, were killed, the number being estimated at 191; these were mostly on the hills tending their flocks and herds, or collecting the berries of the wild laurel, from which they extracted the oil for burning in their rude lamps, and which some of the poorer classes still use.

The shock of earthquake was so severe that it destroyed the churches and the greater number of the houses of Ponta da Garça, distant nearly a league, and Póvoação, some two leagues away, eighty persons perishing beneath the ruins of the first-named place. Villa Franca also suffered greatly. What terrified the inhabitants, however, more than anything else, were the vast quantity of ashes which fell all over the island during three days and nights, in some parts covering the ground to the extent of from 80 to 96 inches, and in others from 160 to 240 inches, many small houses being covered to the roofs. The ashes fell, not only in St. Mary's, 44 miles distant, but in Terceira, 24 leagues off, some people even affirming that they fell in the distant islands of Corvo and Flores, 240 miles to the westward.* The flames which arose from this eruption were so distinctly seen from Terceira that they sent boats to St. Michael's, fearing that some volcano might have destroyed the island.

The funnel of this crater was in the centre of the lake bed, where it formed a small peak, conical in form, and consisting entirely of ashes and pumice, the action of rain and the repeated attempts made to utilise the soil for agricultural purposes, have considerably truncated this baby crater.

Between this Lagôa Secca and the sea on the south rises the Pico da Vigia, at the foot of which is an immense crater, covered on its inner sides with unusually large blocks of pumice stone, which, with a comparatively small proportion of scoriæ, form the component parts of the whole mountain; its flanks are consequently gashed into deep ravines through the action of rains.

The surface of the crater, which is called "a Cova da Burra," or the asses' grave, is covered with scrub and underwood. Its formation was anterior to the discovery of the island, and its great size, and the vast quantities of expleted matter around, probably mark the site of one of the earliest and most extensive eruptions that ever took place in the island.

About half-a-mile along the road leading from the lake towards the valley is another well of mineral water, known as the "Sanguinhal Source," where, some forty years ago existed a small bathing establishment, known as "os banhos de Sant' Anna," but of which subsequent earthquakes have not left a single vestige. The chief of these springs, once protected by a mural enclosure, has now from neglect broken through its slender bounds and overflowed the site. Its waters, which are warm and not ungrateful to the palate, flow in considerable volume, and are lost in a shallow

---

* Ashes from the burning city of Chicago are said to have fallen on some of the Azore islands, and especially Fayal, on the fourth day of the conflagration.

stream hard by. Three temperature tests were taken by M. Fouqué of the springs nearest the roadway, which ranged 30 to 32 degrees C. (86 to 89.60 Fah.); a fourth, at a distance only of a few metres, showing 38 degrees C. (100.40 Fah.). The professor paid special attention to the principal source of these wells, situated at the end of the neighbouring ravine, the acidulated waters of which leave a distinct ferruginous deposit in their course, and are highly charged with carbonic-acid gas. They present a temperature of 36 degrees C. (96.80 Fah.), and show the following analytical results :—

Bicarbonate of soda	.412
Bicarbonate of lime	.041
Bicarbonate of iron	.044
Chloride of sodium	.060
Silica	.140
Sulphates	traces
	0.697

A litre of this water submitted to evaporation gave a residue weighing 0.543 gramme.

The expenditure of a small sum of money would supply these springs with a stone basin, and utilise them for drinking purposes. They sensibly raise the temperature of the brook already referred to, which seems to flow over several other smaller sources having their rise in its very bed. A pleasant and startling feature along its course are the masses and fields of inhame, the yam, the Indian kale, or tanga, of South Carolina, and taro plant of Australasia (*Caladium esculentum*), which these waters irrigate, the broad umbrageous leaves of rich green lending a semi-tropical aspect to the country. It is difficult to account for the name " inhame," by which this tuber, the kalo, or taro, of the Sandwich Islands and New Zealand, is everywhere known in the Azores.

Ivens and Capello mention a cultivated plant in Central and West Africa which the natives called inhame, it was not, however, the caladium, but a species of potato, which they took to be the *Discorea alata.*

As we know there were many Africans in these islands during their early days of colonization, the plant probably received the name " inhame " from the negroes, who likened it to the vegetable with which they were familiar in their native country.

Whether the influence of iron and other mineral properties of the waters in which they grow imparts a special flavour to these tubers, I cannot say, but certain it is that the Furnas yams are superior to any others grown in the island, and are in high esteem.

The leaves, when mature, attain a height of 4 or 5 feet, and grow with beautiful symmetry and luxuriance. At this stage they are cut down and given as food to pigs, and it is curious to see the village girls up to their knees in the soft, yellow marsh, looking like very Naiads, peeping out here and there from under the leaves, and laughingly piling up huge bundles of surprising weight, which they will afterwards carry long distances home. It is common to meet women and young girls—oftentimes mere children—not only working in the fields, but staggering under loads of firewood, which they have collected on the distant hills—labour which, continued from early years, is the cause of much infertility among them, and renders them prematurely old and wan. Nevertheless, these Furnas girls, during the short period of their girlhood, are justly reputed the handsomest in the island ; and certainly some of them have perfect Hellenic forms, and move about as if conscious of the poetry of motion. Of an evening they may be seen—a pretty but painful sight— wending their way to the fountains, to fill their pitchers of old Roman and other classic shapes, which they carry erect on their heads, without any support whatever. I well remember when it used to be a favourite pastime with the *aurati juvenes* of Ponta Delgada, staying here for the bathing season, to waylay these girls on their return from the fountains, and suddenly smashing the earthen vessel with a well-directed blow from the alpenstock, which everyone here carries, to drench the unfortunate creatures to the skin. The voluntary, and, to these poor girls, rich compensation of a dollar for each broken pitcher and ducking, soon brought them out in troops to undergo the ordeal, until the novelty of such tame sport wore off.

The earthenware vessels referred to above are all of island make, and of coarse manufacture, fictile art in the Azores having made little advance since the days of the Romans.* One of the most characteristic shapes is a jar with a tubular spout at the side, a relic of the tetinæ, or feeding bottles of the Romans, of which examples have been found at Wilderspool, in England. Throughout the Peninsula these singular-looking water coolers are much in vogue, and the natives, by dint of constant practice, hold them at arm's length, and pour a refreshing draught into their mouths without spilling a single drop on their persons.

Quite a feature in Furnas are the flocks of a very handsome species of goat (*Capra ægagrus*, Pall.), with immense antelope horns, gracefully curved, which, in early morning, are driven down from the mountains and go from house to house to supply visitors with delicious milk. Many of these have curiously-sounding bells fastened round their necks, which serve to warn the slumberer that it is time to rise.

The little church in the valley, dedicated to Sant' Anna, was built in 1792. The altar-piece, poor as it is, was the gift of Queen Maria I. The church occupies the site where the hermits founded their convent, which the eruption of 1630 completely destroyed. Vestiges of the hermitage are

* Exception to this must be made in favour of the numerous fancy and extremely pretty articles, in imitation of terra-cotta, made from imported clay, at the recently established pottery works of Snr. Manoel Leite Pereira, at Ponta Delgada, who deserves great credit for his efforts at improvement in this direction.

still to be traced, and even the grottoes, or cells, in which the hermits lived, are pointed out at the back of the church, and to the west of it. In 1843, whilst some excavations were being made on the north and west side, some rude kitchen utensils belonging to the convent were found, and no doubt many more exist in the same locality, the building and all it contained having been suddenly abandoned.

These hermits, three in number, had been chaplains at the hospital of S. José, in Lisbon. On arriving at Furnas they were met by an anchorite, who had been here some time, and where he, like

—————— Honorius, long did dwell,
And hoped to merit Heaven by making earth a hell.

At first their sufferings were very great, from the difficulty of obtaining food, and they had barely completed the erection of their chapel, when it was entirely destroyed by the eruption of the 3rd September, 1630, which covered the valley and surrounding hills with from 10 to 12 feet of ashes. Deserting the desolate spot, these hermits established themselves in the valley of Cabaços, near Agua do Pão, where they passed the remainder of their ascetic but useless lives.

In various parts of the valley of the Furnas, and at considerable depths, magnificent trunks of cedar trees are occasionally found, buried by the eruption and earthquakes of a quarter of a century ago, the timber being in perfect preservation, but the villagers make short work of such *trouvaille* for firewood, and it is difficult, if not impossible, to obtain an entire specimen.

So great was the abundance of large timber trees on the neighbouring heights in former times, that, even in Fructuoso's day, the descents into the valley on the eastern and northern sides, were made through dense and lofty woods of cedar, faya, laurels and other forest trees.

Besides these trunks of cedar, specimens of the more ancient flora of the island are occasionally found in the deeper ravines, consisting chiefly of the myrica, myrtle, and *Erica arborea*, of giant proportions, in a state of lignite, but still preserving their different characteristics.

Scattered about the village are a good many plain-looking and roughly built, and more roughly furnished cottages, let out to visitors for the month or six weeks' "villeggiatura," at rentals ranging from £3 to £5 per mensem, but as they are destitute of all requisites excepting beds, and the rudest of deal tables and chairs, all additional comforts, &c., must be brought from town. Perhaps the temporary privation of luxuries and the Arcadian simplicity of life, adds not a little to the enjoyment of a month's stay in this beautiful valley.

Several native gentlemen, much to their credit, subscribed together the necessary funds for enclosing and laying out a large and central piece of land as a public ornamental garden, and the "Park" now ranks amongst the attractions of the place. In various parts of its miniature lake may be observed the constant escape of gases and the discoloration of the water by some iron spring beneath.

Other Portuguese gentlemen, and foremost amongst them the Count da Praia e Monforte, Dr. Caetano d'Andrade, the Baron da Fonte Bella Jacintho, Viscount das Laranjeiras, Señhor Francisco Machado de Faria e Maia, &c., have done much to beautify the otherwise waste land they owned here; and those fond of quiet may now enjoy many a verdurous and delicious retreat in any of these gardens. On the hill sides around may generally be observed the curling smoke of numerous charcoal fires, lending life and picturesqueness to the scene, and everywhere is to be heard the murmur and ripple of silvery runlets, along which huge zangos or dragon-flies love to course. In their waters grow luxuriant beds of the native agriaõ, or watercress, much used here in soups. There are other streams richly impregnated with iron, which is precipitated and thickly incrusts their beds, transforming every stone into veritable iron pyrites; these streams all aggregating, form the Ribeira Quente or hot river, the largest in the island. It is a curious fact that, notwithstanding its high temperature and mineral constituents, during the spawning season, tainhas, a species of grey mullet and other fish, ascend the Ribeira Quente as far as a point called "Lombo Frio," although a cascade occurs midway, which they successfully pass. The best flavoured and largest eels (*Anguilla canariensis*) in the island, are also caught in this river, as high up as Furnas.

In the depths of the neighbouring plains are to be found some immense rounded blocks of erupted granite, like lesser Tarpeian rocks, which were apparently rolled into their present position by one of those tremendous volcanic eruptions this region has been subjected to.

> And dost thou still, thou mass of breathing stone,
> Thy giant limbs to night and chaos hurled,
> Still sit as on a fragment of a world,
> Surviving all?

These "daughters of Time" generally stand isolated and alone, otherwise they might be taken for roches perché of the Glacial period; the absence, however, of striæ, on their surface, or appearance of moraines in their vicinity, would seem to assign to them a Plutonic origin, although it is quite possible that, in a circumscribed area like this, the frequent and violent changes its surface has from time to time been subjected to, may have entirely effaced and destroyed these physical characteristics. In Terceira, where the surface of the country has undergone less mutability, and notably in the parishes of Doze Ribeiras and Serreta, there are distinct evidences, both in the valleys and higher plateaux, of deep striated furrows and grooves, caused by the moving glaciers.

On the left of the road leading to the caldeiras, or geysers, is the small Convalescent Hospital, built by means of funds supplied by the Miserecordia establishment in town, and capable of accommodating, in its couple of infirmaries, from thirty to forty in-door patients, who are sent here for the baths during the months from June to September.

In 1870, the Camara of Ponta Delgada voted a sufficiently liberal amount for the purpose of maintaining a resident physician here during the six summer months, on whom the duty was imposed of drawing up a report of the effect of the waters upon each of the various cases brought here for treatment, and of otherwise studying the hitherto much neglected science of balneology. These reports, based upon actual results, and prepared, as many of them are, by careful and intelligent medical men, are a useful addition to our knowledge of these undoubtedly valuable springs, and their infinite application. A study of these reports would well repay the trouble, and the Camara of Ponta Delgada would do much towards diffusing in Europe and America knowledge of these waters by periodically publishing them in French and English, as a guide to their use by invalid visitors.

It would seem that most of the patients frequenting the hospital suffer from the various forms of rheumatism so prevalent in this moist climate, and that the warm alkaline waters, in most cases, prove a perfect panacea in these particular ailments, which generally begin to yield after the first half-dozen baths. At this stage, when a radical cure commences to set in, the patient feels an intense aggravation of his sufferings, thinks himself *in extremis*, and can with difficulty be prevailed upon to continue their use to the end. If, however, persevered in, relief soon comes, and after the thirtieth bath, the quondam cripple, in the most acute of cases, regains his activity, and leaves his aches and crutches behind.

It is a singular sight to meet these nondescript peripatetics, wending their way from the baths completely enveloped from head to foot in blankets and wraps, as preventatives against chills, calling to mind the par-boiled patients who are met with at Monte Catini, issuing from the "inferno" of the grotto of Mosumanno.

The sight at the baths is not less remarkable. There the

patients may be seen in groups round the entrance to the bath-houses specially set apart for their use, some on crutches, others too feeble to stand, and lying on mats patiently awaiting their turns, making up a picture vividly suggestive of the " pool, where lay a great multitude of impotent folk, of blind, halt, withered, waiting for the moving of the water," and eloquent of the health-giving properties of these springs.

Owing to the poverty and irregular diet of the poorer villagers, scurfy diseases of the skin are rather prevalent; but these soon yield to a short course of the sulphur waters, which are powerfully efficacious in itch, and even more troublesome cutaneous disorders.

Shortly after passing the hospital, the ground becomes more and more uneven and tussocky, until a sudden bend in the road reveals a gradual depression, broken and contorted beyond all description. It is here, on the crest, sides and concavities of a contracted slope, the soil of which is whitened with efflorescences of sulphur and alum, relieved by brilliant coruscations, here and there, of orange and red, that exist in the celebrated Caldeiras das Furnas, the marvellous polypharmacy of nature. On all sides, as we approach, come the muffled rumble sounds of the angry agency below— a scene which Carlyle might well have had in his mind's eye, when he wrote, " Oh, under that hideous coverlet of vapours and putrefactions, and unimaginable gases, what a fermenting-vat lies simmering and hid!" Right in front of us, enveloped in rapidly-emitted vapour, is the "Caldeira Grande," a boiling well, seething furiously in a bed of loose stones of about 8 or 10 feet in diameter, and protected by a circular wall some 6 feet high. The degree of heat, even at some distance from it, is considerable, M. Fouqué having registered 98.5°C. (208.40 Fah.) in the narrow trough along which the water runs ; but he estimates the temperature at the actual spot where it wells up at the rate of 19 gallons per minute, at much higher, probably above 100° C. (212° Fah.)

—which, however, by the time it reaches the baths, is lessened to 53° C. (127.40 Fah.) The rush of gases is considerable, and they probably increase the violence of its agitation, which makes it impossible to take the temperature at the source.

M. Fouqué's tests for the character of these gases gave the following results:—

Carbonic acid	988.90
Sulphydric acid	9.50
Azote	1.46
Oxygen	0.14
	1,000.00

An evaporated litre of this water left a dry residue weighing 1.818 grammes. After the super-oxidation of the sulphate of soda, the weight of the dry residue was equal to 1.767 grammes, which, when dissolved, gave:—

Carbonate of soda	0.707
Sulphate of soda	0.025
Sulphate of potash	0.016
Chloride of sodium	0.646
Sulphuret of sodium	0.064
Silica	0.285
Silicate of soda	0.024
	1.767

The same objectionable system, elsewhere noted, of the channels, or ducts, of these waters to the baths, and their respective reservoirs, being all exposed to the air, obtains here; and unless the waters be quickly used, decomposition rapidly takes place, and their properties are rendered nugatory, or greatly lessened. In the case of the Caldeira Grande, one of the ducts traverses the tunnel leading to the new bathing establishment, and is covered along this distance, only that portion of the water not required for immediate use is collected in a large open tank, where it is allowed to cool, and is drawn off to the baths as wanted, at a temperature of 28° C. (82.40° Fah.)

Floating on the surface of many of these cooling tanks, where the water has not been drawn off for some time, may be seen the thick, glairy film which all still thermal waters seem to generate.

The next geyser to arrest attention is that known as d'Asmodée, the latest born of these caldeiras. Its bed is in the bottom of a circular pit, some 12 feet deep, whence the water is shot up at rapid and regular intervals, to a height of 3 feet, falling back again into its basin. A conduit carries it to the baths of Snr. José Maria Rapozo d'Amaral, a reservoir above allowing a portion of it to gradually cool.

The violence of the agitation at the mouth of this source, probably also increased by the large quantities of escaping gases, made it impossible to test the temperature, but M. Fouqué estimates it at probably 100° C. (212° Fah.)

Like the water of the Caldeira Grande, it rapidly loses the sulphuretted hydrogen it contains, on exposure to the air, but differs from the former in possessing a much larger proportion of sulphates, and in its extreme alkaline character.

A litre of this water, when evaporated, left a dry residue weighing 1.669 grammes. After the super-oxidation of the sulphate of soda, the weight of the dry residue was equal to 1.636 grammes, from which the following results were obtained :—

Carbonate of soda	..	..	..	.719
Sulphate of soda	..	..	..	.190
Sulphate of potash	..	..	..	.022
Chloride of sodium	..	..	..	.420
Sulphuret of sodium	..	.	..	.060
Silica	..	..	..	.220
Silicate of soda ..	..	..	..	.005
				1.636

Resuming our steps cautiously over the heated and

sibilating ground, pocked all over with fumeroles, which fill
the air with mephitic vapours, we next come to a deep and
yawning pit, known as the Caldeira de Pedro Botelho, or as
the natives prefer to call it, Boca do Inferno, as it is what
they picture the entrance to the pit Tophet to be, and its
appearance is certainly repelling in the extreme. Very little

BOCA DO INFERNO, OR, CALDEIRA DE PEDRO BOTELHO.

water exists in the Caldeira, but what there is, is shot
upward two or three feet with even, recurrent spurts, and as
in the case of the Caldeira d'Asmodée, falls back again into
its awful abyss. It emits large quantities of gases at each
pulsation, accompanied, too, by loud and measured sounds, as
of blows from a heavy sledge hammer. The water is
intensely acid, and remarkable for the predominance of
sulphates, and for the presence of alum and sulphate of
lime, which M. Fouqué thinks are derived from the action

of the free sulphuric acid on the rocks enclosing the geyser, which they decompose; the sides of the pit being covered by a fine grey silicious mud, and, as there is a wide belief amongst the peasantry as to its efficacy for topical use in cases of stiffened joints and skin diseases, the cuticle impressions of collectors from distant parts of the island may be seen upon the soft plastic clay in places it would appear impossible and most dangerous to reach—so eagerly is it sought for.

A sample of this mud from which all traces of sulphate of lime had been eliminated, presented these results on analysis:—

Silica	61.23
Alumina..	25.41
Peroxide of iron	0.92
Lime	0.51
Manganese	8.47
Potash	1.33
Soda	0.41
	98.28

The thermometer, quickly plunged into a bucket of this muddy water taken from the mouth of the Caldeira, indicated 98·5° C. (208.40° Fah.), but the temperature is probably higher.

A litre of evaporated water gave a dry residue weighing 1.003 grammes, which on analysis showed—

Sulphate of soda	.651
Sodic alum (supposed anhydrous) ..	.087
Sulphate of lime	.034
Sulphate of iron	traces
Silica	.300
Chlorohydric acid	.012
Sulphuric acid	.003
	1.087

The belief in the curative properties of muddy deposits of mineral waters is widely shared in by people on the Continent, and doubtless gave rise to the famous mud and peat baths of Abano, St. Amand and many of the German spas. It was no uncommon practice with the better class in this island, some forty or fifty years ago, to treat certain pulmonary diseases by burying the patient in fresh earth up to the chin, for several hours every day. Unfortunately we have no record of the results of so violent a remedy. I believe that sand baths are still a feature in some parts of the Continent. As may be supposed with this superstitious peasantry—very Ossians in their powers of invention—such localities as these are the "haunts of light-headed fable," or happy hunting grounds of elves and gnomes, and many are the dire accounts told of mysterious disappearances and occurrences attributed to the agency of the Evil One and his minions inhabiting the Boca do Inferno. One of their pretty legends is, that this caldeira had been purposely placed across the path of travellers by the Author of all Evil, as a trap to destroy them; that once upon a time a holy hermit named Pedro Botelho, overtaken at night by a storm of wind and rain, which obscured his way, tumbled headlong into its fiery gulph, but that the raging waters, recoiling at touch of so saintly a man, gathered force for one great effort, and hurled him back again, safe and sound !

Bryson tells us that turf, when brought into contact with the gases of geysers, causes violent disturbance, owing to the irritant organic elements it contains, and the natives here have certainly discovered this law, for to summon the fiends of the Pedro Botelho Caldeira, they crowd its mouth with tufts of grass, when the pulsations are loudly intensified, and even flames have been said to appear, but this I never saw, nor believe.

This caldeira is an unfailing barometer to the Furnenses, indicating with accuracy the atmospheric changes that occur. When rain or wind threatens, the noise it emits rises from the soft beating of the waves to the thunder of the storm ; but when the weather clears and sunshine returns, the sounds emitted relapse to the soft murmur of the ripple on a sandy shore, at regular and never-ceasing intervals. Not only is this caldeira affected by the weather, but the waters of all the others are said to boil with greater violence when the wind is strong from the south-east, east, or north-east. One of my companions, after a great deal of difficulty, succeeded in " catching " the sound of this geyser in a microphone he brought for that purpose. Imperfect as the experiment was, the noise sounded like the " Crack of Doom," and so frightened one of our donkey-men, whose curiosity we indulged with a hearing, that without uttering a word he fled terrified from the scene, and nearly succeeded by his wild description of the awful sounds he had heard, and the ten thousand *demonios* he felt sure were after him, in creating a stampede amongst the villagers.

The explosions which accompanied the formation of the formidable Pedro Botelho and Asmodée Caldeiras were very alarming, and the feeling of insecurity which the throbbing earth inspires is calculated to suggest that, as we stand over this fizzing and hissing spot, it might be our fate to be hoist on such a natural petard, or else swallowed up by a subsidence of the apparently thin crust separating us from the fiery cauldron below ; but the fear is a purely imaginary one, the numerous safety valves around guaranteeing us against anything so tragic. The slightest upturning of the soil reveals layers of sulphur crystals in acicular and other beautiful forms, which crumble at the touch, and crowding each other and rising indiscriminately all about, are hot and cold springs of greater and lesser volume, sometimes alternating with jets and whisks of hissing gases and mud puffs, honey-combing the ground. Each spring, however, preserves its own individuality, and all flow to swell the Ribeira Quente—a perfect ocean of mineral wealth completely lost. Picking our way along, for there are many miniature Bocas do Inferno hereabouts, and past the side of a small circular caldeira, whose edges are carefully banked up by the natives, for in it they prepare the vime or osier twigs with which they make the delicate and graceful baskets the valley is famous for, we regain the path, and a little beyond are the dilapidated misturas baths, so called from the mixture of sulphur and iron waters. We next reach the perennial Agua Azeda, a fountain flowing from a rude spout fixed in the side of a low hill. This water is of the ferro-saline type, delicious to the taste, and tonic in its effects. This most valuable spring was for a long time regarded by the natives as a sort of "aqua tofana," of which it was death to drink; but they now know better, and it has become a custom with most bathers to take a tumbler of this water after their ablutions, and the appetite it invariably engenders augurs well for its beneficial effects. The quantity of iron it contains is so considerable, as to stain its channel a deep ochre, although nothing could be clearer, or more sparkling than when first drawn. It is highly charged with carbonic acid gas, which clings thickly to the sides of a glass, as in the case of "Apollinaris"; its solvent properties upon urinary calculi are said to be considerable.

After a thunderstorm, the quantity of gas is so increased as to fairly realise the idea of a " windy suspiration of forced breath," when a tumbler-full is tossed off. Undoubtedly the best time to take this pleasant dietetic water is at or before meals, when its beneficial effects are more readily felt.

Its temperature is 16° C. (60.80° Fah.), and it flows at the rate of 11⅔ gallons per minute. A litre submitted to ebullition lost 930 cubic centimetres of gas, composed of—

Carbonic acid	..	..	..	..	890
Azote	..	..	..	..	35
Oxygen	..	..	..	..	5
					930

equal to—

Carbonic acid	..	..	..	..	95.7
Azote	..	..	..	..	3.7
Oxygen	..	..	..	..	0.6
					100.0

A litre of this water evaporated left a residue weighing 0.334 gramme, which gave—

Bicarbonate of soda	..	..	..	.170
Bicarbonate of lime	..	.	..	.010
Bicarbonate of iron	..	..	..	.008
Sulphate of soda	..	..	..	.040
Sulphate of potash	..	..	..	.004
Chloride of sodium	..	.	..	.067
Silica	..	..	..	..	.091
				0.390

The sulphurous acid and sulphuretted hydrogen exhaled from these numerous solfataras mutually decompose each other, and cause the sulphur they contain to be precipitated around the orifices. The ground in many places, therefore, is one mass of beautiful sulphur crystals, and the rapidity with which the substance appears to be deposited would promise to repay the trouble and expense necessary for collecting and distilling it, the abundance of wood in the neighbourhood facilitating the operation. Every year flower of sulphur, in considerable quantities, is imported from England for application to the vines and other purposes; but as a slight risk attends the setting up of the simple apparatus requisite, no Portuguese can be found willing to incur the first risk. If, however, some bolder spirit proved the speculation a remunerative one, all possessing the necessary funds would flock to set up distilleries. Meanwhile, for ages past, a promising industry has remained altogether neglected.

With regard to the cause and origin of thermal springs and the formation of sulphur deposits, Mr. Charles, W. Vincent, F.C.S., in a paper read before the Society of Arts, in January, 1873, "On the sulphur deposits of Krisuvik, Iceland," gives some interesting and valuable information, portions of which I here reproduce, as they are quite applicable to the solfataras of St. Michael, and explain much of the mystery connected with this curious phenomenon. "It is somewhat to be regretted," says Mr. Vincent, "that no one amongst the numerous eminent men—men accustomed to experimental investigations and acute observers—who have since traversed this region, should have investigated the question of the origin of these hot springs and sulphur deposits from the point of view which was thus displayed by these careful and painstaking philosophers. The conclusion they drew from their investigations is, that the hidden fires of Iceland dwell in the crust of the earth, and not in its interior ; that the boiling springs and the mud cauldrons certainly do not derive their heat from the depths of our globe, but that the fire which nourishes them is to be found frequently at only a few feet below the surface, in fermenting matters, which are deposited in certain strata. By their theory the gases from the more central parts of the earth penetrate these beds by subterranean channels, and so set up the chemical action, producing fermentation and heat, these channels also forming the means of inter-communication between the separate sites of activity, and equalising and transferring pressure. To return to their facts : They further observed that the heat is invariably found to be greater in the blue and blueish-grey earth ; that these earths almost always contain sulphuric acid ; that they contain also sulphur, iron, alum, and gypsum ; and lastly, that finely-divided particles of brass-coloured pyrites are visible throughout the whole of the beds when heat exists. Lastly, not only does the heat increase and diminish in various successive layers of the earth, in the neighbourhood of the active springs, but the locality of the heat, as might be expected from their previous observations, travels very considerably in different years. At present it appears to be doubtful whether the sulphur results from the decomposition of metallic sulphides, by heat and water combined, or by sulphuric acid formed by the oxidation of sulphurous acid. In the one case, the whole action is so far within our reach, that it should not be an insurmountable difficulty to establish the point as to whether the whole action does not depend on the percolation of water into beds of pyrites surrounded by other beds which are non-conductors of heat. The other view, viz., that the sulphur proceeds as sulphurous acid from a lower depth, is, on account of the more complicated action required, far from being as satisfactory to my mind as the more simple supposition above. It is also an element in the question of much importance to discover whether the beds penetrated by the water are already heated, whether the water is heated before it reaches the sulphur-bearing strata (the clays containing pyrites), or whether both are not alike cold till they have been for some time in contact."

Sir Henry Holland, who also visited the Solfataras of Krisuvik, adds the following:—" The theory of these sulphureous springs (if springs they may be termed) at Krisuvik is an interesting object of inquiry. They are situated in a country decidedly of volcanic origin. The high ground on which they appear is composed principally of the conglomerate or volcanic tufa, which has before been noted. The source of the heat which can generate permanently so enormous a quantity of steam must, doubtless, reside below this rock; whether it be the same which produces the volcanic phenomena may be doubted, at least if the Wernerian theory of volcanoes be admitted. It certainly seems most probable that the appearances depend upon the action of water on vast beds of pyrites. The heat produced by this action is sufficient to raise an additional quantity of water in the form of steam, which makes its way to the surface, and is there emitted through the different clefts in the rocks. The sulphates of lime and alumina, appearing upon the surface, are doubtless produced in process of time by these operations. In corroboration of this view it may be observed that the quantity of steam issuing from the springs at Krisuvik is always greater after a long continuance of wet weather, and that whenever earthquakes occur on this spot it is during the prevalence of weather of this kind."

Another and very reasonable theory for the occurrence of these springs is the fact of heated columns of steam rising from great depths, when passing through cold, spongy and mineralised strata, becoming condensed before reaching the surface, issuing with varying degrees of temperature and impregnated according to the mineral properties of the beds they pass through.

No sylvan scenes are to be met with in the immediate vicinity of the caldeiras, for the noxious vapours have killed all vegetation near at hand, some stunted yams only making a desperate effort for existence. These fetid-like gaseous emanations, rising from solfataras in general, though unbearable to the majority of people, and fatal to the vegetable world, are, nevertheless, on the authority of competent observers, found to be positively beneficial to those habituated to them, and the glow of health conspicuous in the people of this valley would seem to bear out this opinion. To those accustomed to these caldeiras from childhood, these exhalations are not only tolerant, but positively enjoyable, and the lower animals, especially cattle and horses, often seek their neighbourhood to escape from the torment of flies, for no insect can live within their influence.

In the midst of the Caldeiras are several earthy mounds,

formed by regular and divers-coloured layers, from 1 to 2 inches thick, singularly decomposed, acted upon, as they have been for ages, by caloric and the various evolving gases, in the cooler portions of which there have been formed thin deposits and sheets of hard siliceous sinter of beautiful opalescent colours. Between these layers, leaves of ferns and small plants growing on the mounds are found encrustated with a preserving coat of silica. These are the nearest approach to fossiliferous substances I have ever met with in the island. When hardened by age, these layers appear to consist of a white suffaceous clay, in which the leaf impressions show very perfectly and appear of immense age.

An alkaline fountain, the medicinal virtues of which the peasants have long held in such high esteem as to bestow upon it the name of " Agua Santa," or, Holy Water, rises to the right of the pathway leading from the Misturas baths. Its volume is computed at the rate of 1 gallon per hour. The water is strongly opalescent, and possesses a temperature of 88° C. (190.40° Fah.) It is unique in containing a larger proportion of silicate of soda than any of the other waters, and in being almost destitute of gaseous elements.

The peasants have great faith in the efficacy of this water in ophthalmic complaints, and it is regrettable that no records of its effects are available. M. Fouqué's analysis of the water gave the following :—

Carbonate of soda	..	..	..	.120
Sulphate of soda	..	..	..	.036
Sulphate of potash	..	.		traces
Chloride of sodium	..	..	..	.180
Silica	..	..	,.	.134
Silicate of soda ..	..	..	..	.212
Bicarbonate of lime	..	..	..	traces
Sulphuret of sodium	..	..	..	.024
				0.706

Another acidulated water, which usage has prescribed as beneficial to drink when bathing, is that known as the Padre José spring, close to the pathway leading to Snr. Amaral's baths; its temperature, however, of 51° C. (123.80° Fah.) scarcely renders it as pleasant as the Agua Azeda, but it is richly mineralized, and a close study of its effects would doubtless reveal valuable results from its systematic use. It flows in considerable volume, estimated at 1⅔ gallons per minute.

The imbibition of mineral waters by the Portuguese generally follows the bathing, instead of preceding it as at all the most frequented watering places in Europe, and no regular professional advice and system is followed in their use.

A litre of this Padre José water, submitted to ebullition, lost 102 centimetres of gas, made up as follows :—

Carbonic acid	86.3
Azote	12.0
Oxygen	1.7
	100.0

and a detailed analysis gave—

Bicarbonate of soda	.214
Bicarbonate of lime	.031
Bicarbonate of iron	.020
Sulphate of soda	.114
Chloride of sodium	.113
Silica	.201
Sulphydric acid	traces
	0.693

At the foot of the geyser hill flows the yellow Ribeira Quente stream, just such a river as poets have vainly paved with sands of gold, collecting all the waste waters of these caldeiras, and conspicuous for miles around by the bright colours of its water.

Any individual may erect a bath-house here, conditionally upon his also providing one for the public use, and, until recent years, it was mainly due to private enterprise of the sort that any accommodation at all existed. Such baths are still known by the names of the persons who long since erected them; thus we have, " os Banhos do Barão das Laranjeiras, Visconde da Praia," "Morgado Gil, Snr. J. M. Rapozo d'Amaral and others. As, however, these half-dozen buildings were altogether inadequate for the number of visitors and hospital patients frequenting the valley, the Lisbon Government, urged by the then Civil Governor, Felix Borges de Medeiros, very wisely determined upon erecting a suitable range of buildings on a scale worthy of such a magnificent collection of sanative waters. They accordingly instructed their engineer, the late Snr. Ricardo Ferraz, to draw up the plans for the very creditable establishments now existing here, and which would by no means disgrace any of the Continental watering-places. The site occupied is close to the old Quenturas baths, and the ridge separating them from the caldeiras having been pierced by a tunnel, access is now made easy from that side, as well as from the village, by a handsome carriage drive running parallel with the Ribeira Quente river.

The original plan of the building is for 30 baths and dressing rooms, but only about one half of these are as yet fitted up. These new baths are a great advance upon the old ones, a handsome smooth yellow limestone bath, cut out of a solid block and having all the appearance of marble, replacing the old gigantic stone troughs to which bathers were condemned of old.

The waters supplying the establishment are limited to two kinds, the sulphur, and the iron; the former, drawn from the Caldeira Grande, and the latter from the Quenturas source close by; the respective waters being always " on tap " in the baths, so that a bather, at a moment's notice, can be accommodated with either.

The apartments are well proportioned and neatly fitted up, each bathroom having its dressing room attached. The attendants are civil and obliging, and to these a small gratuity is given upon completing the course, as no charge whatever is made for the use of the baths.

The iron waters are naturally tonic in their effects, but less pleasant than the sulphur, than which nothing can be more delightful, and if taken moderately warm, at a temperature between 90 and 95 Fah., are invigorating and bracing. This sulphur water is indescribably soft and unctious, highly detersive—whitening the skin to an extraordinary degree—and it may well be said that in using it " on devient amoureux de soi-même."

To properly enjoy this water, however, the example of a few of the old habitués should be followed, and baths taken in the older and less pretentious buildings nearer the source, and where consequently the water has not undergone such exposure to the atmosphere. In these old dingy troughs it is certainly stronger and more pedetic, than when it reaches Snr. Amaral's, or the new baignoire. The soft feel of this sulphur water is probably due to the very large quantity of silica it contains, dissolved by the action of the sulphuric gases. A short distance to the west of the new baths stand the old Quenturas baths, formerly much frequented by patients from the hospital, but now altogether abandoned. Near to them are numerous acidulated iron springs of greater or less degrees of heat, precipitating their chief mineral constituents and oxidising their channels a bright yellow, and the largest of these wells up at a rate of 38 gallons per minute at a temperature of 48° C. (118.40° Fah.), and is drawn off into reservoirs for use as required. Some of these appear to have been constructed over small gaseous sources, which constantly bubble to the surface in large quantities, thus tending to preserve the mass fresh and sweet. The water from the main source is also much charged with carbonic acid gas, and indeed is only second to the Agua Azeda in this respect. A litre of this water, submitted to ebullition, lost 200 cubic centimetres of gas, composed of—

Carbonic acid	192.5
Azote	6.0
Oxygen	1.5
	200.0

An evaporated litre left a dry residue, weighing 1.014 grammes, which, on analysis, showed—

Bicarbonate of soda	.956
Bicarbonate of lime	.008
Bicarbonate of iron	.008
Sulphate of soda	.026
Silica	.192
Chloride of sodium	.111
	1.301

Nearer the village are some other springs and baths, known as " Os banhos do Laureano," or " Banhos d'Agua Ferrea," still much frequented by native visitors. The chalybeate which supplies them, like that of Quenturas, is in strong contrast to the sulphur waters, being hard and rough to the feel, and contracting the pores of the skin; they are, however, stimulating, and have long been celebrated for their efficacy in cases of sterility.

These waters are very like those of Quenturas in their constituents, but, unfortunately, were not analysed by M. Fouqué.

With unrivalled facilities at hand for the easy establishment of vapour baths and inhalation rooms of almost every temperature, it seems a pity that the wealth of sulphuretted hydrogen and carbonic gas, so useful in various stages of bronchial and rheumatic affections, should be entirely lost. Much, too, remains to be done with the neglected but stimulating douche, and the constant flow of sulphur and iron waters invites the erection of the delicious piscinas or swimming baths, so common on the Continent.

At Perpignan, Panticosa, Sicily, Ischia, the Lipari Islands, many of the German spas, and Switzerland, " vaporaria " and " salles d'aspiration " have for many years formed an important part in the water-cure system, and in many instances with marked beneficial effects.

To use these Furnas waters only empirically, as is done at present, is to slight the great gift which nature has bestowed on mankind here.

In erecting the new baths, and sending a medical man for a few months every year to chemically investigate the properties of the wells, the government have certainly taken a step in the right direction; but the importance of the question would seem to call for a wider and more systematic study of the sanative qualities of these wonderful springs.

Nearly ninety years ago, Beckford recorded Dr. Ehrhart's indignant outburst at the manner in which patients were allowed the indiscriminate use of the Caldas da Rainha waters, and as the salutary caution implied is equally applicable at the present time, I transcribe what the irate physician laid down in forcible but amusing language : " I found many of them (the patients) with galloping pulses excited almost to frenzy by the injudicious application of these powerful waters, and others with scarcely any pulses at all. The last will be quiet enough ere long ; and considering what dreadful work these determined Galenists drive amongst them, with their decoctions and juleps, spiced boluses, and conserve of mummy, and the devil knows what, I expect a general gaol-delivery must speedily take place, and the souls of these victims of exploded quackeries be soon released from their wretched bodies, rendered the worst of prisons by a set of confounded bunglers."

Although visitors to the Furnas may in these days escape the infliction of " spiced boluses and conserve of mummy," it would nevertheless be well if those suffering from chronic affections or tendency to congestion were to consult the native medical man for the time stationed here, before committing themselves to a regular course of any of the waters, and more especially the powerful sulphur ones.

Time was, and that not very long since, when phlebotomy, like the handkerchief round the negro's head, was regarded in this island as a panacea for maladies (typhoid and other fevers included), but " on a changé tout cela," and patients may now with perfect safety place themselves in the hands of such native medical men as Drs. Hintz Ribeiro (brother of the talented Minister of the Interior), Rosa, the medical officer in attendance at the Miserecordia Hospital, and several others, who have been trained in the modern schools of medicine and surgery of Lisbon and Coimbra. Indeed, I have known of some very difficult surgical operations performed with perfect skill and success by Dr. Rosa upon some of my countrymen and countrywomen, whose gratitude to him is expressed in no stinted terms. Before dismissing the subject of the Furnas geysers, with their wild chaotic surroundings, I cannot refrain from strongly urging upon those of my readers who have not as yet witnessed these remarkable phenomena to spare no effort to do so, for their sight is a perfect revelation.

The earliest account received in England of these hot springs is that of Thomas Turner, as related by Purchas (4 vol., 1625). He says, " In Saint Michael, one of the Açores, they ascend vp in a forenoones journey vnto a hill into a chappell, wherein they need a fire in summer for the cold: there being, a little off, three springs, the one whereof casteth vp waters in a continual boyling with a terrible noise, and of great heate, the second of heate intolerable, which in short time scaldeth any living thing

R

to death, the ground also hote to stand on : but the water calme.   The third is warme, and a fit bathe."

The founders of the village of Furnas seem to have been the two anchorites already referred to, who, crossing over from Portugal, and abandoning all things worldly, here took up their abode in the early part of the seventeenth century. The wilderness they had chosen, and the austerities they practised, recommended these holy men to the notice of the then donatario, the Count da Camara, who had a chapel and monastery erected for them.   It was not until many years after they were driven from the valley by the occurrences of 1630, that shepherds gradually resorted here with their flocks, and that regular habitations were established. These were followed by the Jesuits, who afterwards possessed considerable demesnes in the valley, on which they appear to have systematically kept large apiaries, for part of their annual revenues consisted regularly of a pipe of honey—an eloquent testimony of the abundance of wild and cultivated flowers, yielding their sweetness in this favored spot.

The place is still famous for the beautiful clear honey-comb to be had in the season from some of the cottagers, but for want of proper attention the industry has fallen off.

The village has a population of some six or seven hundred souls, mostly wretchedly poor, who occupy themselves chiefly in cultivating the small plots of land which some of them possess; but the soil is weak, and makes them poor returns. They, however, raise milho, kidney beans, flax, and, in the more marshy places, large quantities of yams.

A small, snow-white cheese is made here from goats' milk, which, when quite fresh, is extremely palatable.

One of the most delightful spots at the Furnas is the Tank, now the property of the Count da Praia e Monforte, a nobleman enjoying a rent roll equal to one of the wealthiest of our English earldoms, and who has recently rebuilt and greatly improved the residence.

As far back as 1770, Mr. Hickling, a former United

States consul, had tastefully laid out the grounds—suscep-
tible, from their natural situation, of being made into the
perfect Eden they now are—and imported a large number of
ornamental trees from the States and Europe. Upon his
death, the property passed to the late Viscount da Praia,
the father of the present owner. This benevolent gentleman, who was known in the island as the " Pai dos
Pobres," also possessed remarkable taste, and to him is
chiefly due the credit of bringing the gardens to their
present condition, and of introducing the numerous and
rare trees they contain. It was here that William Hickling
Prescott, the American historian, and Consul Hickling's
grandson, spent a part of the year 1816, and from the old
house wrote to his sister:—" In this delightful spot I have
enjoyed some of the happiest hours that I have spent since
I quitted my native shores." In such a retreat as this, a
man may well throw off the acerbities of a, perhaps, over-
wrought mind, and find peace and health, induced by the
surrounding beauties and pure atmosphere he breathes.

At the foot of the Alegria heights, on the western side
of the valley, exists a circular hollow, about ten feet deep,
filled to within a few inches of the surface with beautifully
clear water, which never increases or lessens in volume,
welling up continually from a sandy bottom, with such
force, and apparently accompanied by so much gas, as to
cause the pool to eject a heavy alpenstock thrown vertically
into it. Similar hollows, always perfectly circular and
funnel-shaped, were formed in the plain of Rosarno, in
Calabria, by the earthquake of 1783, and no doubt this, the
only one which I have been able to hear of in the island,
was caused by a similar occurrence. These remarkable
wells have been known to dry up as suddenly as they have
appeared, and, the pits being filled up, their sites are no
longer discernible.

Following the gilded course of the Ribeira Quente river
on its way to the sea, where it debouches at the little fishing

village of the same name, we come, about a mile from the geysers, to the Caldeira do Esgite, or "dos Tambores," on the very brink of the stream, actively emitting considerable quantities of vapour, accompanied by loud hissing and rumbling sounds, like the rapid beating of numerous drums, from which it derives its name. The spot itself is difficult of access, but as looked down upon from the old high road (to Povoação) opposite, is picturesque to a degree, the barren spots near the geysers contrasting with the prodigal verdure beyond them. From these heights the direction of the little river, with its crisping wavelets, may be traced for miles, its banks here and there fringed and overshadowed by the graceful salix.

Nothing can exceed the exquisite beauty of the scenery along the new road to Povoação, a small town some eight or nine miles distant, situated on the south-east coast of the island, for the whole way runs over hills from 1,000 to 2,000 feet high, all clad in pine, chesnut, and other timber trees, and past sheer precipices revealing richly cultivated valleys below. Every now and then a break suddenly opens up the view of the distant sea with its specks of fishing boats, each successive step presenting some scene of which the eye never wearies.

Povoação itself is interesting as the first spot the early colonists trod upon, and where they erected the first rude chapel built in the island. The site is now occupied by the ancient Ermida of Santa Barbara, which suffered so much during the earthquake of 1882. The place, as viewed from afar, presents a snug and *riant* appearance; its broad, rich valley, shut in on all sides, except the south, by high mountains, and its three or four long lines of cottages or "lombos," running up from the coast and intersecting the plain. In its upper end, and charmingly situated in the midst of well-cultivated lands, stand the imposing-looking country residences of the Camara and Machado families, and still higher up—a dot of white among the clouds—the little eyry-like mirante or look-out of the Baron Jacintho, from which a superb view can be enjoyed :

> To us it seemed some happy haunt
> Of freedom and content—
> A little world, shut out from care,
> And all disquietment.

Here some good quail shooting can be had, and occasionally a red-legged partridge may be flushed, but these are fast disappearing. Game birds in these islands are extremely shy, owing as much to the perpetual warfare carried on against them by native sportsmen—many of them unerring shots—as to the perhaps still more destructive ravages of that bird of rapine, the hawk (*Falco buteo*), which can be everywhere seen high in the air, or preening his wings on some forest tree, watching for his victim either in field or poultry yard :—

> Around, around, in airy rings
> They wheel with oarage of their wings.

These destructive birds have been known to fly in at the open window of a room in which two men were seated, in chase of a hen which had entered there.

Although so fierce and rapacious, this powerful buzzard possesses a troublesome and implacable foe in the little arvelinha or arveloa, identical with the wagtail (*Motacilla alba*) ; it generally hunts in bands of six to a dozen, mobbing the hawk when flying, and with passionate sibilations fastening itself firmly underneath his wings. Mr. Bates, in his charming work on the " Amazon," mentions a similar characteristic on the part of the diminutive Bem-te-vi, assailing the black eagle, Caracára-i, and Mr. Wallace, in his " Malay Archipelago," notices similar onslaughts on hawks and crows by an equally small bird found in the Moluccas, the *Tropidorhynchus subcornutus*. Several very pretty cascades are to be seen at Povoação, amongst others the " Grota do Intrudo," and in the hills behind, specially the "Mata dos Silvados," 2,000 feet above the sea, are several others of lesser volume, but equally beautiful. It is here, in these almost inaccessible and perpetually moist ravines, that the beautiful *Woodwardia radicans, Dicksonia culcita, Pteris arguta,* and *Capillus veneris* (or maiden-hair) ferns, can be seen to perfection, completely covering the steep declivities in canopies of green.

The people of Povoação, owing to the larger proportion of Moorish blood coursing through their veins, are rather a fine race of swarthy-looking men, and generally better to do than in many other parts of the island, the soil being richer, and enabling them to raise heavy crops. They have also extensive pastures which maintain large herds of cattle. Their love of order and justice is proverbial, "long rope and short shrift" being their verdict in criminal cases. As exemplifying their impulsive character, Cordeiro relates a story of a man, who, shortly after the foundation of the colony in 1444, ran off with his neighbour's wife; caught and brought before the Moorish judge, the latter, on hearing the case, at once exclaimed, "Forcarte, forcarte, e depois tirarte inquiricione" ("Hang him, hang him, and then try him.")

Povoação is a good *point d'appui* for excursions to various parts of this wild and little frequented side of the island. A very fair road leads through the valley of Povoação to the Pico do Passo, 3,040 feet above sea level, and on to the Pico da Vara, 530 feet higher still, and the loftiest point in St. Michael's, the views from which are unsurpassed.

During the severe winters, Pico da Vara surprises the islanders by showing its cusp covered with snow, which, however, rarely outlives the day.

Povoação is also within easy distance of Fayal da Terra; thence past Pico de Nunez. 2,220 feet high, to Agua Retorta, and the bold basaltic headland of Lombo Gordo, 1,347 feet high, where magnificent cliff scenery can be enjoyed. This grand and elevated coast line may be followed round to

Nordeste and Maya. The land around Nordeste was formerly very fertile, and immense crops of wheat were raised—so much so, that the inhabitants obtained the privilege at their earnest request of supplying provisions to the náus arriving from the East Indies, for which they declined to receive any remuneration whatever. King Manoel, in consequence, raised the place in 1514 to the dignity of villa or town; but its prosperity was of short duration, for the second earthquake of 1563 buried its rich soil under thick layers of pumice set free from some neighbouring heights, and from which they cannot be reclaimed. Owing to lesser contact with strangers, the inhabitants of these places are unsophisticated and shy, but invariably respectful and obliging.

At Ponta do Arnel, on the north-east extremity of this coast, a dioptric beacon has been placed, 37° 49' 20" north, and 25° 8' 30" west of Greenwich; the light is white and fixed, flashing every two minutes, and will illuminate two-thirds of the horizon (240°). In fine weather, the fixed light can be seen eighteen miles off, and the flashes twenty-five miles.

The focus of light is 67m. 5 above sea level at mean tide.

Back at the Furnas, shorter but equally enjoyable trips may be made to Pico da Vigia, which frowns upon Ribeira Quente, to the heights of Alegria, the Cascada da Briosa, the Cascada das Camarinhas, and other places.

At Jeronymo's Hotel, a large and spacious apartment is devoted to music and dancing, where of an evening visitors as well as members of the club, as it is called, congregate and enjoy these innocent amusements.

> Adeos Furnas, vou deixar-te,
> E' lei do fado cruel;
> Para sempre abandonar-te,
> Meu amor de S. Miguel.

Chapter XIII.

> Sink me the ship, Master Gunner—sink her, split her in twain !
> Fall into the hands of God, not into the hands of Spain !
>
> *Tennyson.*

The new southern road from Furnas to Ponta Delgada runs along the shores of the lake and Snr. José do Canto's wood, and is a perfect triumph of engineering skill. It entirely avoids the old route past Ponta Garça and the coast, but hugging the mountains—always at a great altitude—follows a zig-zag course, passing in places along the very brink of precipices, 1,000 feet deep, and through steep and narrow gorges, cut through the immense masses of pumice, and descends at a gradual but perceptible incline, all the way to Villa Franca, not a single village or hamlet being passed the entire distance (some nine or ten miles) of this first stage of the journey.

No words can adequately describe the grand and ever-changing scenery met with at every step along this road, green on either side with thick beds of moss and graceful over-hanging ferns, and past a country, from ravine to hill-top, thickly clad with beautiful timber trees and lush vegetation. Certainly, this southern route, along which a carriage may be driven from beginning to end, is undeniably the most varied and interesting of the two approaches to Furnas, for, besides the inland beauties it reveals, the long stretches of exquisite coast views it presents are unrivalled in any part of the world. An alternative choice of reaching the valley from the city is by sea, as far as Ribeira Quente, in one of the fast-sailing lateen-rigged boats for which this village has always been famous. These rakish-looking craft are generally employed in carrying charcoal and firewood to Ponta Delgada, bringing back supplies for the small villages around. Given a fair land-breeze, the trip may be accomplished in three or four hours, and the fatigue and heat of the land journey are greatly lessened by this sea route. Against it are the chances of being becalmed, the necessity, as a rule, of starting at midnight, and the loss of the inland scenery. This last objection may, however, be obviated by landing at Villa Franca, where either carriages or donkeys may be had to complete the journey.

Ribeira Quente is within two hours ride on donkey back of the Furnas; but the landing-place, owing to the surf which beats against this part of the coast, is difficult of access; even in perfectly calm weather, passengers have to land on the boat-men's backs, luggage and other impedimenta being carried on shore in like manner, before the craft can be placed high and dry. Owing to the absence of protecting cliffs, the little village of Ribeira Quente is almost every year threatened with destruction from the inroads of the sea, which, in 1880, carried away a dozen cottages, and seems to be ever gaining on the beach. This, however, must not be construed as sustaining the theory of these islands subsiding; on the contrary, although the progress of elevation is so gradual as to be scarcely perceptible, there are yet signs that it is continual. In Madeira too, the intervening beach between the Banger column at Funchal, created since its erection in 1798, is pointed out as a proof of the elevation of the land there also.

In 1679, during the night time, a band of Algerine Moors landed at Ribeira Quente and the little bay of Agriaõ hard by, from two three-masted "xebecs," and crossing the hills at the back, descended at day-break into the valley of the Furnas, capturing all the live-stock they could meet, and pillaging the villages around, successfully carried off their spoil to their ships.

As the road approaches Villa Franca, and becomes almost level, patches of orange gardens with their green selvages of protecting fayas are passed; and, immediately afterwards, we enter the "Villa" itself, an imposing looking town with its large church, municipal buildings and hospital, its numerous dwelling houses, clustering together as if for mutual protection.

Every now and then, when digging out the foundations of new buildings, parts of the buried town are uncovered, and *trouvaille* of various kinds met with; amongst other things, quaint earthenware vessels and amphoræ filled with silver and copper coins, of the 16th century, in perfect preservation, and interesting to the students of numismatics, have been unearthed.

I was fortunate enough to secure several specimens, both of pottery and coins, and feel confident that if a more systematic search were made, the amateur archæologist and collector of "curios" would reap an interesting, if not rich harvest.

After the almost entire distruction of Villa Franca on the night of the 21st October, 1522, the terror-stricken inhabitants were desirous of abandoning the locality for good, but their captain donatary, Ruy Gonçalves, and the municipality of the town, ordered large quantities of cedar and other trees to be cut in the Valley of the Furnas, where they then abounded, and had these distributed gratis to the more needy sufferers, thus inducing them to rebuild their habitations on the same spot.

A sketch of the early history of this place having

already been given, it will suffice here to mention that Villa Franca is happy in the possession of a newspaper, an omnibus, which runs once or twice a week to the city, an assembly or club house, a band of music, and boasts 5,937 electors. It has also a pretty square, planted with trees, known as "Praça de D. Luiz," in front of its excessively unsightly church, dedicated to San Miguel, and which was much damaged by the earthquake of 1630, when the entire roof fell in. An interesting circumstance in connection with the subsequent repairs of this church may be noted in the fact of the massive beams and joists used having been cut from the huge cypress trees, which, as already related, were common in the island on its first discovery. Those used on this occasion were also brought from the valley of the Furnas. This is the last authentic period recorded of these magnificent trees being still in flourishing condition, and from the great distance from which they were transported, they were probably the last in existence at that period in this part of the island.

From the boles occasionally unearthed at the Seven Cities and Furnas, there is little doubt that these splendid trees on its first discovery inhabited a high belt of country extending east and west along the axis of the island. The probable dearth at that time of solid timber suitable for building purposes, and the simultaneous introduction of those enemies to the young forest tree—the goat and hog— which, with cattle, are said to have increased astonishingly and become wild, doubtless account for the rapid and total extinction of these grand denizens of the forest, and with them probably of interesting plant and insect life.

Padre Cordeiro, in his "Historia Insulana," casually mentions that the beams and roofing of the church of Santo Ignacio de Loyola, now forming a chapel to the palace of the civil governors of Terceira, were constructed from cedars brought from the island of Flores, where at that time the tree was said to flourish better; a proof of its distribution over the entire group—of itself a very re-markable fact—for both Flores and Corvo are distant about 120 miles from the nearest of the other seven islands.

Padre Andrade, in his "Topographia," says that Terceira, when discovered, was densely wooded with heavy timber; all the old churches and other buildings were roofed with cedar wood. A tradition has it that the immense beams, even now to be seen supporting the roof of the cathedral in Angra, were cut at the very spot now occupied by the old square, showing that these beautiful trees must have flourished on that island as late as 1570, when the Sé was first commenced.

At S. Roque, in the island of Pico, was still to be found about the same period abundance of that beautiful wood called teixo (*Taxus baccata*, L.), but which, like the cedar, has long since become extinct.

Besides the assertions of Fructuoso and Cordeiro, we have that of Linschoten, who resided long at Terceira about the latter end of the sixteenth century, to the effect that, in his day, the cedar was the commonest wood in many of the islands. About this he says:—

"The island, Terceira, hath great store of excellent kinds of wood, specially cedar trees, which grow there in so great numbers that they make scutes, carts, and other grosse workes thereof, and is the commonest wood that they vse to burne in those countries, whereby it is the wood that with them is least esteemed, by reason of the great quantity thereof. Saint George hath likewise many cedar trees and other kinds of wood, that from thence are brought vnto Terceira, and sold vnto the joyners, which for that occasion dwell only in Terceira. These joyners used to turn out fine pieces of work, as desks, cupboards, chests, and other such like, supplying the Spanish fleets.

"There is a certain kind of wood in island Pico, situate and lying twelve miles from Terceira, called teixo, a most excellent and princely wood, and therefore it is forbidden to be cut, but only for the king's own vse, or for his officers. The wood is as hard as iron, and hath a colour within as if it were wrought like red chamlet, with the same water, and the older it is, and the more vsed, the fairer it is of colour."

In various parts of Terceira, and more especially in the vicinity of Santa Barbara, are occasionally found immense cedar trees embedded in deep ravines and valleys, still in perfect preservation; such a find is a God-send to the poor villagers, who instantly cut the bole up for fire-wood, always in these islands a short commodity amongst them.

As late as 1607 Sir Arthur Gorges writes, "Fayall is so called of 'faya,' which in the Portugues signifieth a beech tree," wherewith that island is said to abound, but yet I saw there more store of juniper and cedar than of any wood or timber.

Midway between Villa Franca and Furnas stands the Pico dos Cedros at an altitude of 2,240 feet, doubtless so named from the cypress trees, or cedros as the islanders called it, formerly abounding on its heights. A steep road, not much frequented and consequently not of the best, leads to this Pico from Villa Franca, and at a spot two-thirds of its distance branches off to the Lagôa do Congro, a tarn buried deep in profound solitude, where in the winter those fond of shooting, and who have the courage to visit and stay a day or two in this, then moist, neighbourhood, have a chance of bagging a few brace of wild duck and common snipe (*Scolopax gallinago*). The views around are extremely pretty.

On one side of the Praça de D. Luiz stands the new Casa da Camara, on the ground floor of which may be seen the prison, with its iron-grated windows, enabling the inmates, employed by the compassionate public in their various avocations of tailoring, boot making, &c., to hold unrestricted converse with their sympathetic friends outside.

Villa Franca produces very fine oranges, grown chiefly in

the hollows and sheltered valleys, so frequently met with here, the greater abundance of triturated matter in the soil from the surrounding hills (especially oxide of iron), and the warmer and drier climate, maturing the fruit quicker than in any other part of the island; and it is the first, as a rule, to find its way into the London markets.

Some ten or twelve schooners, conveying about 80,000 flat boxes of oranges, were, during average seasons, despatched to England from its little port.

In these sheltered and fertile depressions of Villa Franca, the sugar-cane was once cultivated to a large extent, and several " engenhos " for the manufacture of sugar were erected here ; but the subsequent cheaper and increased productions in the Brazils and West Indies, combined with the scarcity of firewood in the island, killed this industry, which, as we have seen, was then followed by the pastel, then the grape, and on the " oidium " attacking the vines, by the orange, cereal, sweet potato, and pine-apple cultivation.

During the season 1884–85, Villa Franca exported to London and Bristol 22,573 flat boxes of oranges, 334 packages of tangerines, and 21,171 pine-apples, the value of these exports amounting to £3,800. The previous season of 1883–84, the shipments of oranges alone amounted to 42,798 flat boxes, which shows how seriously this fruit trade is declining, the diminished shipments arising chiefly from so many of the old trees affected with the " molestia " having been rooted up.

In the bay, and at a distance of a short half-mile, stands the Ilheo de Villa Franca, a small trap islet, the highest point of which on the south-west side has an elevation of about 400 feet above sea level. A few yards on its southern head rises a huge detached (probably by the action of the sea) block—like a grim sentinel on guard—adding picturesqueness to the view. The islet is of easy access in boats and worth visiting, if only to enjoy the panorama it presents of the town and surrounding country, which, at this part, possesses many of the characteristic beauties of Madeira, as viewed from the sea. Owing its origin to some remote subaqueous eruption, the rock in its interior presents the appearance of a circular hollow cone, some thousand feet in diameter at top, down the northern wall of which the lava stream flowed, cutting it in two, and admitting the sea into its funnel, where six fathoms are now sounded.

This entrance, its only means of access, is from 20 to 30 feet across, with two fathoms of water at high tide in the narrow channel and permitting of small craft taking shelter within its miniature breakwater, where they may ride in perfect shelter from the severest storm; but it is of little practical use. The diameter of the basin is some 300 feet.

The rock is everywhere rent in deep fissures, some a foot or more in width, and reaching to its base; these rents are the chosen abode of innumerable crabs, many of them of large size. The face of the islet is covered with drusic cavities wrought by the erosive action of the heavy seas beating against it, and almost covering it in winter. In these crevices countless numbers of starlings seek shelter, and may be seen in perfect clouds of an evening wending their way to their safe and undisturbed retreat. On closely examining these masses of tufa, they will be found to be also perforated and honeycombed below water, but from a very different cause, the holes being made by echini inhabiting these shores, the generally soft nature of this tufa rock offering them no impediment.

Round the Ilheo quantities of large cray-fish may be caught, and those fond of fishing will find this an excellent pastime, for the finny tribe are both numerous and in great variety.

In 1582, a very remarkable naval engagement took place off Villa Franca, the results of which were fraught with grave consequences to the island, and indeed to the entire archipelago. As the account has never appeared in any

English publication, it may interest my readers if I give a short *résumé* of the circumstances which led up to and followed an engagement which brought the whole of these islands under the yoke of Spain.

The death of the Cardinal King, Dom Henrique, in 1580, without issue, was the signal for plunging Portugal into the throes of civil war. Amongst the many pretenders to the vacant throne, were Philip II. of Spain, who claimed through his mother, the Empress Isabel, daughter of the deceased king, Dom Manuel of Portugal; Dom Antonio, the Prior of Crato, an illegitimate son of the Infante Dom Luiz, and nephew of the deceased monarch, Dom Henrique; The Princess Catharina, of Braganza, daughter of the Infante Dom Duarte; Alexander Farnese, Duke of Parma, who claimed in right of his mother the Princess Maria, eldest daughter of the Infante Dom Duarte; and the Duke of Savoy, the son of the Infanta Donna Brites. The Pope also laid claim to the crown, as heir to the deceased Cardinal King.

Of these, the only two who showed any disposition to try the force of arms in support of their pretensions were Philip of Spain and Dom Antonio, who had caused himself to be proclaimed king, in June 1580. The former lost no time in marching an army of his veterans into Portugal, under the command of the Duke of Alva, to oppose which, a multitude of untrained and badly armed peasants were led by Dom Antonio, only to be utterly routed and dispersed at Alcantra on the 25th August. Once more gathering his shattered forces together, the unfortunate Portuguese prince essayed the fortune of war at Aveiro with even more disastrous result, his followers being again quickly dispersed, he himself seeking safety by flight into France. Meanwhile, Philip, having annexed Portugal to his already unwieldly dominions, called upon the Portuguese colonies in Africa, India, and Brazil to recognise his authority, which they did; the Azores alone, led by Terceira, stedfastly refusing, professed allegiance to Dom Antonio. Before I proceed with the details of the sea fight off Villa Franca, the result of which consolidated the sway of Spain over the whole of Portugal for a period of 60 years, it will amuse my readers to learn the issue of an attack made by the Spaniards upon the refractory island of Terceira, and the manner—unique in the annals of warfare—in which it was repulsed.

Early in the morning of the 25th July, 1581, the inhabitants of the village of S. Sebastiaõ were alarmed at the sight of a squadron, consisting of seven large Spanish war galleons, anchored off the little bay of Salga; the operations for landing a hostile force being actually in progress. Hastily summoning some companies of militia, and collecting behind a neighbouring knoll a large herd of the semi-wild cattle from the surrounding pastures, the islanders quietly awaited the massing of the Spaniards on the beach. When this had been accomplished the Terceirenses advanced close up to the foe, as if to the attack, when suddenly opening out into two long columns, and leaving a wide open space between, the herd of cattle were sent thundering down the centre goaded on by picadores on horseback. So unusual and unexpected a charge threw the Spaniards into the most complete disorder, and being at once set upon by the islanders scarcely a man escaped to the ships; several guns, which had been landed, falling as spoil to the conquerors.

Having succeeded in gaining the sympathies of the court of France, Prince Antonio was enabled by midsummer of 1582 to equip a formidable expedition for a descent upon the Azores, and subsequently the coast of Portugal; for Saint Michael's, never very stable in its political leanings, had shortly before given its adherence to Philip. Antonio's fleet, commanded by the Count of Vimioso, consisted of 60 sail, some of considerable size and powerfully armed, carrying altogether a fighting force of 10,000 men, almost all French, under Marshal Estrosse, and numerous French noblemen. Arriving off the island on the 14th July, and receiving a refusal of surrender, they proceeded to cannonade the forts and towns along the coast for the space of three days, after which some 3,000 men were landed without any opposition at a rocky point between Alagoa and Rosto do Caõ. These were quickly followed by Dom Antonio himself, with 2,000 additional men; the formidable force overrunning the entire island, which they proceeded to sack and pillage, with the exception only of Villa Franca, which had pronounced in favour of the prince. People, too, were butchered in cold blood, for we have records of some 200 peasants ruthlessly slain in defending their women from outrage and their chattels from robbery. Churches even were broken into, and despoiled of their massive silver ornaments and vessels, which were carried off; and the work of rapine and plunder would have been greater, had not a powerful Spanish fleet, numbering forty sail, under the Marquis de Santa Cruz, appeared off the island on the 21st. This fleet is said to have had 6,000 soldiers, besides marines and sailors, on board.

By the following day, Dom Antonio had re-embarked the whole of his men, with the exception of a small French detachment, left on shore to watch the castle of S. Braz, into which the governor of the island, Martin Affonso de Mello, had thrown himself, on the landing of the French, with the handful of regulars at his disposal. It was, however, decided by his leaders that Dom Antonio should not risk his person in the coming engagement, but retire, with a suitable escort, to the stronghold of Terceira. This he accordingly did, laying himself open, by this act, to the severe criticism of the historians of these events.

For three days the hostile fleets did little more than watch each other, occasionally skirmishing, until, on the 26th, the leading and then the admirals' ships, became engaged at close quarters, the fight growing furious, and continuing for upwards of five hours. Late in the day, the brave Marshal Estrosse was killed, whilst heading a boarding party against the Spanish admiral's galleon, the "Madre de Dios." The Count of Vimioso also lost his life in another gallant effort to retrieve the day, for several of his ships had now been sunk, others crippled, and those remaining making all haste to get away. So severe had been the struggle that the Spaniards were unable for three days afterwards to follow up their advantage.

One thousand two hundred Frenchmen, besides several of their leaders, are said to have been killed, and a good many taken prisoners. Of these latter, Santa Cruz immediately ordered thirty nobles to be decapitated on a scaffold erected in the market place of Villa Franca, fifty-three of lesser grade to be hanged, and, as an earnest of what they might expect in the event of sedition, the Marquis caused one of the chief magistrates to lose his head, and several of the leading inhabitants to receive minor punishments. Leaving a force of 3,000 men in the island, Santa Cruz sailed for Terceira, finding it well prepared for defence, and considering his forces inadequate for its capture, he returned to the Tagus, from whence he again set out on the 23rd June of 1583 with a fresh expedition, consisting of 97 sail, and having on board some 13,000 men. These arrived off Terceira on the 24th July. The whole of the force on landing, two days later, were met by the islanders, who once more assayed their wild-cattle ruse ; but the wily Spaniards, being this time prepared for this original mode of warfare, opened a central avenue for the passage of the animals, and falling upon the astonished Portuguese, put them to the rout.

Upwards of 300 pieces of cannon fell into the hands of the Spaniards, and for three whole days the entire island was sacked, and unspeakable cruelties perpetrated. Terceira was now destined to become the centre of Spanish dominion in these waters for 60 long years to come.

At the end of the previous November Dom Antonio had left the island and returned to France, where he died some years later in almost abject poverty.

It is interesting to Englishmen to remember that Elizabeth recognised this unfortunate prince as King of Portugal, and in consequence of Philip's designs upon England, sent Drake, Norris, Frobisher, Burroughs, the Earls of Essex and Cumberland, and others, to ravage the Azorean seas, which then became the happiest of hunting grounds for English privateers; innumerable rich " caraks " and " caravels " from the West Indies and India being captured. The immense booty thus secured may be estimated from the two following instances, mentioned in Astley's collections.

Sir Robert Cross, during a cruising voyage, in 1592, took, a little to the west of Flores, a huge carak, estimated at 1,600 tons, homeward bound from the East Indies. Her cargo consisted of " pepper, cloves, maces, nutmegs, cinnamon, green ginger, benjamin, frankincense, galingale, mirabolans, aloes, zocotrina, camphire, damasks, taffatas, sarcenets, altobassos (that is, counterfeit cloth of gold), unwrought China silk, sieaved silk, white twisted silk, curled cypress, book calicos, calico-lawns, broad white calicos, fine starched calicos, coarse white calicos, brown broad calicos, brown coarse calicoes. There were also canopies and coarse diaper towels, quilts of coarse sarcenet and of calico, carpets like those of Turkey; whereunto are to be added the pearl, musk, civet and ambergriece. The rest of the wares were many in number, but less in value—as, elephants' teeth, porcelain vessels of China, coco-nuts, hides, ebon-wood, as black as jet, bedsteads of the same, cloth of the rinds of trees, surprising both on account of the matter and artificial workmanship. All these commodities being valued by men of judgment, at a reasonable rate, amounted to no less than one hundred and fifty thousand pounds stg., which being divided among the adventurers (whereof Her Majesty was the chief) was sufficient to content all parties." It is curious to see Queen Bess here designated as the chief adventurer and participator in the spoils of this expedition.

In July of 1592, Capt. Thos. White, on his return to

England from Barbary, in the " Amity," fell in with two Spanish argosies, which, after a stout fight, he captured, finding them "laden with 1,400 chests of quicksilver, with the arms of Castile and Leon fastened upon them, besides a great quantity of bulls, or indulgences, and ten packs of gilded missals and breviaries, sent on the king's account; also an hundred tuns of excellent wines, designed for his fleets; all which the English brought, shortly after, into the Thames up to Blackwall.

" By the taking of this quicksilver, the King of Spain lost, for every quintal of the same a quintal of silver, that should have been delivered him by the masters of the mines (in Peru), which amounteth to six hundred thousand pounds; and the two millions and seventy-two thousand bulls, for living and dead persons (designed for the provinces of Nova Hispania, Yucatan, Guatemala, the Honduras and the Philippinas), taxed at two rials the piece, besides eighteen thousand bulls at four rials, amounted in all to one hundred and seven thousand seven hundred pounds; so that the total loss to the King of Spain was seven hundred and seven thousand seven hundred pounds."

The enormous wealth of some of these cargoes, obtained by the Spaniards, who were justly stigmatised as "hostes humani generis," through the cruel sacrifice of thousands, nay, millions of lives of the unhappy aborigines they had conquered, may be estimated from the fact that Van Linschoten, who resided for a long time in Terceira, and whose statements are confirmed by several Portuguese writers of that period, " saw the entire quay of Angra covered, from November, 1589, to March, 1590, with chests of silver to the value of 5 millions of duckats," equivalent to about £5,000,000 sterling of the present time, and this out of only two caracks recently arrived from the Spanish West Indies, and irrespective of a large quantity of gold, pearls and other precious stones and articles of value not mentioned or accounted for.

Nor were the repeated depredations of our sailors upon Spanish trade in these latitudes unattended by some glorious fighting, as witness the noble defence made in August of 1591, by Sir Richard Grenville, in his ship the " Revenge," a second-rate vessel of 500 tons burden, with a crew of 250 men, and carrying less than 40 guns, against a whole Spanish Armada of 15 ships, part of a fleet of 53 sail in all, commanded by Don Alfonso Bassan, brother of the Marquis de Santa Cruz, sent from Ferrol to the Azores to convoy a large number of richly laden argosies daily expected from the Spanish main, and which Lord Thomas Howard was endeavouring to intercept.

By some unaccountable means, Sir Richard Grenville found himself isolated and deserted by his chief, Lord Thomas Howard, who went off with five other ships. However, nothing daunted, Sir Richard engaged the Spaniards single-handed, continuing the fight for fifteen hours, and before being mortally wounded had succeeded in sinking two of the enemy's ships (one of 600 tons), and disabling several. Of his crew of 250 men, Sir Richard lost 100 killed, almost the whole of the remainder being wounded, the Spaniards having 400 killed and many others crippled.

In the " argument " to his remarkable " Tragedie of Sir Richard Grinuile, Knight, based upon this celebrated fight, and written in 1595," Gervase Markham gives a very concise account of it, which it may be interesting to reproduce :—

" Sir Richard Grinuile, lying at anchor neere vnto Flores, one of the westerlie islands of the Azores, the last of August (1591), in the after noone, had intelligence by one Captayne Midelton of the aproch of the Spanish Armada, beeing in number fiftie three saile of great ships, and fifteene thousand men to man them. Sir Richard, staying to recouer his men which were vpon the iland, and disdayning to flie from his countrie's enemy, not beeing able to recouer the winde, was instantlie inuironed with that hudge

nauie, betweene whom began a dreadfull fight, continuing
the space of fifteene howers, in which conflict, Sir Richard
sunck the great 'San Phillip of Spaine,' the 'Ascention of
Suiel,' the 'Admirall of the Hulks,' and two other great
armados; about midnight Sir Richard receiued a wound
through the bodie, and as he was in dressing, was shot
againe into the head, and his surgion slaine. Sir Richard
mayntained the fight, till he had not one corn of powder left,
nor one whole pike, nor fortie lyuing men; which seeing,
hee would have sunke his owne ship, but that was gaine
stood by the maister thereof, who contrarie to his will
came to composition with the Spanyards, and so saued those
which were left aliue.

"Sir Richard dyed aboard the 'Admyrall of Spayne,'
about the fourth day after the battaile, and was mightlie
bewailed of all men."

The Spaniards had little leisure, however to gloat over
their hardly-won victory and the rare capture of an
English fighting ship, for scarcely had the homeward-
bound argosies reached the rendezvous at Corvo and Flores,
where they were joined by the king's ships above mentioned—
the entire fleet now reaching the almost incredible number
of 140 sail—than the most terrific storm which has ever
visited this archipelago overtook them, scattering them in all
directions, and wrecking 107 of them; amongst these the
" Revenge."

Linschoten in his " Discours of Voyages into the East
and West Indies," translated from the Dutch, in 1598,
gives the following very graphic particulars of this terrible
cyclone : —

"The Spanish Armie (*i.e.* Armado), staied at the Island
of Coruo till the last of September (1591) to assemble the
rest of the fleet together; which in the end were to the
number of 140 saile of ships, partly comming from India,
and partly of the Army (*i.e.* Armado), and being altogether
ready unto saile in Tercera in good company, there

sodainely rose so hard and cruell a storme, that those of the
island did affirme, that in man's memorie there was never
any such seen or heard of before : for it seemed the sea would
have swallowed up the islands, the water mounting higher
than the cliffes, which are so high that it amaseth a man to
beholde them ; but the sea reached above them, and living
fishes were thrown uppon the land. This storme continued
not only a day or two with one wind, but seauen or eight
dayes continually, the wind turning round about, in all
places of the compasse, at the least twice or thrice during
that time, and all alike, with a continuall storme and
tempest most terrible to behold, even to us that were on
shore, much more than to such as were at sea ; so that only
on the coastes and cliffes of the Island of Tercera, there
were above twelve ships cast away, and not only upon one
side, but round about it in every corner, whereby nothing
els was heard but complayning, crying, lamenting, and
telling here is a shippe broken in pieces against the cliffes,
and there another, and all the men drowned : so that for
the space of 20 dayes after the storme, they did nothing els
but fish for dead men, that continually came driving on the
shore.

"Among the rest was the English ship called the
'Reuenge,' that was cast away vpon a cliffe neare to the
iland of Tercera, where it broke in a hundred peeces, and
sunke to the ground, hauing in her 70 men Gallegos,
Biscaines, and others, with some of the captiue Englishmen,
whereof but one was saued, that got vp vpon the cliffes
aliue, and had his body and head wounded, and hee, being
on shore, brought vs the news, desiring to be shriuen, and,
therevpon, presently died. The 'Reuenge' had in her
diuers faire brasse peeces, that were all sunke in the sea,
which they of the iland were in good hope to waigh vp again."

"On the other ilandes the losse was no lesse then in
Tercera ; for on the iland of Saint George, there were two
shippes cast away ; on the iland of Pico, two shippes ; on the

Iland of Gratiosa, three shippes, and besides those there came euerie where round about diuers peeces of broken shippes, and other things fleeting towards the ilands, wherewith the sea was all couered most pittifull to behold. On the iland of S. Michaell, there where four shippes cast away, and betweene Tercera and S. Michael, three more were sunke, which were seene and heard to crie out, whereof not one man was saued. The rest put into sea without masts, all torne and rent; so that of the whole fleete and armado, being 140 ships in al, there were but 32 or 33 ariued in Spaine and Portingall, yea, and those few with so great miserie, paine, and labor, that not two of them ariued there together, but this day one, and to-morrow another, next day the third, and so on one after the other to ye number aforesaid."

The old hatred of the Spaniard caused these unfortunate islands (then garrisoned by the troops of Philip II.) to be on several occasions attacked and ravaged by some of Elizabeth's famous captains, and as we pass through Villa Franca, we are reminded of one of these descents, which took place in October, 1597, a few brief particulars of which from Purchas may be found interesting :—In the summer of the above mentioned year, a formidable fleet, consisting of no less than 120 sail, of which 60 were good men-of-war, the rest being transports, and having a field force on board of 6,000 men (besides sailors), with 10 pieces of artillery, had been quietly and secretly collected at Plymouth, and victualled for a four months' cruise. The object of the expedition was the capture of the most important of the Azores group, and especially of Terceira, and to place garrisons in this and some of the other strongholds of the archipelago.

The famous Robert Devereux, Earl of Essex, was commander-in-chief with Lord Thomas Howard, a son of the Duke of Norfolk, as his Vice-Admiral; his Rear-Admiral being Sir Walter Raleigh. The land force was commanded by Sir Charles Blunt, assisted by Lord Mountjoy, Sir Francis Vere, Sir George Carew, Sir F. Gorges, &c. Besides these the Earls of Rutland and Southampton, the Lords Audley, Gray, Rich, and Cromwell were noblemen employed in this service.

The fleet, which was divided into three squadrons, set sail from Plymouth on the 9th July, 1597, but had scarcely proceeded sixty leagues on the voyage, when it was overtaken by a terrible storm, lasting four days, which compelled it to put back into Plymouth much damaged. Disbanding all but 1,000 of his land forces, the Earl, with Lord Howard, and Sir Walter Raleigh, again set sail on the 17th August, and after cruising along the coast of Portugal, reached Flores, the most western of the Azores, on the 11th September. Here a council of war was held, at which it was decided to capture all the islands, the dispositions made being the following :—The Admiral and Rear-Admiral were to take Fayal. Lord Howard and Sir Francis Vere were to undertake Graciosa. Lord Mountjoy and Sir C. Blunt St. Michael's, whilst Terceira was to be reserved for the combined action of the fleet.

With this intent Sir Walter Raleigh arrived off Fayal on the 17th September with his squadron, but after waiting four days for Lord Essex, who never arrived, he proceeded to land with 460 men and 30 or 40 captains at a place four miles to the N.W. of Horta; the landing was feebly disputed, and the loss trifling, the troops marching at once upon the town, which surrendered without a fight. The island was now theirs, with the exception of two forts, which still held out, one of which was between the invaders and the town.

Sir Walter Raleigh very gallantly led his men to the foot of this fort, with no other weapon than his leading staff, and was soon shot " through the breeches and doublet sleeves in two or three places." Besides some who were hurt, two of his train had their heads shot off by cannon balls.

"It was a very fine fortification, all of stonework with curtains, flankers and ditch very artificially cast." It was soon abandoned by the 200 Spaniards who guarded it, and occupied by the invaders.

On the 22nd September the Earl arrived with his fleet, but being ambitious of gaining honours, highly censured Sir Walter, who had many enemies on board the Earl's ship, for what he had done, and threatened him with dismissal, but by the friendly intervention of Lord Howard, the Earl's displeasure was overcome.

Having carried away all the ordnance in the forts, the Earl embarked all his men, and on the 26th September sailed for Graciosa, where the chief men came off, proffering submission; from thence they proceeded to St. Michael's and anchored in the roads. Here a council was held on board Sir Walter's ship, at which it was decided to take the town and loot it, the Earl himself proceeding to search for a safe landing place. Sir Walter meanwhile lying as near the town itself as possible with his whole fleet, threatened it in a manner thus described by Sir A. Gorges: "We that were left under command of the Rear-Admiral in the best ships before the towne of Saint Michael's, did all the night give them perpetuall alarums, with shot, drummes, and trumpets, in such boats as were left, sometimes in one place, sometimes in another, alongst the shoare, where the Spaniards kept their *Corps de Guards* and fiers, who were often in great amazements, calling and running to and fro, thinking verily that we were landing in that place or about it."

During the night the Earl, accompanied by all his officers and 2,000 men, embarked in boats and pinnaces and landed at daybreak at Villa Franca without any resistance; most of the inhabitants abandoning the town on their approach. Here they found such abundance of fruit, wines, and victuals of all kinds, and such quantities of wood, wheat, and salt, that for six days they were busily engaged in conveying the latter on board ship. The Earl's intention was to have marched upon Ponta Delgada, which would have fallen an easy prey to the combined attack of the ships and troops, but rough weather setting in, the whole fleet, consisting of "four score sayle of good ships," was brought round to Villa Franca, and the troops embarked with considerable difficulty.

On the 9th October, 1597, the islanders were much rejoiced at seeing this formidable force set sail for England—no subsequent attempt having been made at molesting them.

Villa Franca is noted as the birth-place of Bento (or Benedict) de Goes, one of the greatest of mediæval travellers, and of whom Col. Youle, in his essay on the geography of the Valley of the Oxus,* thus writes :—" Goes was a truly noble character, and a man whose name would have occupied one of the highest places in the history of geography, had he survived to tell his story in a complete and intelligible shape."

Ritter was the first to draw the attention of the geographical world to the remarkable travels of Goes, and Dr. Caetano d'Andrade has done his countrymen good service by gathering together the particulars of this little-known journey, and publishing them in the " Archivo dos Açores " in a connected form. From this account, taken from the diary kept by Goes, we learn that the great traveller was born at Villa Franca, in 1562. At the age of 26 he was serving as a private soldier in the Portuguese forces garrisoning Goa. His religious tendencies, however, induced him, in 1588, to abandon the military service and join the Jesuit Fathers as a lay brother. Some time afterwards he accompanied a mission to the Emperor Akbar, at Lahore, and acquitted himself with remarkable skill before the Great Mogul in debate, and his defence of the Christian religion.

Some years subsequently, the General of the Indian Missions, recognising in Goes a man of no ordinary stamp, whose thorough knowledge of Persian fitted him for such

---

* See " Sources of the River Oxus," by Capt. John Wood.

an enterprise, determined upon sending him on a journey of exploration into the then mysterious Cathay, and to report upon its capabilities as a mission field. The route the explorer was to take was laid down by the famous St. Francis Xavier, and was to be from India through Eastern Turkestan to the frontiers of China.

Having secured the friendship of the Emperor Akbar, Goes, travelling in the guise of an Armenian merchant, and under the name of Abdullah Isai, finally started from Agra on the 2nd October, 1602, accompanied by two Greeks, a deacon named Leo, and a merchant named Demetrius, also by an Armenian named Isaac.

The expedition arrived at Lahore on the 8th of December following, where it joined the annual kafila or caravan for Kabul, numbering some 500 persons, besides an escort of 400 men, who joined them at Jelalabad by Akbar's orders. On the 15th February, 1603, they crossed the Indus near Attock, and proceeded *via* Peshawur, through the Khyber Pass to Jelalabad and Jigdilik, reaching Kabul at the end of six months time. Here the two Greeks refused to proceed further upon so perilous a journey, the cold having been very severe on the mountainous country of Hazara and the Himalayas, and the tribes in the Khyber causing much trouble and loss of life. Goes, however, continued on his way with the Armenian Isaac, and taking the direction of Charekar, crossed the Hindú Kush by the Parwán Pass and the village of Tangeran ; continuing to the north, until striking at Talikan the caravan route crossing the valley of the Oxus from west to east. Previous to reaching Talikan, Goes mentions the Galchas, remarkable for their light-coloured hair and blue eyes ; probably the same people similarly described by the Bhuddist missionary, Huentsan, in the seventh century, as inhabiting the Bolor range.

The exact route followed by the expedition from this point to Badakhshan is very obscure, but ultimately emerging at the gorge of Tangi-Badakhshan, after repulsing the repeated attacks of robber tribes, our travellers arrived at Charchounar, the Karchu of Ritter, from which in ten days they reached Serpanil; probably the Sir-Pamir or top of Pamir of the natives, supposed to have been visited by Marco Polo in 1277, by Wood in 1838, and by Sir Douglas Forsyth in 1874. Twenty days march from this place, the highest table-land in the world, brought the expedition to the mountainous province of Sarcil, remarkable at that time for the density of the population; thence, they reached, at the end of two days, the summit and pass of the Chichiklik range, where many members of the caravan died from the excessive cold, Goes himself narrowly escaping. Six days were here occupied in crossing the deep beds of snow before gaining the banks of the river Tangitar.

Continuing their journey through a most inhospitable region, they reached the city of Yakrik at the end of fifteen days, having lost so many beasts of burden as to compel Goes to proceed alone on a five day's journey to Yarkund, from whence he sent back to his companions supplies of animals and food; the caravan, a few days later (November, 1605) entering the city after ten months travel from Lahore.

Goes appears to have been well received by the Khan Mohammed Eddin, and remained in his capital a whole year.

He had the good fortune to meet in Kabul a sister of the Khan of Kashgar, who was returning from a pilgrimage to Mecca, and had been plundered of all she possessed by robber tribes on her way to Khotan; at her invitation, Goes visited the latter city, six days from Yarkund, where she received him very hospitably, presenting him with some of the famous jade from the neighbouring mines.

Leaving the capital of Kashgaria on the 14th November, 1604, the newly equipped caravan proceeded past Ilchi and the desert of Gobi to Aksu, and thence to Kucha, where they were detained a month, leaving again for Tchalis in the province of Karachar (Karakash?), which they reached after twenty-five days journey. Here Goes met a returning caravan from Cathay, and from its members obtained information which convinced him that Cathay was but another name for China. Some of the merchants of this caravan told him that in 1601 they had been in the capital of Cathay, where, during their three months stay, they had lived with Father Ricci and his companions. Goes knew that Ricci, the head of the Jesuit mission at Pekin, had preached Christianity in China ever since 1583, and delighted at the information obtained from these merchants, determined upon leaving the bulk of the caravan at Tchalis, and with a limited escort proceeded on his way, arriving at Kamul or Hami on the 17th October, 1605, where he was hospitably received and remained a month. It is here that the western caravans strike due south across the great desert which separates them from China; the track is infested by roving Tartars, and Goes mentions the road as strewn with skeletons of murdered travellers.

Nine days of almost continuous and most weary travelling, brought our hero to the threshold of his goal, the fortified town of Kia-yü-Kuan—for centuries the western gate of the desert. After the lapse of twenty-five days, permission was granted him by the governor of Chen-si to pass the Great Wall, and enter Chinese territory, one day's march bringing him to the city of Sou-tcheou, which he entered about the end of 1605, and was awarded quarters in the Mohammedan part of the town. His first thought was to send off a letter to Ricci at Pekin, which, however, never reached its destination. A second epistle, written in the spring of 1606, met with better fortune, but was only delivered in November of that year. Ricci had, however, heard of the approach of the adventurous Goes, and had dispatched one of his native converts to accompany him to Pekin; but delays prevented the guide from reaching Sou-tcheou before the end of March, 1607.

During this lengthened period Goes had been compelled by the authorities to confine himself to the Mohammedan quarter of the city, almost a prisoner, and this, combined with many privations and petty annoyances, so undermined his health, that in spite of the reassuring letters from Ricci, this remarkable man passed away on the 11th April, 1607, in his forty-fifth year, there appearing to be cause for suspicion of his having been poisoned by his Mohammedan companions from Yarkund, who at once commenced to plunder his baggage and destroy his diary, in order to efface the evidence of debts they were owing him. Fragments of this precious document were, however, saved at great personal risk by the faithful Isaac and the native guide; both of whom, after much delay and vexation, succeeded in leaving at the end of five months' time for Pekin, which they reached in safety and deposited the mutilated diary with Father Ricci, who, with the assistance of the Armenian Isaac, at once proceeded to fill up the missing gaps, preserving the narrative as we now have it.

From Pekin Isaac was sent by the Jesuit Fathers to Macao, whence he embarked for Malacca, ultimately reaching Bombay, where he resided for some years.

It is impossible to read the account of these extraordinary travels of Bento de Goes, and his untimely end, without a thrill of intense interest. No dangers or suffering, however great, were able to make this devoted man swerve for one moment from the path of duty.

In 1880, Dr. Caetano d'Andrade, who at that time represented Villa Franca in the Cortes, expressed the hope that a fitting monument should be erected in the town in memory of the man " who had immortalised his name, enlightened science, ennobled Portugal, and shed a ray of glory upon the corner of the earth where he was born"; but up to the present time this praiseworthy suggestion has not been carried out.

CHAPTER XIV.

> Farewell to the land where the clouds love to rest,
> Like the shroud of the dead, on the mountain's cold breast;
> To the cataracts' roar, where the eagles reply,
> And the lake her lone bosom expands to the sky.
> *Walter Scott.*

A MILE from Villa Franca, the land again becomes high, and reveals in superimposed layers, alternating in singular regularity, its basaltic, trachytic, and trachydoleritic formation, with here and there immense masses of tufa, mostly formed by ancient submarine eruptions. Overlying these again, are the thick mantles of ashes, pumice, and lava excretions from the more recent sub-aerial volcanoes, their sombre colours relieved by layers of that bright red granulated earth and volcanic product known as puzzolana. The excellent macadamised road runs at the foot of these cliffs, past a long sandy stretch called Praia, from whence the Count of that name derives his title. Much money was once expended upon the house and estate, but of late,

T

unhappily, both have been greatly neglected, and the place is little better than a ruin. In the grounds, watered by the Ribeira da Praia, which comes down from the Lagôa do Fogo, are some extremely fine dragon trees (*Dracæna draco*), brought over some 40 years ago by the late Viscount, from the Canary Islands, and which appear to thrive here equally well. Although easily raised from seed, this is said to be the slowest grower known, trees of 400 years old being barely a foot in circumference.

Humboldt estimated the great dragon tree in the valley of Orotava at 10,000 years old ! The sun, although invisible in other parts of the island, seems ever to shine here, and the hot and sultry climate, the sandy beach and soil around, gives the place so arid an appearance, as to make it resemble some corner of African desert transported here, in striking contrast with the surrounding fertility. Crossing a solid and picturesque stone bridge, spanning at a considerable height the Praia ravine, and affording a charming peep of the Serra d'Agua de Pao in the background, with its hill-tops wreathed in ever-changing mist, we next arrive at the old village of that name, prettily situated at the base of the hills, and inhabited by a race of people characterised in former days by many peculiarities. They are said to have originally belonged to the best blood of Portugal, and it is more than probable that their idiosyncrasies and naïve dialect are traceable to the exclusive habits and long-continued custom of intermarrying of this little community ; that they were brave was proved at the storming of Benahamad, when two brothers and their retainers, all natives of this place, voluntarily joining the troops in India, so distinguished themselves as to win high praise from the Viceroy, upon whose recommendation the king, D. Manoel, offered to confer the habit and cross of the military order of Christ upon the elder brother, but he, modestly declining the honour for himself, begged that it might be bestowed instead upon the "Nossa Senhora" of his village, who he said had protected him through so many dangers, which was accordingly done, and to this day N. S. dos Anjos, of Agua de Pao, may be seen décoré with the red ribbon of the order, and, like Bideford Bridge, is an esquire.

The economical propensities of these people are carried to an absurd extent; all natives of these islands of both sexes, of the working orders, go about bare-footed, except on Sundays and high days, when the better-to-do amongst them don boots and shoes. On such occasions as these, or when attending a distant procession or market, the people of Agua de Pao would put on one boot or shoe, carrying the other under their arm. A new coat, also, they would turn inside out, so wearing it until almost threadbare; if asked why they did so, the reply would be, " to save and preserve the article." These vagaries naturally brought upon them much chaff and ridicule, so that few are now seen practising them.

One of the most telling pleasantries directed at them by their more astute countrymen, was the apparently meaningless query " a porca ja furou o pico," the origin or meaning of which I could never discover, but probably possessing as much significance as the parallelogram so effectually hurled at the old lady of Lower Thames Street; they are, nevertheless, still very sensitive to the remark, and reply with the choicest Agua de Pao expletives, which would put to the rout the veriest of Billingsgate fish-fags. Some of the words they make use of are now quite obsolete in the language; and, altogether, these villagers are in many respects an interesting link between the past and the present.

The etymology of the word Agua de Pao is very obscure, but probably refers to some waterfall (of which there are several in the neighbouring hills), resembling at a distance the trunk of a tree, and for which the early settlers mistook it.

While passing through these island villages one cannot but remark upon their interminable length, their one street

being overcrowded with urchins of both sexes, in the most
paradisaical attire, who, with troops of sucking pigs, squirm
all over the place; but if we peer into their cottage recesses
we will observe, however poor their owners may be, the
gaudily decked out "presepios," or high altars, containing
under glass cases the favourite family Penates; these are
"Nossa Senoras," or "Meninos Jesus," generally made out
of worthless china dolls, gorgeously arrayed, and on whose
festival days high jinks occur.

From Agua de Pao, the road runs along the pretty and
sheltered valley of Caloura, named after the novitiate monks
of the Caloiro order, who had a monastery and broad acres
here—long since, like all the rest in the island, secularised.

This district was ever famous for the wine it produced;
and even now, notwithstanding the ravages of the oïdium
in other parts of the island, a very pleasant light wine, much
like Vin de Grave, is made in some quantity under the intelligent direction of Senhor Agostinho Machado, who has
paid much attention to viticulture. Indeed, the numerous
rocky or biscouto slopes and depressions from Villa Franca
to Ponta Delgada, were formerly rich wine districts.

Two miles beyond is the considerable village of Alagôa,
or Lagôa, having a population, including its outlying districts, of 10,764, and situated in one of the most fertile
parts in the island, where cereals and oranges are cultivated in large quantities. In the middle of the fifteenth
century a number of Capuchin monks took up their
residence here in a large monastery, now occupied by public
officers. It now possesses a spirit distillery on an important
scale, which cost £15,000 to set up. The initiative in its erection was taken by the enterprising firm of Bensaude & Co.,
and the establishment gives employment to a good many
villagers, returning an excellent per centage upon the
capital invested—so much so, that a rival still quite as
large has been set up at a place called Santa Clara, on the
outskirts of the city. The articles used for distillation are

maize and other cereals, also the sweet potato, of which latter large quantities are now cultivated for the purpose; the windfalls from the orange trees too, which were next to valueless and formed an unimportant portion of the yearly crop, are now purchased for the distillery at the rate of 600 reis per large box, or about 2s. 2d. per 1,000.

This distillery produced, in 1883, 31,123 gallons of spirits, on which a duty was paid of £864—the whole of it being shipped to Lisbon.

A drive of three-quarters of an hour from Alagôa brings us to the city, and it is along this strip of coast line that most of the pine-apple houses are to be seen, the warm and sheltered situation favouring the cultivation of this fruit.

A visit to Pico da Pedra, a mountain 1,260 feet high, and easily reached from this point, affords the unique spectacle of a perpendicular cavity on its northern flank, 140 feet long, and 110 feet broad, supposed to have been formed by the sinking of the crust into an immense "blister" after the cooling of the lava.

At the suburb of Calhetas is the huge new jail, apparently large enough to lock up the whole of the inhabitants of Ponta Delgada, and a standing libel upon the statistics of crime; for, to their credit, the islandry send but few tenants to occupy its well ventilated and proportioned wards.

By its side is a small bay, celebrated for the sickening sight which every now and then it presents, schools of the common dolphin (*Delphinus delphis*), called by the natives "bôdos," and numbering from 50 to 200, and in size averaging from six to eight feet in length, very frequently allow themselves to be driven like a flock of sheep by fishermen in boats from distances of two or three miles out, into this or other adjoining bays, where they are slaughtered with long knives, by men who dash into the water and swim after them, attacking the bewildered fish in their own element, or harpooning them from the surrounding rocks, their warm blood spurting in incredible quantities, and dyeing the sea for a quarter of a mile around. On such occasions, men, women and children crowd the shore, almost as delirious with excitement as the savage Spaniards at a bull fight. It is impossible to depict the horrors of such a scene. There cannot be a question of its inhumanity and brutalizing effect, and the Camara would show its enlightenment by compelling the slaughter of these bôdos by other means—perhaps, detonation—or, at any rate, in less frequented localities.

The flesh of this fish is melted down for oil, and must be remunerative, for a speculator gave £50 (just as they were) for 111, which I once saw driven into this bay; not a bad afternoon's work for the dozen fishermen engaged.

The dolphin has an elongated snout with two rows of beautifully shaped conical teeth, too regular to appear formidable, and which they have never been known to attack with. When harpooned in the open, the dolphin never, like the whale, dives to the bottom, but swims with astonishing rapidity on the surface of the water, and in a very short time will carry in tow a large fishing boat with three or four men in it almost out of sight, until loss of blood ends its agony. The creature's tongue is much esteemed here, and the flesh even is sometimes eaten. They cause immense destruction to the sardinha, pilchard, and mackerel tribes, and on that account meet with little mercy at the hands of the fishermen. The neighbourhood of these islands is a favourite resort of the spermaceti whale (*Physeter macrocephalus*), many American ships plying about in search of the huge cetacea, as far as the feeding banks near the west coast of Ireland, and midway between the Açores and America. There are depôts at S. Miguel and Fayal, where some of these vessels often land during the short whaling season as many as 250 barrels of sperm oil; but, with few exceptions, the islanders do not engage in this industry, although many ship as sailors on board the American vessels and are much sought after by the masters for their daring in pursuit of the fish, as well as for their quiet behaviour on board.

It is this cachalot that produces ambergris (so much valued in perfumery), a substance supposed to be a biliary calculus found in the intestines of the whale. A good deal of it is now and then brought to these islands, but at once bought up for the American market. As many as 150 sperm whales are said to be caught off the islands in the year. Occasionally the Greenland whale (*Balæna mysticetus*) is seen here, but not often. The bottle-nose whale, however (*Hyperoodon*), is common in these seas.

In the season of love desperate battles oftentimes take place between male sperm whales. I myself, many years ago, witnessed for a length of time and with the aid of a powerful telescope, such an encounter, far out to the S.E. of S. Miguel; and it is a fact that the bodies of captured whales often show deep and ugly tooth-scars, which whalers attribute to fights for supremacy.

Perhaps nothing is calculated to impress a person on landing at Ponta Delgada, fresh from the traffic-congested and bustling streets of London, that "busiest hum of men," than the quiet serenity of the apparently deserted city; the noiseless tread of a large proportion of the bare-footed population contributing much to this, until a rapidly-driven carriage (for these "bolecîros" are perfect Jehus) comes tearing along over the large cobble stones with which the streets are paved, making a noise as of a thousand chariots.

Outside the precincts of the town, a relic of the past may occasionally be seen, and more often heard, in the rough country carts, probably introduced and used in Portugal by the Romans. They consist of a solid flat frame-work of strong wood with ponderous pole, all in one; the lynch-pin, also of wood, being not too firmly wedged and fixed into the centre of the two equally solid wheels, almost as solid and heavy as the stone discs still used in the Central Provinces of India, and revolving with them, makes, in so doing, an indescribably creaking noise, heard far and wide. These Luso-Romano carts are always drawn by two or more oxen yoked by means of a heavy wooden frame, and they are said to like the " singing " noise of the vehicle. Round the floor of the cart are placed uprights which support a wattled structure holding the contents, and in these receptacles heavy loads of grain and produce of all kinds are carried. No less remarkable are the immense ox-goads, or aguilhadas, used by the drivers.

As there are no springs to break, these cheap and easily-constructed carts were most serviceable in a broken country, where the roads were once execrable ; but, with recent improvements in this respect, these lumbering conveyances are rapidly giving way to a very light and serviceable mule cart, now to be everywhere seen. The charmingly executed etching of an " imperio " contains a good illustration of one of these ancient vehicles, and the usages they were sometimes put to.

Carriages, both open and closed, are plentiful in Ponta Delgada, and on moderate hire. Most of these are now made in the island, the springs only being imported from Lisbon and France ; for the import duties on carriages of any description are enormous.

Now and again and generally in out of the way places, the old-fashioned sége is seen—another relic of a bye-gone age ; a compromise between a modern hansom-cab, and an ancient Sedan chair. Swung high on two wheels, and drawn by a pair of horses, postillion fashion, the sége had heavy leather curtains in front, completely shutting off the occupants from view, when closely drawn. An old friend of mine, who resided here some 40 years ago, never tired of relating an amusing little anecdote which befell himself, and which illustrates the customs of that time and the vast social advances which have since been made. A lady and her daughter were suddenly met by my friend riding in one of these carriages, when the latter catching sight of the stranger, hastily exclaimed, " Oh minha mãe, minha mãe, aqui vem um homem!" ("Oh, mother, mother, here comes a man!")—when bang went the curtains, to the utter bewilderment of the unconscious intruder; but *tempora mutantur*, and the charming young island ladies of to-day no longer treat the men as if they were *feræ naturæ*.

Victorias are much in vogue, and if only the Government would lower the present prohibitive duties, many private families would import more of these elegant carriages.

No traveller in any part of Portugal can fail at some time or other to meet "Nosso Senhor," as the Host or last sacrament to some moribund wretch is called. The priest, arrayed in a gorgeous chasuble, preceded by a white-frocked acolyte, ringing in slow time a peculiarly toned bell, to announce the dread approach of the santissimo, walks under a canopy of red damask, held over him by four supporters, and in his hand bears a silver vessel containing the sacred emblem of consolation; by his side walk one or more acolytes carrying censers, also a number of choristers in white surplices; and, filing along on either side of the road for some distance, walk members of some irmandade in scarlet stoles, each holding a long wax candle; thus the procession proceeds slowly, chanting in measured time, and at intervals, a dirge-like hymn.

The villagers, when apprised of the passing of the Host, generally strew the ground with aromatic leaves and scented flowers, that they may

> Return the sweets by nature given
> In softest incense back to heaven.

All turn out and reverentially kneel and repeat their "Ave Marias" as the procession passes.

If anything were calculated to frighten a dying man into eternity, I can imagine nothing more effective than this slowly approaching visitation, seeming to announce from afar his coming dissolution.

During Lent, groups of from thirty to eighty men join in a romaria, called " visitar ou correr as casinhas de Nossa Senhora," and visit all the chapels and churches dedicated to the Virgin throughout the island. They travel on foot, with handkerchiefs tied round their heads, slowly intoning " Ave Marias," each group electing a chief, who directs the ceremonials of the visits.

Of all people I have come in contact with, these poor island peasantry are the most innately religious. Would that they had more conscientious instructors! A time-honored custom exists here during the three days of the " Intrudo " or carnival, so gaily celebrated on Sunday, Monday and Shrove Tuesday, of squirting water from windows and verandahs on to all passers by, by means of india-rubber syringes, many of which are most artistically got up, and generally have silver spouts. The plan adopted is this : the fair inamorata finds means of letting her Adonis know that she and some chosen friends will repair at such and such a time to the house of kind-hearted senhora so and so, who, regardless of broken windows and spoilt furniture, but mindful of her own youthful days, allows her young friends to run riot for the nonce. Hither, monsieur and his companions, arrayed in top boots and waterproofs, proceed to accept the challenge, and with half-a-dozen boys holding trays full of bright-coloured wax limas (so called from their resemblance in shape to the lime), filled with water, return the ladies' showers, by hurling at them these water-laden missiles, which, breaking at the slightest impact, saturate anything they touch. When the weather is fine, and the combatants on both sides numerous, the fun runs high. On these three days many hospitable houses are thrown open, and large numbers of the hosts' friends and acquaintances drop in *incognito* during the evening; thus going from house to house, all wearing masks or dominoes, and all joining in the dancing going on. These meetings and balls are invariably well and decorously conducted, and most enjoyable from the absence of the usual constraint.

A relic of this curious custom of throwing water on passers-by is, I believe, still preserved at Howden, in Yorkshire, for on the day preceding Ash Wednesday, the fire engines of the town are drawn round to the different public pumps and everyone passing within range is well wetted. After some time spent in this fun, a holiday is made of the day by the inhabitants.*

The costumes of the peasantry of the Açores, although less graceful and calculated to set off the figure than some of those of the provinces of Portugal, are nevertheless characteristic, and some exceedingly peculiar. The dress of a well-to-do St. Michael's farmer consists of coarse island-spun stuff, the trousers hempen and mostly white, the short "Eton" jacket, either blue or black, sometimes profusely semé with buttons; all splendour, however, being concentrated in the waiscoat, which is generally of some bright imported material, the shirt front being elaborately embroidered.

His head-covering is the singular carapuça, unique in its extravagant design, yet not altogether devoid of utility, for its immense frontal brim of half a foot in depth, terminating in crescent shaped cusps, shades the face and even chest from the sun; from the close-fitting body of the hat (devoid at the back of any brim) falls a cape-like covering of fine cloth, effectually protecting the wearer's neck and shoulders from wet, advantages which may possibly compensate for its great weight. The origin of the "carapuça" has ever been a mystery, and for some time its singular name conveyed but an abstract idea to my mind, until dim memories of half forgotton lessons in zoology returned, and

---

* The Hindús throw a farinaceous powder, dyed red, called "gulál," on each other during the "Holí," the great festival held at the approach of the Vernal Equinox.

referring to the friendly and well-thumbed glossary, the following word occurred—"carapace"—a protective shield of crab, lobster, and many other crustacea.   It would really

ST. MICHAEL'S PEASANT AND CARAPUÇA.

seem as if some wag of the sixteenth century had coined the word carapuça, to spite and poke fun at those who used so hideous a covering.

It is singular how, in the size and form of their carapuças, the people of the various, and particularly remoter villages in

St. Michael preserve a species of ethnographical distinction, which extends to the entire group, the carapuças, especially of St. Michael, Terceira, and Madeira, differing so entirely as if they belonged to different planets, and a very interest-

WOMEN IN "CAPOTE E CAPELLO."

ing and good-sized volume might be written upon the strangely varying headgears of the inhabitants, both male and female, of this archipelago, the only exception being Graciosa, the inhabitants of which use a straw or felt hat or a cap.

The capote and capello of the women also differ in every island, according to the taste and caprice of their respective inhabitants. The capote is an ample cloak reaching to the feet, and made of dark blue cloth—infinitely too hot for such a climate as this, except on a cold wintry day. Surmounting this is a ponderous hood, the " capello," of the same material, kept expanded by means of whale-bone, and in which the head is completely lost. These capotes, being of a dark color, give the streets of the town a sombre and " subfusc " appearance whenever a large gathering of the better-to-do lower class takes place. A much more pleasing effect is created by the mixing together of the poorer people or country women, who, from poverty, affect a simpler, but brighter dress, and yet their great ambition is to possess a " capote e capello".

I took some pains to find out the origin of these singular head-dresses, but was unable to arrive at any satisfactory solution of the subject in the islands themselves, the universal answer to inquiries being that it " has been the custom to wear the capello and carapuça from time immemorial "; and as in no other part of Portugal are they worn, or even known, we must seek elsewhere for an explanation, and may possibly find it in the pages of Planché.

At the time when a good many of these islands were peopled by Flemings, it was the fashion in Flanders for ladies to don the towering fabric known as the " hennin," in shape very similar to that of the capello of St. Michael, though made of a light gauze-like material. Modifications of this appeared in Paris about 1429, and, amongst others, the " escoffion cornu," or horned head-dress, which much resembles the island carapuça.

Viollet-le-Duc thus describes the escoffions worn in l'Ile de France, 1415 :—

" Ils se composaient d'une coiffe de mousseline empresée formant couvre-nuque et venant joindre ses pans saillants et roides au sammet du front. Sur cette sorte d'auvent, qui donnait des reflets très doux et clairs à la peau, se posaient les cornes assez semblables a deux valves d'une coquillage ouvrant. Ces cornes étaient plus ou moins richement ornées de broderies, de passementeries, de pierres et de perles. De l'intervalle qu'elles laissaient entre elles, s'échappaient, en gros bouillons, un voile de gaze ou d'étoffe très légère et transparente."

It seems strange that a fashion which would appear to have been a purely feminine one in Flanders and France, should have become modified and adopted in the shape of the carapuça by the hardy Azorean peasant, and, more remarkable still, that in St. Michael's, the very island in the whole group where no Flemish blood mingles with its population, the fashion should have been carried to a really ridiculous extreme, the cusps attaining true " longicorn " proportions.

At St. Giles' church, near Torrington, Devon, is still to be seen a brass memorial to the memory of "Alyanora Pollard," dated 1430, with an example of a horned head-dress.

Like the peasantry of France, these islanders are industrious and thrifty; in the ordinary way, labourers earn 10d. a day, and, during harvest-time, as much as 1s. 8d. to 2s. 2d.; women and strong lads earning 5d. per day. In some country places wages are still paid in kind—generall about a gallon of maize per man per day. Contracts fo labour in kind are also not infrequent; for instance, separating the maize from the cob, for the sake of the latter, for purposes of fuel, &c.; beating out the lupin seed for the straw ; making a wicker basket or hamper for the quantity of maize it will hold. This last expression recalling the old Arabic law, which condemned the slayer of a camel to pay a fine amounting to the quantity of wheat necessary to cover the carcase.

The Azorean peasant is a prodigious bread-eater; indeed, he carries out the old adage, "Tudo compão faz o homem são." On rising at day-break, he at once sets about preparing the "açorda d'azêdo," by mixing onion, garlic, vinegar, lard, and a pinch of saffron, all boiled in sufficient water to moisten the half of a maize loaf. About 8 o'clock he partakes of a second breakfast at the spot where he may be at work, consisting of a bit of salt fish, washed down by spring water; at noon he again eats his salt fish and bread, and on returning home in the evening he takes "en famille," the last meal, consisting of bread and chopped greens, the whole boiled with lard, salt and red peppers. At these meals a strong man eats a loaf and a half of maize bread a day, made from two kilos of flour; his wife's first occupation of a morning being to grind sufficient grain for the day's consumption.

A very pleasant way of eating the maize is in the form of bôlo, or bôlo da sertā, especially when hot for breakfast. Instead of being baked in the oven, the dough is made into a disc, the size required, and rather less than an inch thick, and slowly toasted over the fire in an earthenware sertā, a round sort of frying-pan, used also for roasting coffee, &c.

The islanders are not so superstitious as their kinsmen in Portugal, but they believe in "feiticeiras," or witches. Nearly all young cattle and colts have a pouch fastened round their necks, containing various ingredients calculated to drive away evil spirits from them, and if you look carefully behind the door of cottages and dwelling houses, you will often see the form of the cross made by plastering on the gum of tragacanth, to prevent the "arch fiend" from establishing a footing therein, the device so successfully adopted by Faust in the play, by means of the pentagram sign. Mushrooms are here discarded, and looked upon as the "paõ do diabo," or devil's bread.

A very curious belief exists that the fern, known here as "feito de S. Joaõ" (*Osmunda regalis*) produces a very beautiful flower on the night of the festival of St. John, which, however, no one has ever been fortunate enough to see, but which would assuredly bring unheard of wealth to the person finding it. A priest, they say, robed as if to perform mass, would be the most likely one to come across this floral treasure, if he were to proceed at midnight to the spot where these ferns grow ; this belief is also common in Portugal.

The popular treatment of certain ailments is oftentimes suggestive of the African's fetich practices. To cure erysipelas, a black puppy dog is bled, or blood is drawn from the comb of a black hen, and when mixed with the pulp of abobora (pumpkin), is laid on the affected part; the remainder is then hung up in the chimney, and never again noticed. To cure varicose veins in the leg, the pulp of the abobora is laid on, and then thrown to a pig, the flesh of which must not be eaten by the person treated ; they have other most singular nostrums for diseases they cannot understand.

The peasantry firmly believe that the last twelve days of December are the faithful forecast of the twelve months of the ensuing year, and that the events of the new year will be regulated by the way the wheat maize and beans shall germinate. These, at Christmas time, they place in dishes of water for that purpose; should the prognostic be unfavourable, they go about their field-work in a half-hearted way, and without faith in the future year.

Although the peasantry possess surnames, they rarely, if ever, make use of them, preferring "alcunhas," or pseudonyms, which they are passionately fond of bestowing, and which have been known in course of time to altogether supersede the inherited patronymics, until the latter are completely lost. On the western side of the island, and more especially at Bretanha, a very singular custom exists of giving the sons, as surnames, the Christian name of the mother ; thus, there are many men there whose only names are Antonio Claudina, João Carlota, Manoel Jacinta, &c., &c. This peculiarity was first observed by Snr. Arruda Furtado, who says it is confined to

v

this part of the island. Perhaps in no country in Europe could such singular names be met with as in Portugal; one of the late port captains of Ponta Delgada, had as his surname, merely the letter O', and in the rua da Lapa, in Lisbon, there is a business firm established under the title of Espirito Santo & Co. (Holy Ghost & Co.), the principal having no doubt received the baptismal name of Espirito Santo. Another one trades under the name of Christo & Irmão. Numerous singular instances of the kind could be adduced.

The utmost importance is attached by the peasantry to the spiritual office of " compadre " and " madrinha "— God-father and God-mother, and if brothers and sisters act in this capacity, the appellation of " brother " and " sister " ceases from that moment, and they address each other as " compadre " or " madrinha," and however much two God-fathers may hate one another, they invariably raise their hats when passing each other's dwellings, saying—" Deus salve a casa do meu compadre ! "

The women of these islands are extremely clever at all kinds of ornamental needle-work, and excel in beautiful embroidery and lace in all conceivable designs, which their poverty compels them to sell at what appear to be absurdly low prices, thus enabling people to indulge in the most princely pillow-cases, toilet covers, and even towels, bordered in deep, elegant work.

The Azorean lavadeira, or laundress, is the cleverest of all her troublesome kind, and has achieved the secret of sending linen home as white as it is possible to get it; in this she is greatly assisted by a usually bright, hot sun, but chiefly by the " barella " process.

Linen to be washed is put into the large open wicker basket of the country, and a thick wood-ash lye spread over it, then boiling water is every now and then poured over this, and allowed to percolate slowly through ; after a sufficient soaking, the things are taken out and thoroughly washed in running water, and although violently beaten and rolled against the abraded surface of large stones, the destruction is less than the boiling process of our laundress tribe at home, and the alkaloid properties of the barella lye, infinitely more effectual.

The disadvantage of long residence in isolated islands like these, is the mental atrophy into which the people are liable to lapse, in the absence of some deterrent stimulus. This we ourselves observe nearer home in the Channel Islands. Here, however, if only to judge from the perpetual warfare carried on in the newspapers, which the frequent changes of Government and elections assist, wits appear sharp enough; indeed, it would be difficult to find in a limited community like this, the young generation of both sexes so well educated and talented.

Many of the leading Portuguese statesmen, poets and writers, have been furnished by the islands (and especially St. Michael's), and amongst them in our own day may be mentioned the late Duke of Avila, Dr. Philomeno de Mello da Camara Cabral, Antero do Quintal and his brother, Pedro, Theophilo Braga, Dr. Ernesto Rodolpho Hintz Ribeiro, Dr. Caetano d'Andrade Albuquerque, Dr. Ernesto do Canto, Snr. José do Canto, and many others I could name, who would be men of mark in any country. Neither are they behind-hand in musical genius, both vocal and instrumental, as witness the first-class amateur concerts held at the theatre whenever some charitable purpose calls for support. The charming illustrations in this book by my friend, the Baron das Laranjeiras, speak eloquently of the self-taught talent there exhibited, and there are innumerable other instances of marked intelligence and culture, which, considering the remote position of the islands, are as creditable as they are surprising.

The pernicious custom of frequent intermarrying of relations is very prevalent in Portugal, and particularly in these islands, leading to lamentable results. 550 B.C. the Greek poet, Theognis, warned his countrymen of the physical and moral degeneracy attending this practice, in the following noble lines :—

> With kins, and horses, Kurnus! we proceed
> By reasonable rules, and choose a breed
> For profit and increase, at any price ;
> Of a sound stock without defect or vice.
> But, in the daily matches that we make,
> The price is everything: for money's sake,
> Men marry : women are in marriage given ;
> The churl or ruffian, that in wealth has thriven,
> May match his offspring with the proudest race:
> Thus everything is mix'd, noble and base!
> If then in outward manner, form, and mind,
> You find us a degraded, motley kind,
> Wonder no more, my friend! the cause is plain,
> And to lament the consequence is vain.*

The Kalmucks have a wholesome horror of close inter-marriages, one of their best remembered proverbs being that "The great folk and dogs know no relationship." The Circassians and the Samoyeds of Siberia adhere strictly to this rule, with results beneficial to the physique of their hordes.

One of the axioms laid down by Confucius, and inculcated from time immemorial upon the mind of young China, is that ceremonies amongst nations are the symbols of virtue; if there be any truth in this assertion, the Portuguese must be the most model people in the world, for in this respect they are devoted disciples of the great Chinese philosopher.

Lord Carnarvon's high tribute to Portuguese politeness, as he found it in the upper and aristocratic classes in 1827, is still true in many respects in the present day. "If," said he, "I could divest myself of every national partiality, and suppose myself an inhabitant of the other hemisphere, travelling solely for my amusement, noting men and manners, and were asked in what country society

---

* "The Works of F. Hookham Frere," vol. II., p. 334.

had attained its most polished form, I should say in Portugal."

Probably no nation in Europe excels them in politeness and good breeding, an attribute traced to the influence of the Moors, the most chivalrous of people, who conquered and held Portugal for four centuries. They are great sticklers for etiquette; every lady in this country, of whatever rank, expects to be addressed as " excellency "; men too, if of the better class, and of slight acquaintance, vie as to who shall out-excellency the other. Thus is a distinction said to have been first used in the time of Constantine, and to have been addressed only to princes distinguished in war, now applied in Portugal to almost all classes. Outside this polite society, the less exalted " vossa senhoria " is used, more especially, by servants and menials to their masters and betters; these latter, addressing the former as " vossa mercê," or its contraction "vossê," and more often by the familiar "tu." The absurdity of some of these forms are however better exemplified in the superscription of letters, which take the style of " Illustrissimo e Excellentissimo Senhor Fulano de Tal," an address once given only to kings.

Some fashions still prevail here amongst the men, which at first sight appear to us strange. On gala days, a most funereal suit, made of black cassimere or doe-skin, is considered the " chic " thing to wear, and when a man " pops the question," he goes in a carriage and pair, arrayed in dress clothes, to formally interview and obtain the sanction of the lady's parents; he is also married in the same costume; for, here, as in the centres of civilization, some men seem to think with Teufelsdröckh, but in a manner peculiarly their own, that clothes give them— " individuality, distinction, and social polity."

It is customary for gentlemen to enter a reception room with both gloves on, it being considered a breach of etiquette on these occasions to extend the ungloved hand to the host, in happy forgetfulness that the most civilised sovereigns in Europe, and consequently their subjects, expect and require all who approach them, even the fair ones, to respect this piece of decorum.

À propos of gloves, Chateaubriand gives a *bon mot* of Charles the Tenth. As a " chevalier of the orders " the count assisted at the coronation at Rheims, when " Charles having some difficulty in removing his gloves to take my hands, said, smiling, in answer to my gentle remonstrance, ' Chat ganté ne prend point de souris ' "—(the gloved cat catches no mice).

A curious habit obtains in Portugal, both amongst men and women, of allowing the nail of the little finger, and very often the thumb, to grow to a prodigeous length, as a proof that they are removed above the necessity of manual labor ; this is distinctly a relic of barbarism, and only worthy of preservation amongst Tapuyas, Brazilians, and Chinamen. In Deut. xxi., 13, occurs an early instance of a woman paring her nails, as a sign of servitude. A Portuguese aphorism has laid it down that a woman should, during her life-time, only leave home three times—to be christened, married, and buried; and the native ladies would appear to follow out this precept in a great measure, for they are seldom seen abroad, and when they are, it is generally under escort of their mothers or other discreet relatives. Some of the more enlightened families, however, following the example set by the English, are gradually breaking through these old-fashioned notions, and may be seen proudly defying the ogling centres outside the gossiping " boticas."

No peculiarity of the Portuguese has been more criticised by foreigners than their habit of seclusion, and the rare occurrence of a stranger being entertained at their houses. Such a thing as a dinner party, except in the case of men dining together, at some hotel or restaurant, in celebration of some event, is quite unknown ; not that these people are misanthropes, for they enjoy their club-life and quiet serões (family kettle-drums), at each others' houses, but they dread criticism in what they conceive to be their weak point. The social habit of dinner parties has as yet barely taken root in Portugal, and then only in the limited upper strata of society.

They seem to have thoroughly taken to heart Talleyrand's warning to his young countryman, who declined to play cards; this amusement, accompanied by rather heavy stakes, generally occupying their evenings, until they "game away the sun before it rises." Gambling, in its true sense, however, is a thing of the past here.

When paying money to an islander, nothing will induce him to count it in your presence, but he goes away apparently satisfied that the amount is exact; soon, however, you hear him in your saguaõ, conning over the dollars, serilhas, and vintens, one by one, and should any of these be found wanting, up he comes again vociferating wildly until satisfied —a singular contrast of dignity and the converse.

The Portuguese gentleman, however poor, is proud as Artabanes, and cannot brook the criticism of a stranger on his weaknesses—hence his reluctance to entertain him.

An amusing illustration of this shrinking of the islanders from intercourse with foreigners was afforded during one of my visits to the island, by the arrival in the harbour of a beautiful yacht, with her owner, the Marquis of A— on board. His Lordship was said to possess less pluralities, but double the income of the King of Portugal; consequently none of the native gentlemen had the courage to show him the slightest civility.

The health officer, who had put off early in the morning to give the yacht pratique, arrived alongside during the process of deck-washing and surprised the Marquis on his way to his matutinal tub, and coolly standing barefooted on deck. The circumstance was at once reported as a nine days' wonder, and accepted as another proof that all Englishmen are eccentric.

The want of attention in this instance did not, however, proceed from ill nature or selfishness, but from a shyness and diffidence at contact with so great a personage, and fear of any shortcomings in the attention offered.

Sir Thomas and Lady Brassey on their recent visit to the island in the " Sunbeam" would have fared equally badly had not one or two of the foreign residents, and the courtly Conde da S—a come to their rescue ; to their credit, however, be it said, that if applied to, the native gentlemen instantly throw their houses and grounds open to the stranger, and offer such profuse kindness and attention as to make his experience memorable.

A very ancient Portuguese custom is to exclaim, "Viva!" or " Dominus tecum ! " (God be with you!) upon a person sneezing. In Ireland, on similar occasions, the practice still exists of saying, "God bless you." It was common among the Romans, and is said to refer to a plague of olden days, which commenced by violent sneezing.

Such eastern customs as clapping hands when calling at a house, in the absence of a bell, and the servants saluting you with a " Muito boas noites" on bringing in the lights of an evening, are still kept up. In the streets, too, the singularly shrill " Pish ! " used by rich and poor alike, when calling after anyone, is heard at every step, certainly a mode of attracting attention requiring less effort, and pene-trating further than our blunt hallooing.

Time was (during the reigns of Dom Dinis and Dom Affonso V.), when to be engaged in commercial pursuits was, as regards the fidalgos or upper ten, considered not only a disgrace but a crime, punishable by severe penalities, indeed, the nobles were not allowed to tarry in commercial cities longer then three days; now, however, scarcely a single nobleman in Portugal exists who is not more or less connected with mercantile pursuits, and if there be money to be made, it is not even considered *infra dig.* for anyone of these to keep a retail shop. Thus, the tradesman of Ponta Delgada, unlike the generality of his countrymen, is a very " sleuth hound " in the pursuit of gain, and is very

often a superior personage. Tempted by the abolition of
entail, which gave him some little capital, the younger son
of a respectable family will now often embark in trade,
displaying no little skill and acumen in his transactions.
Unfortunately the scope presented to him here is limited to
a degree, and the orange business, into which he is likely,
sooner or later, to be drawn, has, hitherto, only proved a
snare and a delusion, and a good deal of his small patrimony
has been hopelessly sunk in these unfortunate fruit speculations. Indeed, were accounts to be strictly investigated,
a good deal of money would be found to be owing to
merchants in London, for although, unlike that preux-
chevalier, their great countryman, Dom João de Castro, who
was able to raise a loan of 20,000 pardaõs from the traders
of Goa, upon the simple security of his whiskers, an opera-
ation only excelled in its facility by that of the ancient
Gauls, who readily lent money upon the understanding that
it was to be repaid in the next world, or the eagerness
with which " General " Booth's followers accept his offer of
"five per cent. in this world, and ninety-five in the world to
come," still, our island friends have had too many facilities
given them for embarking in this ruinous business, and their
debts will probably have to be paid in the same manner as
those of the ancient Gallic money-lender, or the apostle of
the Salvationists.

It is probably owing to this respectability of their
owners, that some few shops in Ponta Delgada, like the
Casa Havaneza of the Lisbon Chiado, are regularly resorted
to by swell loafers, who meet there as at a club, to hear the
last *verba novissima*, or to abuse the Government.

When thus congregated, a lady, whether native or foreign,
would need to be imbued with no small amount of courage
to run the gauntlet of these clustering, ogling, and criticising
beaux, and if an English or American lady chance to pass by,
observations scarcely complimentary to her feet, which
these facetious exquisites are pleased to compare to ' ferros

d'ingomar' (box irons), would in all probability be made.
The Portuguese frankly admit that our countrywomen carry
off the palm for facial superiority, but, such is their perversity, nothing will induce them to recognise the fact,
allowed by the whole of Europe, that of all women in the
world, the high-bred English lady also possesses the smallest
and prettiest foot compatible with its natural use.

The Portuguese are rabid politicians. In Lisbon there are
no less than eighteen papers published every day of different
political shades—"Regeneradores, Progressistas, Indepen-
dentes, Republicanos, Miguelistas, Dissidentes," etc., besides
fifty-five weeklies, fortnightlies, and monthlies, all greedily
devoured. Ponta Delgada follows suit with thirteen dailies
and monthlies, all written in "high falutin" style.

> Here, as elsewhere they find
> 'Tis sweet your foe to aggravate,
> With epigrams that defamate.

When the mail steamers come in, a little fleet of boats is
observed to put off, each with a dark visaged, mysterious-
looking individual, who, regardless of the manifold duties he
has to perform, button-holes the unlucky captain for information as to the latest decree or act of tyranny of the
Government. Solitary men are seen in retired nooks,
savagely perusing the *Journal de Noticias*. Presently, the
wealth of the language is expended in virulent abuse of the
said Government, and of everyone else not of their party,
for perfect liberty of the Press not only exists here and
throughout Portugal, but is oftentimes abused, and the
tomahawk is ever held aloft; the wonder is, that in a small
community like this, the respective editors, ever crossing each
others' path, in more senses than the literal, and meeting
round friendly corners, should be able to keep the peace,
when their political keynote is ever " guerra al cuchillo."

Until quite recently, banking establishments were here
unknown; the only means of keeping money—which gene-
ally consisted of the formidable Spanish pillar, or old

Brazilian dollar—being in cellars dug out for the purpose, or strong rooms carefully propped and strengthened, for it was no uncommon occurrence for an accretion of many thousands of pounds sterling worth of silver to be found in such places after some old Crœsus had gone over to the majority. Some few years back, however, a perfect mania for banks seized the commercial centres in Portugal, and at the present time there are no less than six or seven branches, or agencies, of Lisbon banks in Ponta Delgada. The chief of these are the Banco Lisbôa e Açores (agents, Ben Saude & Co.); Banco de Portugal (agent, Francisco Xavier Pinto); Banco Lusitano (agent, Clemente Joaquim da Costa); Banco Nacional Insulano (agents, Tavares and Irmão); Companhia Geral de Credito Hypothecario; Companhia Geral Agricola e Financeira and Banco Ultramarino (agent, Antonio José Machado)—at any of which cheques and bills on London can be negotiated, or current accounts opened, and at some of them the luxury of a cheque book may be enjoyed.

The island currency is rather puzzling to strangers who have made themselves familiar with the intricacies of the Lisbon coinage, for there a sovereign costs 4$500, whereas here, you have to pay 5$625 for it, a difference of 25 per cent.; in other words, island money is worth a quarter less than that of Lisbon; the former is called "dinheiro fraco," and the latter "dinheiro forte."

As in Portugal, however, the £ sterling is here a legal tender, and almost everywhere in the islands accepted as equivalent to 5$600.

The circulation in Portugal of our sovereign began with the introduction of the guinea, which in 1812, at the request of the Duke of Wellington, became a legal tender at 3$733. When the guinea was called in, habit and convenience caused the £ to replace it at 4$500, an arrangement welcome alike to the Government and the people in such close commercial intercourse with England, and above all to that ubiquitous creature, the British tourist.

A Lisbon wag, reflecting the sentiments of his country-men, once wrote:—

> Mas soberanos amarellos,
> E d'aquelles de valer,
> Que os amigos Ingles' manes
> Nos vieràm cá trazer.

The smallest Portuguese monetary value existing, how-ever only nominally, and the unit upon which all calcula-tions are based in Portugal and the colonies, is the "real," plural, "reis." Five of these make up the cinco reis, the equivalent of our farthing coin; ten, the dez reis, or half-penny; twenty, the vintém, or penny-piece; and fifty, the old pataco, patacão, or dump. Small as is the real, there was a coin called the seital, worth only a sixth part of a real, 120 making up a penny, and which were common in Portugal down to the reign of Sebastian; these, like the maravedis of Spain, were doubtless a relic of the Moorish conquest. Of silver coins, 120 reis make up the "seis vintens," or sixpence; 240 reis, the "serrilha," or shilling; 600 reis, the half-dollar piece of seis tostões; and 1,200 reis the dollar-piece. For convenience in calculations the decimal, though purely nominal (in the islands), value of tostões (= 100 reis) is much used, articles being bought and sold at so many tostões. 1,000,000 reis make up the conto de reis, equal in island currency to £178. 11s. 5d.* Contos de reis are, when written, separated from milreis by a double point, and mils, or milreis, from reis by a single point or crossed cypher, thus :—

> 0$001 = 1 real.
> 1$000 = 1 milreis.
> 1:000$000 = 1 conto de reis..

Based, as it is, upon the decimal system, calculations in this currency are easy and readily understood by the people.

---

* The conto on the Continent is worth £222. 2s. 1d.

The new Portuguese silver coinage is gradually being introduced into the islands, but is very often refused, the natives preferring the old " peseta " pieces (of 5 reals) minted by the Governments of Spain two and three centuries ago, now obsolete, even in that land of slow progress. So worn are these pesetas and half-pesetas, known here as serrilhas and meias serrilhas, that the inscriptions on them are generally illegible.

It seems singular that, in spite of the bitter hostility which has always animated the Portuguese against the Spaniards, and in which the Azoreans form no exception, that this old Spanish currency should by force of habit be so tenaciously clung to by the islandry. The amount of gold and silver coin turned out by the Lisbon mint during the short epoch of Portugal's material prosperity, known as the "idade de oiro," or golden age, and which reached its culminating point in the first decade of the sixteenth century, was quite equal to the requirements of the country, but the vast sums annually remitted then, and in subsequent years, to Rome; the calling in and substitution of the national coin by the Spanish, during the sixty years usurpation; the hoards subsequently carried away by the French in the beginning of this century, and the drain for a lengthened period caused by the increasing requirements of the Brazils and other dependencies—made silver, and especially gold, so scarce in the mother country that little could be spared for these much neglected islands, where a tendency naturally arose to hoard the little there was, and carry it away to Lisbon, where a premium was paid for it, which made matters worse; it was therefore, with a view to retaining coinage in the islands, and to prevent its remittance to Portugal, that the depreciation in exchange of 25 per cent. was established.

The currency in Madeira is now the same as that of Portugal, and no doubt in a few years that of the Azores will be equally assimilated, as it should be.

The following are the various coins in circulation in the Azore Islands :—

SILVER.

				s.	d.
60 reis	=	1 reale	=	0	$2\frac{67}{100}$
120 ,,	=	2 ,,	=	0	$5\frac{1}{7}$
240 ,,	=	4 ,,	=	0	$10\frac{2}{7}$
300 ,,	=	5 ,,	=	1	$0\frac{85}{100}$
600 ,,	=	½ dollar	=	2	$1\frac{71}{100}$
1,200 ,,	=	1 ,,	=	4	$3\frac{42}{100}$

All old Spanish coins.

The Brazilian dollar of the old coinage has a special currency in the Azores, of 1,200 reis = 4s. $3\frac{42}{100}$d.

COPPER.

20 reis	=	$\frac{85}{100}$ of a penny.
10 ,,	=	$\frac{42}{100}$,,
5 ,,	=	$\frac{21}{100}$,,

LISBON MONEY (SILVER).

				s.	d.
60 reis, worth in Azores 75 reis		=	0	$3\frac{21}{100}$
120 ,, ,, 150 ,,		=	0	$6\frac{42}{100}$
240 ,, ,, 300 ,,		=	1	$0\frac{85}{100}$
480 ,, ,, 600 ,,		=	2	$1\frac{71}{100}$

COPPER.

			s.	d.
40 reis, worth in Azores 50 reis	=	0		$2\frac{14}{100}$

GOLD.

		£	s.	d.
1,000 reis current in Azores 1,250 reis	=	0	4	$5\frac{67}{100}$
2,000 ,, ,, ,, 2,500 ,,	=	0	8	$11\frac{14}{100}$
5,000 ,, ,, ,, 6,250 ,,	=	1	2	$3\frac{85}{100}$

All Spanish and Brazilian dollars of the new coinage are not current in the Azores, but are exchanged at the rate of 1,000 reis, or 3s. $6\frac{85}{100}$d.

The American dollar is also exchangeable at the same rate. The American gold eagle of twenty dollars is exchangeable generally at $23,000 or £4. 2s. $1\frac{14}{100}$d.

The English sovereign, as we have seen, is current by law for 5$600.

The above calculations are based upon the exchange of 5$600 per £ sterling, but 90 d/s bills are often sold at 5$675, which would slightly reduce the value given.

A sovereign coin can frequently be sold, and especially during the busy winter months, at 5$700; drafts on Lisbon are also then at $1\frac{1}{2}$ to 2 per cent. premium, but when the demand again falls off, they can be bought at a slight discount.

The par of exchange is 25 per cent.; that is to say, if you want in Lisbon an order to receive in the Azores 100$000, you pay for it there 80$000; but, if on the other hand, you want to remit to Lisbon from the islands, 100$000 of their money you pay for it 125$000 of the island currency.

There are also notes of the Bank of Portugal circulating in the Azores for 10$000 and 20$000 of island currency, or, respectively £1. 15s. $8\frac{7}{100}$d. and £3. 11s. $5\frac{11}{100}$d.; but these are not legal tender, although accepted in all public offices. Sometimes they have been sent to Lisbon, and the bank there gives 8$000 and 16$000 "dinheiro forte," charging $1\frac{1}{2}$ to 2 per cent. commission, sending them back again to the islands. Vessels putting into these ports in a damaged condition, known all the world over as "lame ducks," and as universally looked upon as legitimate plunder, are compelled by usage to accept any advances or disbursements made them for repairs or supplies, at the exchange of 5$000 per £ sterling, which represents a large gain to the island consignee when serious amounts are involved. The crusado was coined by Affonso V., to commemorate the Crusades to the Holy Land against the Turk, in which Portugal took so conspicuous a part. The gold crusado was worth 500 ducats.

After the discovery of India and Brazil, Dom Manuel, who succeeded to the throne in 1495, caused a coin to be struck bearing the ambitious design on one side of a globe or sphere, and on the reverse a crown with the word MEA; these were gold pieces called "espheras."

The pluralities of the King of Portugal were in keeping with the pretensions put forward on the above coin. In 1531 we find our Henry VIII. thus addressing John of Portugal :—

"To the High and Mighty Prince John, by the Grace of God, King of Portugal and of Algarve on this side, and beyond the sea in Africa, Lord of Ghinea,* and of the conquest, navigation and traffique of Æthiopea, Arabia, Persia, India, &c., our most deere and well-beloved brother."

Perhaps the most interesting coin circulating in the Peninsula and Brazil, on account of its ancient associations, is the well-known pillar dollar, evidently copied from a Phœnician coin found on the site of the numerous colonies of these people in Spain or Portugal; for many of the coins dug up at Tyre bear the pillars of Hercules, with the tree of knowledge in the centre and the serpent twined round it, and in the combination of the two pillars and the serpent probably lies the origin of the universal dollar sign—$.

With the exception of coins bearing Greek or Carthaginian inscriptions, circulating only in the seaboard colonies of these people, we find no purely Lusitanian coins prior to those struck in 81 B.C., by Quintus Sertorius,† a famous Roman rebel general, who, joining the Lusitanian and Celtiberian tribes, with a few of his own disaffected Romans, succeeded for some time in establishing a powerful independent sovereignty with Evora as his capital.

---

* Martin V. first bestowed this title of "Lord of Guinea" upon the King of Portugal by special bull.

† Quintus Sertorius was, according to Plutarch, invited by the Lusitanians to take the command among them. "For they wanted a general of his reputation and experience to support them against the terror of the Roman eagles ; and he was the only one on whose character and firmness they could properly depend." This invitation to Lusitania Sertorius accepted, and took his voyage from Africa thither.

In this town, and also in Almeida, silver and copper coins, bearing the effigy of Sertorius, have been found. After his suppression by the Romans, we have none but Roman coins, dating from the time of Julius Cæsar to the advent of the Goths, excepting some struck by towns such as Merida, but always bearing on one side the inscription " Emerita Colonia Augusta," and on the reverse the head of Augustus or Tiberius. Thousands of gold, silver, and bronze coins of the Roman empire have been found at Evora and its neighbourhood.

The Romans having been defeated and driven out of the Peninsula by the Goths under Uric (A.D. 466), the founder of the Gothic kingdom of Spain, we find at Evora and Merida, where they established their power, many Gothic coins bearing the effigies of their numerous kings, from Leovigild to Roderick, the last of their line—embracing a a period of 245 years.

In July of 711 A.D., Roderick, at the head of 90,000 Goths, met a still more formidable army of Moors under Tarik ben Zẽeyad, who had landed at Gibraltar from Tangiers, on the 30th April, 711. After a sanguinary battle, in which Roderick was slain by Tarik, the whole of Spain and Portugal was subjected by the Moors, who introduced all over the Peninsula various coins, amongst others the maravidis, which so long outlived the Arab dominion of 400 years in both countries.

Affonso Henriques, the first king to rule over the whole of Portugal, is said to have issued coins bearing his effigy ; but these must have been few, for they are exceedingly scarce, if indeed any have been discovered. Native numismatists point to the gold coin of Sancho I., 1185, as the most ancient of the Bourgoyne dynasty ; then follow those of the house of Avis, the Spanish rule from 1580 to 1640, and finally of the present Braganza sovereigns.

In every town, or even village of any size in Portugal and in these islands, there was always to be seen a " casa da roda," or species of foundling hospital. The poor little waifs, whether illegitimate or not, were placed, generally in the dead of night, in a cylindrical box let into the wall, standing on end and turning on a pivot, the open side of which always faced the street ready for the little strangers; a bell was gently rung, the wheel was turned round, and the child, now branded as " enjeitado," the forsaken or rejected, was for ever lost to the wretches who brought it into the world. It is said that this "roda dos expostos" was instituted in order to do away with infanticide, which at one time attained serious proportions in Portugal; but if we examine the death-rate in these national baby-farms, we find that the mortality amongst the children averaged at least fifty per cent. Instances were not uncommon in this fecund climate of parents in moderately well-to-do circumstances abandoning to the " roda " one or more of their legitimate offspring. I am far from agreeing with those who hold that this turning box is the most demoralising machine ever invented. Human nature scarcely needs this incentive to vice, but what more particularly arrests our attention with regard to these establishments was the appalling rate of mortality which blighted them. The primary cause of this was due to the niggardly contributions of the Government, who were responsible for their support; hence the huddling together in foul, confined places, not large enough for a tithe their number, of these unhappy children, who were, moreover, deprived of proper and sufficient food, and condemned to general neglect.

What is here required is a more liberal contribution on the part of the Government towards the support of these institutions, aided by private subscriptions, and that every " casa dos expostos " should be thrown open at every time of day to the inspection of visitors. Some of the native ladies too, who seem to shun these hospitals as if they contained the plague, might be induced to form committees of supervision, and see that the nurses do not neglect their duty; thus could these establishments be rendered of infinite use to the state for recruiting, colonising and other purposes, and a means of alleviating untold misery and wretchedness.

Although the existence of the roda has been doomed, and its abolition decreed, to satisfy the susceptibilities of the public, the institution will still continue under another name, probably " Asylo da infancia," where the same mismanagement will continue.

The existing analogous institution, supported mainly by voluntary contributions, contained in 1881 1,015 children, 193 having been admitted that year. The mortality amounted to only 10.443 per cent., and the expense for the year to £2,000.

The present law, however, compels the mother, if possible, to father her illegitimate child.

It has been well said that the Portuguese language represents the history of the successive conquests of the country.

The earliest and perhaps the best treatise on the language is that of the learned Duarte Nunes de Leaõ, published in 1606, and in which he gives 207 Arabic words as then used in Portugal. The Moors came into the country in the beginning of the 8th century, and supplanted the Gothic Latin then in vogue by their own language. Many of these Arabic words are distinguishable by the prefix of the article " al " (meaning *the*), or " xa," or by ending in " x."

One of the commonest and most used, yet ugliest, of these Arabic derivations is " oxala "* (*let us hope*, or more

---

* I have not been able to trace this expression directly to the Arabic, from which it is evidently derived. In that language, however, are the phrases : " hakkta'ālā " (*God is great*), and in " shā allā hu taālā " (*God willing*). In the Persian, which has many Arabic words, owing to the same causes which led to their introduction into Portuguese, there occurs a phrase which bears a greater resemblance to the word I have cited, viz., "oxala." The phase is " ai-kāsh," probably an abbreviation of " ai-kāsh-Allāh," signifying *would to God !* The " ai-kāsh," without any strained etymological fancy, might have been abbreviated to " aiksh," and thence to " ax," the " ala " being plainly from " Allāh " (*God*).

literally, *would to God!*) It is made up of the verb "xa" (*to will*), the noun "Allah" (*the Lord*), and particle "en" (*if*).

There are also a number of Persian words, supposed to have been introduced by the Goths, Vandals, and Suevi, who overran Europe from the East, or by the communication which was carried on between Portugal and Persia in the reign of Dom Manuel, and from which rose the title of "Lord of the Commerce of Persia" the Portuguese sovereigns bore.

How much Latin predominated in the language in the middle ages may be gathered from the following apostrophe of Severim de Faria, written in 1624:—

"O quam gloriosas memorias publico, considerando quanto vales nobilissima lingoa Lusitana, cum tua facundia excessivamente nos prouocas, excitas, inflamas; quam altas victorias procuras, quam celebres triumphos speras, quam excellentes fabricas fundas, quam peruersas furias castigas, quam feroces insolencias rigorosamẽte domas, manifestado de prosa, de metro tantas elegācias Latinas," &c.; or the following curious epitaph to be found in João Franco Barreto, published in 1671 :—

Hic jacet Antonius Perez,
Vassalus domini Regis,
Contra Castellanos misso,
Occidit omnes, que quiso:
Quantos vivos rapuit,
Omnes exbariqavit.
Per istas ladeyras,
Tulit tres bandeyras;
E febre correptus
Hic jacet sepultus :
Faciant Castelani feste,
Quia mortua est sua peste.

A language which can produce eight different substantives to signify the same thing (adagio, proverbio, rifão, exemplo, sentença, ditado, anexim and brocardo), and nine different verbs to express the word abbreviate (abreviar, recopilar, resumir, epilogar, epitomar, compendiar, encurtar, sommar, cifrar) cannot be accused of poverty of expression.

The Spanish historian, Marianna, pays the Portuguese language a graceful tribute, when he says it is pleasing to the ear and elegant; and his countryman, Lope de Vega, the poet, goes even farther, and places Portuguese in the first rank for suavity. Cervantes, the author of Don Quixote, eulogising the Valencia dialect, adds that only Portuguese can compete with it in softness and sweetness.

To account for the very numerous Latin derivations in Portuguese, we must go back to the Roman conquest. All the conquered cities in Spain and Portugal were governed precisely in the same manner as those of Italy; all contracts and legal documents were considered invalid unless drawn up in Latin; every means were taken to teach and force the people to use the language, and with such success that it became general throughout the Peninsula. Notwithstanding the Gothic invasion, which impaired the Latin, and subsequently the Moorish irruption, which again modified and altered the language, the influence of the Romans had become too deeply impressed upon the thrice subjected tribes to be easily eradicated—and till the latter part of the fifteenth century all charters and documents, dates on monuments, &c., were reckoned from the Roman conquest, 38 B.C.—the Christian era not coming into general use until 1480.

For the large admixture of French words in the language, we also find an explanation in the early history of the country.

---

* With the death of Bermudes III., in 1037, the dynasty of the Kings of Leon expired, and this ancient sovereignty was united to Castille in the person of Ferdinand of Navarre, son of that Garcia III., who, notwithstanding his great valour, was surnamed the "Trembler." This family possessed the four Christian thrones of Spain, which were reduced to three in 1038, by the death of Gonzales of Sobrarva. At this time the Moors still possessed Andalusia, Granada, Murcia,

When Count Henry of Besançon joined the Court of
King Alfonso of Leon,* in 1095, at the instance of Philip I.
of France, he was given a daughter of the Leonese king in
marriage, and the government of the outlying Lusitanian
conquests, extending at that time from the Minho in the
north to the boundary of the Moorish kingdom of Badajoz
in the south. This province he held at first as a fief dependent on the crown of Leon, but, gradually throwing off
his allegiance, he extended his dominion by conquest, leaving
it greatly enlarged to his only son Affonso Henriques, the
second prince of the house of Bourgoyne, who, in his turn,
by successfully driving the Moors out of the country, consolidated the kingdom of Portugal as we now find it.
In the train of these French princes came numerous
retainers from Burgundy and Provence, who, settling in the
country much as the Normans did in England, and following
the practice at court, where the French dialects were for a
length of time used, influenced in no small degree the
language of their adopted country; to such an extent was
this carried, that a modern Portuguese travelling in
Provence might imagine himself, on hearing the patois

part of New Castille, and all the sea-coast from Barcelona to the mouth of the
Tagus. The war with the infidels was renewed by the new king of Leon and
Castille, whose frontier was even extended to the Mondego; and the Arab princes
of Saragossa, Toledo, Cordova, and Seville, were compelled to pay him tribute. On
Ferdinand's death in 1065, his kingdom was divided among his three sons. Sancho
had Castille; Alphonso, Leon and the Asturias; Garcia, a part of Portugal with
Galicia. Little variety characterizes the history of these states, until 1081, when
Henry of Besançon, a soldier of fortune, received the hand of Theresa, Alphonso's
natural daughter, and as dowry, whatever he could wrest from the Moors in
Portugal, which had hitherto been governed by Castilian lieutenants, was resigned
by Alphonso VI., 1095, to his son-in-law, Henry of Besançon, whose son Alphonso,
after the glorious victory over the Moors at Ourique, was saluted king on the field
of battle, 1139; but Castille did not willingly allow the assumption of the regal
title until the Pope had decided in favour of the new monarch. His territory lay
between the Minho and Douro. In 1147, he became master of Lisbon, and dying
in 1185, was succeeded by his son, Sancho I.—*White.*

there spoken, to be in some corner of his own native Lusitania..

The Portuguese language, as we have seen, is chiefly derived from Latin, Greek, and Arabic roots, the former predominating. As spoken in Lisbon and Coimbra, it is soft and pleasant to the ear, especially when used by the more refined classes; some authorities going so far as to say that the mode of pronunciation at the university approaches to euphuism, as they there say "aialma, aiaula, setióras, novióras," etc., for "a alma, a aula, sete horas, nove horas," etc.

I have somewhere seen it stated that the inhabitants of ocean-girdled islands are gifted with poetic instincts, and that the effect of a moist climate on the larynx of the throat softens and modifies the voice; here, however, is perhaps to be found the exception which proves the rule, except in the case of the first named gift, for a harsher or more discordant language than the Azorean Portuguese it is difficult to match—it is the language of the middle ages before the refining influence of Camöens and educational tastes toned down its defective sounds. Undoubtedly, the language bears a greater affinity to its parent Latin than Spanish, or even Italian, the purity of its preservation rendering it one of the easiest languages to acquire by those who still remember something of their Latin grammar.

The greatest difficulty exists in the pronunciation, which arises from the nasal sounds given by the letter *m*, to words preceded by an *a*, *o*, or *i*, and by the orthographical sign ˜ or "til" placed over vowels *ao*, *aa*, and it takes many years of practice to acquire the correct rendering of words with such terminations as *aos*, *aens*, *ems*. The dipthongs number some sixteen. Portuguese is essentially a language for men; it is rich in expression and fluency, yet it has not ceased to borrow much from other languages, and, perhaps unwisely, from the English, for it surprises us to find such words as "lunch," "meetings," "speech" (in the sense of oration), "revolver," "rails," "high life," "waggons," "terminus," etc., etc., as of every-day interpolation in newspapers and public speeches. Of all interpolated words one of the most singular is "chicarâ," a cup, taken originally from the Spanish "jicara" of Central America, itself a corruption of the "xicallí" of the ancient Aztecs; the word has since become common, both in Portugal and Italy, where a "chicara de chá," or a "chicchera˙di tè" are usual expressions.

Nothing so much surprises the Continental Portuguese on coming to these islands as the excessive use here of diminutives, which sound to them almost as amusing as Mr. Arthur Roberts' "dotlets and eyelets." Under this habit the numerous Luizas, Marias, Marianas, &c., become Luizinhas, Mariquinhas, Marianinas, &c.

The expression, although conveying an exquisite tenderness, is applied to the most inconceivable things, and is very puzzling to the student of the language.

The habit is not merely confined to ordinary conversation, but permeates the island literature, and particularly the poetry, e.g.—

Casadinha de outo dias,
Sentadinha á janella,
Vira vir um cavalleiro
Com cartinhas a abanar:

Oh meu amor lá de longe
Escreve-me uma cartinha,
Se não tiveres papel
Nas azas de uma pombinha.

Fui-me botar a nadar
No leito de teus peitinhos:
Se me vires ir ao fundo,
Atira-me com beijinhos.

The judicial system in these islands is as follows: All civil suits are in the first instance brought before the Juiz Ordinario, or rural judge, who decides actions relating to moveables up to the value of £1. 15s. 9d.; he also takes cognisance of actions for damages or executions in his own jurisdiction up to the same value, unless the execution be upon immovables, *i.e.*, lands, houses, or tenements, for then the proceedings go before the Juiz de Direito.

Next to the Juiz Ordinario, comes the Juiz de Paz (Juge de Paix) who endeavours, even in the absence of receipts or written documents, to bring the parties to terms of settlement, should none have been arrived at in the Court of First Instance; but if they cannot agree, the case goes to the Juiz de Direito, who decides only upon the documentary evidence, or that of witnesses produced; from his decisions there is recourse to the Relação or Court of Appeal, the judges of which were formally styled Desembargadores, but now they are called Juizes da Relação. All appeals from the other islands come to the Relação or Court at Ponta Delgada. From its decisions, appeal may be made (provided the value of the cause in dispute be not less than £71. 10s.) to the Supremo Tribunal de Justiça (Supreme Court of Judicature) in Lisbon, and there it ends.

In criminal cases there is appeal from the Juiz de Direito's decision or sentence to the two courts above-mentioned, viz., the Relação of Ponta Delgada and the Supreme Tribunal of Lisbon. The sentences on misdemeanors and lighter offences strike foreigners as sufficiently severe. For example, thefts, if over £4. 10s. in value, entail transportation, with nominal police surveillance, to the West Coast of Africa for terms varying from three to more years. The fate of these *degradados*, however, is enlistment immediately on arrival in one of the African regiments, by no means the best of reformatories.

The President of the Supreme Tribunal, in Lisbon, receives £600 a year, and his ten assistants or councillors £470 each, besides what they can make by costs.

The Tribunal for the Islands and Colonies consists of a President, who receives £355 a year; a Vice-President receiving £300; and six Judges, each £295 per annum.

The Judges of the Tribunals of First Instance in the rural districts receive but £90 per annum in addition to fees.

It is highly creditable to the Portuguese bar that, notwithstanding these insignificant salaries, the instances of corruption on the part of the judges have been exceptional and rare. The same may be said of Portuguese statesmen and ministers, who in this respect afford an excellent example to the rest of the community.

The Civil Code of Portugal covers 2,538 articles, some of which are exceedingly complex and curious—affording ample opportunities to the litigants, if so disposed, to prolong a simple suit a whole lifetime.

One of its clauses provides that a woman cannot, unless by settlement before marriage, prevent her husband from administering and enjoying her money, but she may "a titulo de alfinetes," or on the plea of pin money, reserve one-third for her own separate use. The husband, however, cannot encumber his wife's estate without her previous written consent; neither may she contract debts without her husband's sanction. Unless a marriage settlement exists to the contrary, a man cannot will away, as he pleases, more than one-third of his property, the rest being equally divided between his widow and their children. The widow, also, can only deal with the terça, or third of the estate, as she wishes; should she, however, pre-decease her husband, he would have to pay her parents half of all he possessed, a doubly objectionable condition in the case of an unfriendly and perhaps avaricious mother-in-law.

The internal taxation of Portugal weighs heavily upon all classes. The scale charged is not uniform throughout the kingdom, but graduated according to the rank of the town or city. The government has, therefore, never been known to discourage the laudable, but costly ambition of villages to be raised to the dignity of towns, and towns to that of cities. Ponta Delgada, being a city of the third class, pays less than either Lisbon or Oporto.

The following is a list of some of the " sumptuary " and " industrial " taxes levied upon its inhabitants :—

House Rent pays 8 $\frac{4}{10}$ per cent.

					£	s.	d.	
Servants, male, 1 pays	1$960	or	0	7	0	sumptuary.
,, ,, 2 ,,	4$760	,,	0	17	0	,,
,, ,, 3 ,,	13$300	,,	2	7	6	,,
,, ,, 4 ,,	30$380	,,	5	8	6	,,
,, all above 4 ,,	7$560	,,	1	7	0	each ,,
Horses or mules 1 ,,	1$960	,,	0	7	0	,,
,, ,, 2 ,,	4$760	,,	0	17	0	,,
,, ,, 3 ,,	11$480	,,	2	2	0	,,
,, ,, 4 ,,	19$040	.,	3	8	0	,,
,, all above 4 ,,	4$760	,,	0	17	0	each ,,

		£	s.	d.	
Carriages, 2 wheels, drawn by 1 horse 7$140 or	1	5	6	,,
,, 4 ,, ,, 1 ,, 14$280 ,,	2	11	0	,,
,, 4 ,, ,, 2 ,, 28$560 ,,	5	2	0	,,

Armorial bearings, if painted on carriage, 14$000 or £2. 10s. sumptuary.

Medical men and surgeons 22$400 or £4 0 0 industrial.

Music masters (piano) .. 12$600 ,, 2 5 0 ,,

,, (other instruments) 5$600 ,, 1 0 0 ,,

Professors of languages, other sciences, drawing-masters and school-masters 5$600 or £1 industrial.

Servants, horses and mules, in the environs pay 40 per cent. less than in Ponta Delgada, except at Ramalho, which is included in the city.

MUNICIPAL DUES.

		£	s.	d.
A 4-wheeled carriage pays	1$800 or	0	6	5¼
A 2 ,, ,, ...	1$200 ,,	0	4	3½
A cart or other vehicle for loads, drawn by horses, mules or oxen, pays ..	1$200 ,,	0	4	3½
A ditto, drawn by donkeys, pays ..	0$840 ,,	0	3	0

The Contribuição Predial, or land property tax, ranges from 10 to even 17½ per cent. upon the estimated rental, or produce value, according to the abundance or deficiency of the crops, for this charge varies from year to year. The following were the amounts paid for this tax in 1882, by the different townships of the island, upon the rateable value of the property, viz. :—

			£	s.	d.	
1.	Ponta Delgada	52,820$000 or	9,432	2	0	at 5.600 ⅌ £
2.	Lagoa ..	9,200$000 „	1,642	17	2	„ „
3.	Villa Franca ..	9,900$000 „	1,767	17	2	„ „
4.	Povoação ..	5,000$000 „	892	10	0	„ „
5.	Nordeste ..	4,750$000 „	848	4	3	„ „
6.	Ribeira Grande	26,000$000 „	4,642	17	2	„ „

As an index of the agricultural prosperity, or otherwise, of the island during the ten years from 1873-82, the following returns of the property (land and house) tax paid in each year speak for themselves.

Contribuição Predial, 1873–1882, for each 100$000, or per cent. :—

1873.	1874.	1875.	1876.	1877.	1878.	1879.	1880.	1881.	1882.	CONCELHO.
11,5	13,5	14,	13,861	14,380	12,115	11,144	12,589	13,193	12,347	PontaDelgada
13,	13,	14,686	14,	16,285	13,995	12,761	13,972	11,634	13,976	Lagoa.
12,	12,5	12,332	13,	14,872	11,84	11,103	12,627	13,28	11,911	Villa France.
12,	13,	14,	14,	15,586	13,495	12,186	13,416	..	10,792	Povoação.
12,	13,	14,	14,	14,557	12,397	11,393	12,518	13,095	11,683	Nordeste.
12,	13,5	14,	13,5	17,554	14,083	13,467	15,381	15,973	10,778	Ribeira Gde.
				Included in the Concelho of Ponta Delgada.					..	St. Maria.

The tax on the purchase of property is very heavy, amounting to 9,072½ per cent., made up thus :—

8.400		per cent.	
·504	6	„	additional
·168	2	„	on 8.400 for stamp duty
9,072			

If the property pays ground rent, there is besides the above a laudemio (fine on alienation) which ranges from $2\frac{1}{2}$ per cent. to 10 per cent. upon the amount realized. Supposing the purchasing price to be :—

	Rs. 100$000
Add Laudemio at 5 per cent.	5$000
	105$000
,, 9,072 per cent. (on 105$000) ..	9$525
Increasing the purchase money to ..	114$525

The tobacco duty is the most important of Portuguese imposts, and brought the Treasury in 1880-81 £761,440. The sale of the article was formerly a Government right, but in May 1864 a law came into force extinguishing this monopoly and permitting the free cultivation and manufacture of the plant in the islands, in consideration of an indemnity to Government of 70 contos or £15,500 per annum, to be paid by the Azores and Madeira. From 1870 to 1881 the sum of £69,847 was paid by the undermentioned districts on account of this indemnity.

Angra ..	.. £15,006 or	21.33 per cent.
Horta ..	.. 7,458 ,,	10.66 ,,
Ponta Delgada ..	29,689 ,,	42.68 ,,
Funchal ..	.. 17,694 ,,	25.33 ,,

It will thus be seen that of the total amount St. Michael's contributed 42.68 per cent.

In June, 1882, an impost was raised of 200 reis or $10\frac{3}{4}$d. per kilo of tobacco consumed in the islands, in order to meet the above indemnity, which heavily handicapped this otherwise remunerative industry. The law recently passed, however, places the cultivation and manufacture of tobacco in these islands on a much more promising footing.

The total amounts derived by the Ponta Delgada

Treasury, from these various sources, reaches on the average about £46,064 per annum, thus :—

From Land-property tax	.. ..	£19,778
„ Industrial tax ..	.. ..	1,896
„ House-rent and Sumptuary tax		1,152
„ Registration tax	.. ..	7,492
„ Tobacco	.. .. ..	6,666
„ Fish ..	.. .. ..	673
„ Stamp duty	.. .. ..	4,322
„ Water tax	.. .. ..	1,182
„ Contribution from the Break-water dues	.. ..	2,560
„ Sundry receipts	.. ..	343
		£46,064

To which has to be added the duty upon spirit manufactured in the island, the returns of which I have not been able to obtain. If to this sum we add the customs duties upon imports and exports, we arrive at the total revenue of the island, amounting to about £95,000 per annum.

ALTITUDES OF THE MOUNTAINS IN S. MIGUEL ABOVE SEA LEVEL.

	Feet.		Feet.
Pico da Vara	3,570	Pico do Vigario	1,655
Serra d'Agoa de Pau ..	3,070	Serra Gorda	1,570
Pico do Passo	3,040	Pico da Pedra Pomes ..	1,400
Pico do Bartholomeu ..	2,927	Lombo Gordo	1,347
Cumieiras da Lagoa do Fogo	2,916	Pico da Cruz	1,260
Pico da Cruz	2,777	Ponta d'Agoa Retorta ..	1,080
Pico do Carvaõ	2,632	Pico da Maffra	1,052
Pico do Gafanhoto ..	2,345	Pico do Fogo	1,023
Pico dos Cedros.. ..	2,240	Lake of Seven Cities ..	886
Pico do Nunes	2,220	Lake of Furnas.. ..	864
Crater of Seven Cities ..	1,880	Pico Vermelho	858
Pico do Sargulho ..	1,668	Pico das Camarinhas ..	687

MARITIME POSITIONS OF THE AZORE ISLANDS, FROM RAPER'S "PRACTICE OF NAVIGATION."

	Lat. N.	Long. W. (of Greenwich.)
Corvo N. Point	39° 43′ 5″	31° 7′ 2″
Flores N. extremity	39° 31′ 6″	31° 13′ 0″
Fayal W. Point	38° 35′ 6″	28° 50′ 5″
„ Horta	38° 31′ 7″	28° 38′ 5″
Pico E. Point	38° 24′ 7″	28° 3′ 0″
San Jorge S. & E. Point	38° 32′ 5″	27° 46′ 7″
Graciosa W. Point	39° 4′ 2″	28° 4′ 7″
Terceira Praya	38° 43′ 7″	27° 4′ 2″
„ Angra C. House	38° 38′ 9″	27° 13′ 7″
San Miguel, E. or Marquesa Point ..	37° 48′ 3″	25° 8′ 2″
„ Ponta Delgada, Custom House Quay	37° 44′ 2″	25° 40′ 7″
„ West Point, or Ponta Ferraria	37° 51′ 7″	25° 52′ 2″
Santa Maria Town	36° 56′ 6″	25° 9′ 5″
Formigas	37° 16′ 2″	24° 47′ 5″
Dollabarets	37° 13′ 7″	24° 44′ 5″

WAGES.

Men servants from 9s. to 12s. 6d. per month.

Maid servants from 4s. 3d. to 7s. per month.

Field labourers from 8d. to 1s. per day, the average about 9d. per day.

Carpenters about 2s. per day.

Painters from 2s. to 2s. 3d. per day.

Masons about 2s. per day.

Hire of carriage for 2 people, about 6s. 8d. per day.

      „   „   4   „   „   9s. 0d.   „   exclusive of about 1s. 6d. to the driver, and something to eat.

Unfurnished houses, either in Ponta Delgada or the suburbs, and generally with very nice gardens to them, can always be had at rentals ranging from £20 to £40 per annum.

PRICES OF CHIEF ARTICLES OF CONSUMPTION AT PONTA DELGADA.

Bread 1¾d. to 2d. per English lb.

Beef from 6d. to 8d. per English lb.

Butter 10d. to 1s. 3d. per English lb.

Eggs 3½d. to 6d. per dozen, generally 4d.

Fowls from 10d. to 1s. 5d. each, generally about 11½d. each.

Chickens 4d. to 5d. each.

Ducks 10½d. to 1s. 1d. each.

Turkeys 2s. 6d. to 4s. 6d.

Geese 2s. to 3s. each.

Wheat 45s. per qr. of 480 lbs.

Indian corn 35s. to. 36s. per qr. of 480 lbs.

Potatoes 3s. 6d. per cwt.

Sweet ditto 2s. 3d. per cwt.

Muscatel grapes 2½d. per lb.

Sugar, brown 5½d. per lb.; white 7d. to 8d. per lb.; crushed 7d. to 8¼d. per lb.

Common wine made from the Isabel grape 2s. to 2s. 7d. a gallon.

White wine made from island grapes 2s. 7d. to 3s. 3d. a gallon.

Flour 3⅛d per lb.

Tea, good black 4s. 10d. to 7s. 1½d. per lb.

Coffee in berry 1s. to 1s. 2d. per lb.

Port 3s. 5d. to 8s. 6d. per bottle, sherry 5s. 2d., madeira 3s. 6d., champagne 6s. 6d. to 8s. 6d., bucellas 1s. 10d., white Lisbon 1s. 3½d. Spirits—gin 3s., rum 1s. 10d., whiskey 4s. 3½d., brandy 3s. 6d. to 4s. 6d. All without the bottle.

ERRATA.

Page 173 for 30° Fah., read 86°

„ 174 „ 97° „ „ 206.60°

„ 176 „ 95° „ „ 203°

FINIS.

LONDON: Printed by LAKE BROTHERS, 3, Westminster Chambers, S.W., and 7, Suffolk Lane, Cannon Street, E.C.

ISLAND MELODIES.

CANÇÃO ÁS FURNAS.

N'esta | Cintra Michael-ense | N'estes bos-ques se-duc-

tores, No ca-sal que me per-tence Passo a vi-da com sa-

bor. A ven tura que aqui dura No albergue do Pas-

tor Tal mistura de ver-dura Diz es-p'rança Diz a-

mor !

N'esta Cintra Michaelense,
Nestes bosques seductores,
No Casal que me pertence,
Passo a vida com sabor.

A ventura que aqui dura,
No albergue do Pastor,
Tal mistura de verdura,
Diz esp'rança; Diz amor !

Mui brilhantes distracções,
Tem a vida na cidade,
Mas aqui os corações,
Batem com mais liberdade ;
    Aventura, &c.

Este valle é minha terra,
E'minha terra natal,
Mas em bellezas que encerra,
No mundo naõ tem rival
    Aventura &c.

LAGRIMAS.

Com as la-gri-mas nos olhos Com-a

dôr no co-ra-ção Vou votar da tris-te

ly-ra A minha triste can-ção. E sin-

ge-la tão senti-da Como os ais de so-li

dão Mas ar-dente abraza-do-ra Como os

ais do co-ra-ção Mas ar-dente a-bra-za --

do - ra como os ais do co - ra - çào.

Com as lagrimas nos olhos,
Com a dôr no coração,
Vou votar da triste lyra
A minha triste canção.

È singela taõ.sentida
Como os ais de solidaõ,
Mas ardente abrazadora
Como os ais do coraçaõ.

Dentro n'alma foi nascida
Foi a dôr que m'inspirou ;
Foi a fervida saudade
Que no peito me gerou,

Foi a benção derradeira
Que minha mãe me lançou ;
Foi a dôr, a dôr immensa
Que este canto me inspirou.

Minha mãe, primeiro nome
Que ao sorrir balbuciei ;
Minha mãe, doce harmonia
Que jamais olvidarei.

Eu por ella as santas crenças
No meu peito acalentei ;
Mãe e Deus forão os nomes
Que ao sorrir balbuciei.

Que m'im-por-tão des-graças da terra D'essas vagas o louco fur-

ror   Que m'importão o rugir da tor-menta   D'esses

rios fais-cas d'horror.   Que m'importa que o mundo se a-

-cabe   E na   terra só eu fi - co   Rei   Que m'im

porta se o mundo eu de-tes-to   Se des - prezo e   rancór lhe vo-

tei.   Que m'importa se o mundo eu de-tes-to Se des-

prezo e rancór lhe vo-   tei.

Que m'importám desgraças da terra
D'essas vagas o louco furror,
Que m'importa o rugir da tormenta,
D'esses raios faiscas d'horror.

Que m'importa qu'o mundo se acabe,
E na terra eu só fique Rei,
Que m'importa se o mundo eu detesto,
Se desprêzo e rancór lhe votei.

Vinde embora coriscos e raios
Roubai ledas esp'ranças d'amor!
Que este peito de marmore e gêlo
So tem fé no tormento e na dòr.

Tive fé muita fé nesta vida
Crenças mil neste meu coração,
Mas q'importa se seccas mirradas
Ei-las todas cahidas no chào, &c., &c.

A. VIVANDEIRA

Ai que vida que passa na terra Quem não

ouve o rufar do tambor, Quem não canta na força da

uerra, Ai a-mor! Ai a-mor! Ai a-mor! Quem a

vida quizer ver-da-deira È fa-zerse uma vez Vivan—

deira Quem a vida qui-zer ver da-deira E fa-

zer-se uma vez Vi-van-dei-ra.

Ai que vida que passa na terra,
Quem não ouve rufar o tambor,
Quem não canta na força da guerra,
Ai amor! ai amor! ai amor!

Quem a vida quizer verdadeira
É fazer-se uma vez Vivandeira,

Ai que vida, esta vida que eu passo,
Com tão lindo gentil mocetão,
S'eu depois da batalha o abraço,
Ai que vida p'r 'o meu coração!

Que ternura cantando ao tambor,
Ai amor! ai amor! ai amor!

Que harmonia não tem a metralha
Derubando fileiras sem fim,
E depois, só depois da batalha,
Ve'-lo salvo cantando-me assim;

Em taes marchas fazendo trigueira
Mais t'eu amo gentil vivandeira.

&c., &c.

O GUERRILHEIRO.

Ei-lo er-gui-do no to-po da serra. Recos-
ta - do no seu ar-ca-buz, De pe-que-no cria-do na
guerra. Não conhece não vê outra luz.
Vio a ter-ra da patria agredi — da Ergueu

Ei-lo erguido no topo da serra
Recostado no seu arcabuz,
De pequeno creado na guerra,
Não conhece, e não vê outra luz ;

Vio a terra da patria aggredida
Ergueu alto seu alto pensar,
Pula o' sangue, referve-lh'a vida
Vind' ouvir-lhe seu rude cantar.

Era noite, sem lua, sem nada ;
E debaixo do negro docel,
Reluzia-lhe a fronte crestada,
Relinchava-lhe o negro corsel.

Fora noite talhada a sortida ;
Fóra d'horas quem hade valer ?
Pula o sangue, referve-lhe a vida,
Vinde ouvir-lhe seu rude cantar.

&c., &c.

A. SALOIA.

Quero cantar a Sa-loia, quero

cantar a Sa-loia   Ja que outra moda não sei   ja que

outra moda não sei   Minha   mãi   éra Sa-

loia, min - ha mãi éra Sa - loia   Eu com el-la me criei Eu com ella me cri-ei   Sou Sa-

loia tra-go botas, sou Sa - loia trago botas tambem

trago meu manteu, tambem trago meu man - teu tambem

tiro a ca - rapuça, a quem me tira o chapeu, tambem

tiro a cara—puça à quem me ti-ra o chapeu à quem me-tira o cha—peu, Ri-cos a- -mores qu'eu ten-

Allegro.

-ho meu bem—zinho vem do Çéo, Ri-cos a- - - mores qu'eu ten - - - - ho Meu bem zi-nho vem do

Çéo ɩ vem do Çéo ɩ vem do Çéo.....

Quero cantar a Saloia
Ja que outra moda não sei.
Minha mĩi eᵣa Saloia,
Eu com ella me criei.

Sou Saloia, trago botas
Tambem trago meu manteu,
Tambem tiro a carapuça
A quem me tira o chapeu.

Ricos.amores qu'eu tenho
Meu bemzinho vem do Cêɔ,
Eu sou amada d' um grande
Lindos olhos me piscou.

Tambem quiz dar me um abraço
E estas fallas me fallou——
Oh Saloia! da-me um beijo
Qu'eu te darei um vintem——

Os beijos d'uma Saloia
São poucos, mas sabem bem——
Ricos amores que tenho
Meu bemzinho ja la vem——

&c., &c.

670

DATE DUE

DEC 2 2000			
		ILL #	26021877
		DUE: 12-1-07	
ILL 9233607			
DUE 9/26/02			
		Printed in USA

DP702
A87
W3

LaVergne, TN USA
02 December 2010
207174LV00003B/70/P

9 781149 287163